The
Mexicans

The Making of a Nation

VÍCTOR ALBA

PEGASUS   NEW YORK

Published by arrangement with FREDERICK A. PRAEGER, PUBLISHERS
111 Fourth Avenue, New York, N.Y. 10003, U.S.A.
77-79 Charlotte Street, London W. 1, England

Published in the United States of America in 1967
by Frederick A. Praeger, Inc., Publishers
© 1967 by Frederick A. Praeger, Inc.

Maps on pages 142 and 235 reprinted with permission from:
Robert C. Kingsbury and Ronald M. Schneider, *An Atlas of
Latin American Affairs* (New York: Frederick A. Praeger, 1966).

Photographs courtesy of the Pan American Union.

Library of Congress Catalog Card Number: 67–20469

Printed in the United States of America

Author's Note

"MEXICANS ENJOY making a mystery of even their most insignificant acts," wrote Alexander von Humboldt, a German scholar traveling through Latin America in 1803. At the time, the gentleman was a rival of the Liberator of South America, Simón Bolívar, for the favors of a certain La Güera Rodríguez, the Madame Récamier of New Spain (as Mexico was then called). Perhaps it was she who helped the German visitor to understand one of the Mexican's basic characteristics.

It is indeed true that Mexico cannot be understood solely in terms of its physical face or historical exploits. Mexico demands constant interpretation, and Mexican intellectuals devote themselves joyously to this exercise, writing theses on their country and its inhabitants which they disguise as novels, poetry, drama, or essays.

The Mexican's interpretation of himself and his environment

is perforce distorted, however, for he is at once the interpreter and the interpreted. Consequently, I thought that I might usefully attempt an interpretation from without, although after having lived in Mexico for twenty years and having acquired Mexican citizenship nineteen years ago, I base my interpretation also on what I have been able to learn from within. In Mexico, I worked as a journalist (a job that included editing police reports for a newspaper) and as a correspondent for European newspapers on political and economic affairs. Therefore I am not exaggerating when I say that I have come to know my adopted country from within.

It is appropriate, then, for me to dedicate this present volume to Octavio Paz, the poet with whom I have argued most often over the Mexican personality; to José Luis Cuevas, the painter; to my secretary, Angel Villegas, an explosive mixture of pride and patience; to Emilio López, my barber for fifteen years; to various taxi drivers; and to a handful of friends, men and women, who have helped me more than books could ever do to penetrate the mystery that so impressed Humboldt.

V. A.

Washington, D.C.
July, 1967

Contents

A section of photographs follows p. 120.

The Mexicans

1 · The Empty Horn of Plenty

THE EMPEROR CHARLES V never set foot in the New World, but he was always eager to learn about his possessions there. "What is that land like?" he asked a messenger sent by Hernán Cortés to report on the discoveries being made in the territory that is Mexico today.

The messenger picked up a sheet of paper and crumpled it into a ball. Then, opening his hand and letting the paper unfold in his palm, he showed it to the monarch and said, "It's like this, Sire." And indeed that is what it is like.

Seen from the ground, Mexico looks wrinkled and twisted; on the map, its shape is like a horn of plenty. For years, the Mexicans enjoyed the thought that this shape was a symbol, but, more realistic now, they are increasingly aware that the symbol is deceiving.

The Mexican cornucopia stretches across eighteen degrees of

latitude, from the 14th to the 32d parallels, intersected roughly at the middle by the Tropic of Cancer. It lies in the same latitude as the Sahara, Arabia, and Egypt.

Mexico's horn of plenty is almost empty, though not so empty that living conditions there are on a level with those in the Sahara or Arabia. The climate in certain regions of southern Mexico is not unlike that of Guinea; along the Pacific and Gulf coasts, the air is warm and humid, almost like the air of Dakar or even the Mississippi Delta. On the high plateau of the north, the climate is extreme—very hot in summer and very cold in winter, while in the high central region, winter can scarcely be distinguished from summer, so moderate is the climate the year round, and the people divide the year into six months of drought and six of rain.

Because Mexico is the name of one country, we customarily regard it as if it had always been a single entity. But Mexico is more like a continent on which different peoples have lived in various phases of cultural development, some in virtual isolation, inhabiting pockets of land tucked into the folds of the mountains. The many and varied aspects of the Mexicans' culture have constituted the fortunes of anthropologists and the misfortunes of the people. Long before the arrival of the Spaniards in that land of the crumpled horn, Mexico had its own equivalent of Greek innovators, Egyptian irrigators, Roman conquerors, even barbarian invaders.

Then came three centuries of colonial life, plus a century and a half of independence, making Mexico's history many-sided: the history of the *peones* versus the *latifundista;* of the liberal city versus the theocratic rural regions; of those born in Mexico versus those born outside. Yet all these confrontations are only varying manifestations of a single, collective, spontaneous effort to unify the people and their traditions, to unite them wherever they are—on forbidding mountain slopes, in valleys, stifling jungle, or trackless deserts—in any nook or corner where man can live and prosper, and to form an entity with a measure of unity and coherence—that is to say, a nation. It was not an easy thing to do, nor is it now. The habitable enclaves are few and scattered, and one is quite unlike another.

Mexico is bisected from north to south by two mountain ranges. The central plateau lies between them, and steep slopes descend from their heights to either coast. Water flows so rapidly down these inclines that rivers run off and cannot be put to use except at great expense.

Laterally, from east to west, the country is divided by a chain of volcanic peaks that lies near and to the south of the capital city. Nine of them, always snow-capped, tower to a height of 12,000 feet. Wherever the terrain of this volcanic region will lend itself to the hoe or the tractor, the soil is good for cultivation. But such fertile tracts among the mountains or between deserts are few in number.

The ever-present mountains are at once a blessing and a curse. A blessing, because the height makes the uplands habitable; if they were lower, the heat would make work as arduous as it is in the warm stretches along the coast, where sustained physical effort is almost impossible during the most oppressive hours of the day. Conversely, in the cool land at the foot of the volcanoes —more than 6,000 feet high—the vegetation is alpine and cultivated tracts are scarce. In the intermediate area, called temperate, the soil is fertile and the people can summon their energies, even though the climate tends to be hot. Yet even the differences in altitude and the corresponding differences in rainfall are inimical to men. As the currents of warm air rising from the Gulf strike the cold air of the plateau, they yield a frequent and abundant rainfall for six months of the year. The rains in the coastal and Gulf regions are so abundant and encourage such rampant growth that it is impossible to cultivate the soil because the cost of clearing it and protecting farm crops against a too-prolific vegetable and animal life is prohibitive.

After bringing the rain, the winds reach the western part of the country, crossing the two cordilleras on their way. Here they draw the moisture from the soil, which then runs off in narrow, swift-flowing rivers, so that, while the heat is tropical near the Pacific coast, the landscape is often desertlike. Both the excess and the paucity of water bring the Mexican the same result: poverty.

The legendary horn of plenty that is Mexico is, in fact, almost empty. Only 7 per cent of the arable land, amounting to some 5 million acres in all, is capable of yielding a harvest without irrigation. A third of the arable land is semiarid. Half of the land —all through the north, along the coasts, and in Yucatán—is completely arid and must be irrigated before it can be made to yield. Wherever the soil is arable, heat and excessive fertility make cultivation difficult; wherever the altitude furnishes a temperature suitable for work, water is lacking; and wherever water is abundant, effort and money must be spent to hold back recurrent floods. All in all, then, man anywhere in Mexico must make a heavy investment of work, of funds, of ingenuity. In Mexico, nature gives nothing away. The people are more likely to fight

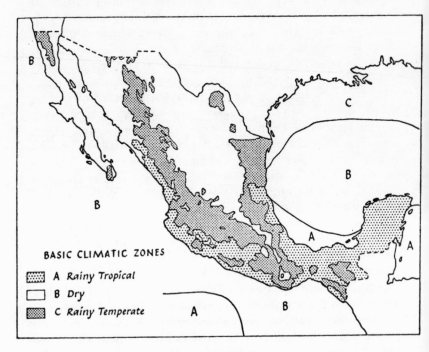

BASIC CLIMATIC ZONES

A Rainy Tropical
B Dry
C Rainy Temperate

Mexico's Climate

for water than for land. Villages quarrel over so many hours of irrigation rights more frequently than over so many acres of land. Yet land is not in great supply. Only about 9 to 12 per cent of the country's surface is fit for cultivation, and in general such tracts lie in narrow valleys or in limited open stretches, perhaps steeply sloped, where mechanization is expensive or impossible. The remainder of the country is jungle, desert, or, in the least unfavorable case, pasture.

Geography is important to a Mexican. It has divided his country into regions and the regions into enclaves. It has made poverty an accepted handicap. Yet, at the same time, it has created a history for the country almost beyond modern man's belief. Distances in the open country are measured in leagues, even today. The league is the distance a mule can travel in an hour carrying a load of 220 pounds. During that hour, the mule may pass through territory now flat and humid, now stony, now high and slippery—along a smooth, open highway or a dangerous trail. The important question is not how far the mule has gone; it is the time taken to cover a distance. People traveling by automobile more frequently count by time elapsed than by miles. Twenty years ago, it took thirteen to fifteen hours to go by car from Mexico City to Acapulco; on the fast highways of today, the same journey has been cut to six hours.

To understand the history of Mexico, distance must be borne in mind always, for it is a history of constant movement through the imposing mountains, frenetically Wagnerian in color and form. A visit to the spot called the Paso de Cortés, several thousand feet above the Valley of Mexico, entails a climb by automobile along a road between Ixtacihuatl and Popocatepetl, the twin volcanic peaks that dominate the city. A look downward from the Paso reveals a superb vista. If the present-day sightseer knows his history, he remembers that Cortés and his 500 men reached this spot only after weeks and weeks of forced marches, first through jungle, then through the cold of the high plateau. Far below them, they could see the immense lake-dotted Valley of Mexico, where the limitless Aztec armies were waiting for them. How did they have the courage to refuse to turn back?

How did they make the difficult descent to the valley and immediately enter into battle?

A knowledge of history also strains the imagination of a visitor to the ranges and deserts of Chihuahua, where hamlets lie far apart and only two small towns break the 200-mile expanse between Chihuahua and the American border. History tells us that during the Revolution, the ragged, barefoot followers of Pancho Villa ranged those featureless plains under the broiling sun, mounted on worn-out horses loaded with weapons and booty, slept through the freezing nights beside their camp-following women and children—yet, they had stamina left to sing and fight.

A trip from Mexico City to Guadalajara, thence to Monterrey, and from there to the Pacific coast would follow the itinerary of Benito Juárez in his incredible peregrinations for his country. Today, automobiles roll along asphalt highways, perhaps pausing overnight at one of the roadside hotels. Juárez traced the same route over and over, riding in a hooded black berlin, imprisoned in a tight jacket and stiff collar, and even managed to work on his papers and write letters as he tried to collect the men he needed for armies that would overthrow the empire of Maximilian.

Geography in Mexico seems to be the implacable enemy of history. Those distances, that overpowering and oppressive heat all through the countryside, the sense of being small and lonely that such a landscape evokes, might make it seem as if nothing ought to have happened, that people must have had to vegetate, helpless to rise above geography. But not so. The people made history and made it with a tenacity and intensity as astounding as the stage on which their saga was enacted. The Mexican horn of plenty is almost empty of wealth, yes; but not of events. And perhaps the explanation of how the Mexicans have been building a nation for centuries out of that string of isolated and unlike enclaves, separated by so many broad zones without life, lies in that very overflowing abundance of event.

No wonder, then, that diversity should be the norm, that the *outré* should predominate over the uniform. There is more than one Mexico. Its history can never be spoken of in the singular. Before and during the colonial period, oppression and servitude were not single; they were several. Similarly, there was not one independence, one reform, one revolution; instead, we must speak of independences, reforms, revolutions—if we wish to understand why today we are coming closer to the possibility of speaking of Mexico in the singular.

2 · Repeated Servitudes

THE FRENCH CANNOT REMEMBER the Gauls, nor do Spaniards keep constantly in mind that among their forebears there were Iberians, Goths, Celts, Greeks, Jews, Arabs, and Romans. But in Mexico, the peoples who inhabited certain sections of the country before the arrival of the Spaniards—the Aztecs, the Maya, the Toltecs—are ever-present, even though the remnants of their ancient civilizations must be sought in museums or wherever their pyramids have been left standing.

Although no racial segregation exists in Mexico and no door is closed to anyone because his skin is dark, the Mexicans are very race conscious. They do not care to be reminded of it, but some of them reveal their feeling in the hallowed phrase: "My grandfather was Spanish, too." Others express it in a steadfast veneration of everything indigenous: women, by wearing the dress of the people, such as the *rebozo* (shawl) and the *huipil* (an embroidered and lace-trimmed jacket or cape), forgetting that the garments are actually of colonial origin; men, by hanging on the walls of their homes clay idols for which they paid a good price but which they pretend to have stumbled upon. Whether or not they know it, carbon-14 would show up such items as bogus. Nevertheless, there are descendants of the prerevolutionary aristocrats who scorn the indigenous and sing the praises of Spaniards and Americans. To be sure, almost all the titles bestowed on their ancestors were created during the nineteenth century by the Spanish queen Isabel II, who became involved in several long drawn-out civil wars. The queen handed out patents of nobility to those who donated money for the purchase of arms. The pope also conferred titles on some owners of silver mines and on the immensely wealthy ranchers who bolstered the Vatican's finances with their remittances after the triumph of Garibaldi. In short, the people with titles are still yearning for the caste society of the days when Porfirio Díaz ruled, and they never fail to point out that President Benito Juárez, a pure-blooded Indian from the south, married off his daughters to Spaniards.

In one way or another, all these actions and reactions form a part of the customs of the country, which anyone living there will discover, somewhat to his astonishment, but which the tourist can seldom perceive.

The man who stands at the foot of the pyramids of Teotihuacán, near Mexico City, offering clay figurines for sale with the assurance that they are Aztec (though in fact he made them and buried them for several months to give them a patina), is the counterpart of the Indian of eight or nine centuries ago who attended religious ceremonies where the vendor stands. The Spanish spoken by Mexicans still retains many words that the conquistadors heard from the lips of the Aztecs of Tenochtitlán. The survival of pre-Hispanic Mexico is evident not only in place names or museums. All Mexicans keep it alive in their minds. The intellectuals build interpretations of the country and of its psychology upon it. Housewives base their behavior toward their servants upon it. Anthropologists, who collaborate with engineers on the massive public-works projects, take it into account wherever they have to displace groups of the population in order to

build a dam, or whenever they plan a highway to connect hitherto isolated regions with the cities. Artists and architects consider themselves in some degree the successors of the men who
constructed the pyramids and painted those red, ochre, and black
frescoes on their walls.

It matters little whether these survivals are real or imaginary.
What does matter is that the Mexicans consider them real and
decisive factors in their personality. He who wishes to offend a
Mexican need only belittle the indigenous contribution to his
history. A Mexican will be openly indignant if the Indians in his
ancestry are criticized, whereas he may greet with indifference
an attack on the Spaniards among his forebears. He will be an-
noyed, too, if the word "Indian" is used instead of the acceptable
indigena. To him, Indians are people who live in Asia, and the
very idea that his forefathers could be related to the Asians is
very displeasing, though he will never say so. On the other hand,
a statement that a similarity can be traced between the Mayan or
Aztec ruins and Egyptian, Babylonian, or Hellenic remains will
evoke a cordial response (outside anthropological or archaeological circles). The theory that Atlantis joined Mexico to the
Old World and that the first "Mexicans" came from the banks
of the Euphrates always rings pleasingly in Mexican ears. I sus-
pect that the Mexicans would be disposed even to accept the idea
that their first ancestors came from the banks of the Indus or the
Ganges if it could be proved that they came by way of the
Mediterranean and across the Atlantic, but not through the Bering
Straits or from Polynesia.

In all of Mexico there is not a single monument to Hernán
Cortés, the Spaniard who conquered Tenochtitlán and laid the
foundations of modern Mexico, the Mexico born of the union of
the indigenous people and the Spaniards. But the vivid presence
of the past shows up in unexpected ways. For example, in 1951,
Eulalia Guzmán, an archaeologist, announced that she had discovered the remains of Cuauhtémoc, the last Aztec emperor, beneath
the altar of the church of Ixcateopan, a small village near the
Pacific coast. Cuauhtémoc, the successor to Moctezuma, had been
captured by the Spaniards and carried off to Honduras, never to
be seen again. As soon as Eulalia Guzmán announced her find, a

veritable battle was fought over the alleged bones of the lost emperor—not a scientific battle, a political battle. Communists, extreme nationalists, and the entire Left vowed that the bones were
authentic; the Right (pro-Spanish in Mexico) maintained they
were fraudulent. In the end, the secretary of education ruled that
a group of responsible archaeologists were to study the question.
When they concluded that the authenticity of the bones could
not be confirmed, they were immediately denounced as "reactionaries," "tools of imperialism," "Malinchists." Journalists-turned-
detectives traced clues in stones and bones to fill hundreds of
newspaper columns; dozens of books on the subject came off the
press. Demonstrations were held and the poor skeptical scientists
were threatened. A pro-Communist candidate for the presidency
went to Ixcateopan to swear on the alleged remains of the last
Aztec emperor his fealty to the anti-imperialist struggle, in defiance of the truth that the Aztecs themselves were an imperialistic
and dominating people.

That purely Mexican adjective "Malinchist," flung at the
archaeologists, is revealing. Malinche was the given name of a
native princess by whom Hernán Cortés had a son. Her people
were engaged in constant warfare against the Aztecs, who had
set out to conquer them and force them into slavery. Malinche's
people quickly joined the newly arrived Spaniards in an alliance
that would help them to continue their struggle against the
Aztecs. Yet the Mexicans of today regard those victims of Aztec
aggression as traitors to their country, and they look upon
Malinche (or Doña Marina, as the Spaniards, ever respectful of
titles, even Indian titles, called her) much as the French and the
Dutch regarded the village girls who fraternized with German
soldiers during World War II. Anyone who adopts a position not
strictly nationalistic is labeled a "Malinchist" and lumped with
those who can see some merit in foreign things or who appreciate
the foreign more than the Mexican. This type of snobbery
abounds and is branded with the abhorred name of the Indian
princess. Yet in a manner of speaking, Malinche is the key figure
in all Mexican interpretations of "the Mexican."

But first it might be well to become acquainted with the plain facts of the origin of today's Mexican, so preoccupied with interpreting himself.

Each time an archaeological discovery is made, each time some scholar declares that an artifact dates back ten, fifteen, or twenty centuries, the press treats the news as a matter as important as politics or sports. Mexicans are always pleased to learn that the age of their country's ancestors has moved another step backward in time. But whatever the experts and carbon-14 may have to say on the subject, nothing certain is known about the period in which the first people settled in what is now Mexico. It is believed that there were tribes already in Middle America twenty centuries before Christ, and that they did not begin to develop an autochthonous culture until about the second century A.D.

The ancients of America made great progress in mathematics and astronomy; they worked out an accurate calendar. But none of the peoples made use of the wheel, even though they knew of it (for clay toys with wheels have been found). They had no beasts of burden. The basis of their diet was corn and the flesh of dogs and barnyard fowl—the Thanksgiving turkey comes from Mexico, where it goes by the Nahuatl name of *guajalote*. People moved about a great deal; it is known that traders traveled from Teotihuacán, near the site of Mexico City, to Yucatán and what is now Guatemala. Each nation, tribe, or group lived on a small stretch of land and developed its own culture with its own characteristics. Of these cultures some archaeological ruins remain, together with traces of a literature preserved in hieroglyphic codices and in whatever the Spanish chroniclers collected from the Indians by word of mouth.

Some of those early peoples lived in clusters around ceremonial nuclei. For example, Monte Albán, in present-day Oaxaca, was the sacred center of the Zapotecs. Other groups gathered in cities of as many as 50,000 inhabitants. Teotihuacán was such a city, with temples, palaces, and even a sewage system. All those cultures vanished, probably because of exhaustion of the soil, invasion by other peoples, and internal dissension. We know that popular uprisings occurred among the Maya in the south and that the nobles were expelled from the cities during one upheaval. Some of the temples discovered in the jungle were supposed to have been built by the exiled noblemen. By the twelfth century, Teotihuacán seems to have disappeared. Invaders destroyed Tula; most of the Mayan cities in Yucatán, Guatemala, and northern Honduras had been abandoned by the fifteenth century, before the arrival of the Spaniards. The conquistadors found only one well-organized nation, the Aztec, firmly installed in Tenochtitlán, which was then a string of islands in a lagoon, now the spot on which Mexico City stands. All around the Aztec capital, and even in remote valleys on the high plateau, other less organized people had been forced to submit to Aztec rule.

The Aztecs had come from the north. According to legend, they moved southward in search of a place to settle promised them by an oracle. They would recognize the spot when they came to it because it would be marked by a three-branched bayonet cactus crowned with two open blossoms. A royal eagle would be perched on the cactus, holding a captive serpent in its claws. These three symbols, the eagle, the serpent, and the bayonet cactus, appear on Mexico's great shield today. The Aztecs named that spot Tenochtitlán, meaning "cactus upon a rock."

The Aztecs were strongly influenced by the Toltecs, who enjoyed a greatly superior culture. Once the migrants had settled in Tenochtitlán, they were ruled by a Toltec nobleman, their first king. This king fathered a large family by Aztec women, and their children became the nucleus of the first aristocracy among the now sedentary Aztecs. The *pipitlin*, or noble class, were permitted to own land; they were given an education and held the offices of command; the king could be chosen only from among them. The *macehualtin* composed the mass of the population, grouped into clans not by blood relationship but by geography for the purpose of cultivating the land in common or of working at their handicrafts. They were given some education, of the type we call technical nowadays, to train them for husbandry or warfare. Among them lived the *mayeque*, who worked the land as serfs, and the slaves. There was little distinction between serf and slave.

The religious beliefs of the Toltecs, which the Aztecs adopted, became in the end a mystical exaltation of war. Their gods were numerous, but to the *tlamatinimes*, who were theologians rather than priests, there was only a single deity manifest under different names. The people, however, worshiped clearly differentiated gods, each with a marked identity, and it was this popular creed that led the Spaniards to conclude the Aztecs were pantheists. Originally the Aztecs had one god, Huitzilopochtli, but they later surrounded him with a lower hierarchy of Toltec gods. One of these Toltec gods was of particular interest to the Spaniards. He was Quetzalcoatl, who embodied the legend of a white god who was to come to them from the east—a messiah, so to speak.

From 1428 to 1440, the Aztecs were ruled by Itzcoatl, an energetic emperor who enlarged his state, terrorized his neighbors, the monarchs of Tlacopán and Texcoco, and formed with them a triple alliance. (The king of Texcoco was a poet named Netzahualcoyotl, some of whose poems have survived.) Itzcoatl then ordered his scribes to write a new history of the Aztecs, according to which the Aztecs were descended from the Toltec nobility, and Quetzalcoatl and Huitzilopochtli were gods of equal rank. The Aztecs, the "Sun People," were destined to conquer other nations in order to provide the sun with human sacrificial victims, upon whom it fed. Some monarchs, less dynamic than Itzcoatl, arranged matters so as to obtain victims for sacrifice by imposing agreements upon nearby subjected peoples: in exchange for ostensible independence, they acquired the right to help themselves to captives taken in so-called "flower wars" (mock wars), where killing was not allowed but seizure of prisoners was, and these captives were sacrificed on the altars of the dominant nation. The Otomis, descendants of those conquered people, are still living wretched lives, handicapped by their long submission.

The question of human sacrifice in ancient Mexico has been the subject of many a debate. Chroniclers and historians maintain that the Aztecs offered human beings on their altars and practiced a ritualistic and religious cannibalism. Some more nationalistic archaeologists and historians consider such statements an insult to Mexico, and they have tried hard to prove that there was no practice of ritualistic cannibalism, though they grant that there was human sacrifice. We shall come across such emotional reactions to the past quite frequently in Mexico.

In any case, it is clear that the Aztecs, in their own way, were as religious as the Spanish Catholics who were soon to conquer them. It might almost be said that everything in Aztec life pertained to their religion. And the human sacrifices can be explained only "in the context of a community in which the aspiration to transcendency covered over a reality that is difficult to conceive in an epoch like ours, which idolizes the mundane."*

Not only in their religion, but in everything else, the Aztecs—as the Romans—tended to be syncretistic, that is, they attempted to harmonize different and even opposing tenets and systems. (They had their Greeks, too, in the Toltecs.) A number of their skills and practices were borrowings from their neighbors: the wearing of featherwork as adornment, a fashion that became the *raison d'être* of an active handicraft; the wearing of amber, as the Maya had done in times past; the adoption of the bright-colored cotton of the Totonacs for clothing; the gold jewelry of the Mixtecs, for glitter; the Huastecs' goddess of love; and the festival in honor of the planet Venus held every eight years by the Mazatecs.

The Aztecs ruled an empire stretching from the Pacific to the Gulf, from the high central plateau as far south as Guatemala. Some 2 million people who spoke different languages and belonged to other nations were living under Aztec domination. Nowadays, this would be called an imperialistic and colonialist state.

With the empire came trade. Merchants began to acquire an importance comparable to that of the nobles and priests. No longer was the thrift of the early period of settlement practiced, no matter how hard the sumptuary laws strove to preserve it. Frugality was for the common people—especially for the peasant, who had neither cape nor feathers, who covered his nakedness with a simple, pajama-like pair of short trousers, lived on corn, and dwelt among his family, knowing nothing beyond his horizon and practicing the monogamy which his economic situation made necessary. The codices and the chronicles make no mention of that peasant, yet he was the only member of Aztec society to survive. The Spaniards did not need the nobles, the

* Laurette Sejourne, *El universo de Quetzalcoatl* (Mexico City, 1962).

priests, or the traders, but they needed the peasants. Possibly the deep differences between the United States and Latin America can be explained largely by that need for the peasant.

At the moment of the Spaniards' arrival, Aztec society was in a state of crisis. Its technical development would permit no further territorial expansion, but the subject peoples were restive over the high tributes they had to pay; the ruling class had lost its driving force. This situation, as much as the people's wonder at the strange horses and their belief that the white strangers from the east might be Quetzalcoatl and his hosts, help to explain the ease with which the Spaniards conquered the Aztec Empire. The conquistadors were aided, too, by the Aztecs' fantastic failure to realize how few conquistadors—only 555 men and sixteen horses —stepped ashore on April 21, 1519, on the beach where Veracruz now stands. The conquered people have left some codices describing their impression of these Spaniards. This is how they saw the strange cavalcade:

> The "deer" advanced, bearing the soldiers on their backs. The soldiers were wearing cotton tabards and were holding leather shields and iron lances in their hands, but their swords were hanging from the necks of their "deer." These "deer" were hung with little bells, many little bells. When the "deer" ran, the little bells made a long noise that vibrates and echoes.
>
> Those "deer" bellow and neigh. They sweat mightily and the sweat rolls off their bodies in streams. The foam from their muzzles falls on the ground like the foamy *amole* [a vegetable soap]. When they run they make a loud noise. From their detonations, it seems then as if stones were falling on the earth. Later, the soil is pitted and scarred wherever they have placed their hoofs. The earth is opened when their hoofs touch it.

At the end of two years, after twice laying siege to Tenochtit-lán, the conquistadors had vanquished the Aztec Empire. Their allies, the Tlascaltecs people, had helped them, but they unhesitatingly used every stratagem to achieve their ends. They laid traps, they tortured Moctezuma and finally murdered him. And Cortés also counted on the terrifying effect of gunpowder: when he embarked surreptitiously on his expedition, against the will of

Governor Diego Velázquez of Cuba, he took with him the newly invented harquebuses, which were completely unknown to the Aztecs.

The conquistadors destroyed everything that might retain even the memory of the Aztecs' religious life. They built their own churches on the ruins of the pyramids and temples. They burned all the codices they could lay hands on. (Fortunately, some of the monks transcribed them beforehand, and, thanks to them, some have survived.) This destruction of everything that bore any relation to the religious life of the Aztecs is in itself a clue to the deep impression it made on the Spaniards. The great intensity of their destructiveness was not simply directed to wiping out superstition and idolatry; it was a strong effort to erase a way of seeing and experiencing life that was much more deeply religious than their own, a road to inner perfection followed by the people as a whole under the aegis of the state. Perhaps it was that very quality of something guided and oriented, so remote from their own religious concepts and mental habits, which frightened the Spaniards, that absence of individual salvation, that submersion of the individual in the collective. Worse than simple superstition, worse than idolatry to them was the spectacle of an entire people dedicated to the salvation of a common, collective soul, instead of the individual effort by each man to save his own soul. In the eyes of a Catholic, especially a Spanish Catholic, that collective soul must have seemed downright diabolical, perhaps the embodiment of the Devil himself.

Virtually nothing was left of Aztec civilization after the conquest. Little by little, the people forgot their Nahuatl language. Today there are some indigenous groups who speak their own languages, but doubtless they are greatly modified from the tongue spoken when the Spaniards came. The idols were destroyed; the priests had escaped or were dead; the new religion was imposed, often by terror, often simply because it filled a vacuum left by the disappearance of the old religion. In any case, Catholicism was incomprehensible to a people unaccustomed to thinking in terms of *you* and *me*, of individual man, who thought rather in terms of *us*, of the collective being. Yet as soon as the Aztec people found themselves without the priests who administered their faith, they lost their religion, and their creed became little more than a superstition. And if their religion was an attribute of the collective soul, that, too, vanished—fragmented by the conquest. But the evangelical monks who baptized the people adapted the ritual and symbols of Catholicism to the prevailing practices of the Aztecs. Virgins and saints were substituted for familiar gods and goddesses. Even today, in villages close to the capital, I have seen Indians venerating images of a village patron saint in preference to an image of Christ. Their old men hold the key to the chapel where the chosen image is kept, and they will not permit a priest to have anything to do with it. Not uncommonly, if such an image is broken, pre-Cortesian relics are found hidden in its base. Today, workmen building new roads may collect a bountiful store of such idols, which are the delight of antiquarians. They are found most commonly underneath wayside and boundary crucifixes. In the stones of the pedestals, workmen find clay figurines from the time of the conquest, hidden there by the Indians (who always knelt and crossed themselves before wayside stations).

In 1964, a magnificent anthropological museum, one of the best of its kind in the world because of its boldness and beauty, was being built in Mexico City. It was decided to set up in the museum garden a huge monolith more than sixty feet high, sculptured in the form of Tlaloc, the god of rain. The stone image had been found in a village not far from the city. But the citizens of the village refused to let their god be taken away. Before they would consent to give up Tlaloc, they must have a well built for them and, as an additional bribe, a school. Not that the god mattered so much to them; they wanted to be sure of having water. Whether technology or the god provided it, they did not care.

When Tlaloc finally arrived in Mexico City, laid out on a special truck and buttressed by hundreds of rubber tires, he crossed the streets by night. Thousands of people were there to see him—standing in a torrential rain. It rained very hard that night, even though it was not the rainy season. People joked about the coincidence, but later, as Tlaloc was being set in place in the museum garden, rain poured down each time he was moved, and the Mexicans began to feel an astonishment not far from superstitious awe, a response they only partly concealed beneath jokes.

Hand in hand with the early mingling of Indian and white blood, as Cortés and his soldiers fathered children by native women of high and low lineage, a cultural blending took place. The beliefs of Indians and Spaniards met and mixed, and their languages also commingled. Spanish quickly combined with Nahuatl and other local languages and ultimately displaced them after absorbing many of their expressions and words. This absorption and eventual disappearance of the native languages is a phenomenon rarely found in history. No colonial empire save the Roman and the Spanish has succeeded in erasing the language of the colonized people. The English in India, the French in North Africa or Indochina imposed their language as an official and cultural medium, but the native languages survived and most of the people continued to speak them. In Mexico, however, promptly renamed New Spain, and in all those southern reaches of America which the Spaniards conquered, Spanish became the spoken language; local languages fell into disuse and survived only in remote regions. Today, Spanish is not merely the official language, as English is in India; it is the *native language* of Mexicans and other Spanish-Americans. Some people explain this by the theory that the Nahuatl language was more difficult to transmit than Spanish, owing to its use of hieroglyphics. Another theory is that more primitive languages are always replaced by more complex ones. But none of these explanations holds true elsewhere: languages with a system of writing more complicated than Latin, or a structure more complex, persisted within the Roman empire. Even the intermingling of the races fails to explain the phenomenon, for Spanish was widely spoken among great masses of pure Indian peoples living out of contact with the white men. Perhaps the explanation must be sought in the absolutist character of the Spaniards themselves and in the work of the missionaries who settled all over the country, teaching Spanish as they taught doctrine.

For several generations, the Spaniards managed to convince themselves that they were making as much headway in changing the culture and way of life among the conquered as they had with language. They failed to realize that they were replacing the native with the Spanish only minimally. Instead, a new culture was arising from the fusion of both, an interaction made the more effective by the blending of the indigenous people with the Spaniards.

For reasons never fully explained, the crossbreeding of Indians with Spaniards in "New Spain"—generally between Indian women and men from Extremadura and Andalusia—occurred more rapidly and intensively than elsewhere in the Western Hemisphere. Perhaps in Peru it happened almost as rapidly. These facts would indicate that the mingling of the races happened more quickly in countries where the Spaniards found a people habituated to a coherent and complex social life, and more slowly and less frequently where the Indians still were living on a tribal level. In such places, time was needed for the Indian masses to adapt themselves to the society imposed by the Spaniards. The colonial period was far advanced by the time this adaptation was made; consequently, as the hour of independence struck, the commingling in the backward areas was less advanced than in Peru or Mexico.

The fact that the Mexican is a mestizo is very important, as we shall see later. Not only does it determine the individual's psychology, it shapes the collective mind as well. One way (among many) of characterizing Mexico's history would be to say that it is a record of the social rise of the mestizo and his march toward political power. That, however, would be an oversimplification. In any case, Mexico demonstrates clearly to what point crossbreeding—or miscegenation, to use the word common in the southern United States—is favorable to national development, perhaps because of the very social and psychological hazards inherent in it, which act as a challenge, thus stirring up attitudes essential to progress.

None of these developments could be foreseen by Cortés as he moved into his palace, built with great haste in Coyoacán, now a residential section of Mexico City. But because he knew his own people and because he himself was an archetypal Spaniard, he no doubt could foresee that he would be confronted with every kind of rivalry and intrigue. Indeed, one denunciation of him followed another, all addressed to the court at Valladolid. In 1529, the king appointed Antonio de Mendoza the first viceroy of New Spain, and with his arrival in 1535, the period of adventure ended. The country became institutionalized; life was harnessed to routine. Thereafter, in the course of three centuries and sixty-one viceroyalties, nothing spectacular marked the history of the colony.

Nothing, certainly, to compare with the voyages preceding the arrival of Cortés, when Hernández de Córdoba discovered Yucatán and Juan de Grijalva landed on the shore he named Veracruz. Nothing to compare, either, with the fantastic history of two other Spaniards, the soldier Gonzalo Guerrero and the priest Jerónimo de Aguilar, who arrived in Yucatán after being shipwrecked in 1512, were captured by the Indians and forced into slavery, but bowed to local customs by marrying Indian maidens. Guerrero helped his captors to repulse Hernández de Córdoba at Yucatán, while Aguilar refused to leave with his fellow-countrymen (though he kept his breviary), choosing to stay with the descendants of the ancient Maya.

Nevertheless, Aguilar joined Cortés when the conquistador disembarked at Tabasco, though Guerrero still remained with the Indians. (One of the local chiefs gave Malinche to Cortés at about that time.) Aguilar served Cortés' expedition as interpreter from then on, although Cortés had brought with him two bilingual Indians captured by Hernández de Córdoba several years earlier.

Nothing in the three centuries of the colony could compare even remotely with the real *folie de grandeur* that inspired the conquest. Indeed, each man had his own delusions of grandeur, so that Cortés had to be constantly on guard against supporters of Cuba's Governor Velázquez among his own men. One of his reasons for burning his ships in Veracruz was to deprive the dissidents of any way of returning to Cuba.

The mind boggles at the thought of his tiny troop of Spaniards, some on horseback, buckled into their armor, grimy and filthy beneath their heavy clothing, toiling ahead through the tropical heat, constantly assailed by mosquitoes and innumerable strange pests, at times under attack by large Indian armies, in-

cessantly on the alert—even against strange foods that tasted
bland and cloying or were heavily perfumed like some of the
tropical fruits. Ever and always they were distrustful of one
another, wonderstruck at what they were seeing and experiencing, yet not so overawed that they were unable to appreciate
the beauty of the Indian women or the courage of the Indian
men. They scaled towering mountains where every breath came
hard; gazed down into impressive valleys, wound their way
through cathedral-like forests, took part in strange festivals and
banquets at the invitation of important hosts who treated them
ceremoniously. They were impatient to get their hands on gold
and to convert the pagans to the true faith, yet they left behind
them at likely spots a handful of soldiers and a few craftsmen to
found a city—a city of twenty or thirty men surrounded by
jungle and people who were an eternal enigma.

Cortés had the good luck to be met by Moctezuma, a credu-
lous, tired emperor who tried to persuade the Spaniards to leave
willingly in return for gifts of great riches. But Cortés installed
himself in the Aztec city and set out to seize power, little by
little, through the use of guile. He was a scion of Extremadura,
where men are tempered early by a hard life, and he showed
stamina as well as extraordinary political and diplomatic acumen
in the coming months—attracting to himself groups of natives
who were enemies of the Aztecs and, at the same time, keeping up
the hopes of the Aztecs through his negotiations with them. Several times he was defeated, but in the end he triumphed, partly
because he liked to attack by surprise. Soon, a captain of the
Aztec army mutinied against Moctezuma, attacked the Spaniards,
and drove them from the city on the night of June 30, 1520,
called Noche Triste. But the Spaniards rallied quickly and with
their allies defeated the Aztecs, laid siege to Tenochtitlán and,
after two months, captured Cuauhtémoc, who had become emperor, and the city surrendered. Cortés did not execute Cuauhtémoc right away, for he knew that he must establish a new country, and he was hoping for his collaboration.

Perhaps the conquest of Mexico stands apart from the conquest
of any other part of the hemisphere because it was accomplished
by Spaniards and Indians *together* and because, from the begin-

ning, both sides behaved, no doubt unconsciously, as if they were bound to go on collaborating in the future. Which they did. For all that the Indians were subjugated and oppressed, they never ceased to play an active role in colonial life. Their advice was frequently sought and their wishes were considered. It is worth remembering that the Spaniards did not automatically consider the Indians an enslaved, base people, and they did not treat them as such. Instead, the conquerors grafted onto the prevailing indigenous society the concepts that ruled Spanish society. Accordingly, princes were treated like princes and were granted Spanish titles of nobility. To the Spaniard, moreover, the Indian was not inferior, only different. If the questions of whether the Indians were human beings and whether they possessed souls and must therefore be converted were moot in the minds of the theologians, for the rough conquistadors there was never any doubt but that the Indians were real men, capable of fighting shoulder to shoulder with them or breast to breast against them. Neither did they doubt that their women were real women, tireless, loyal, and prolific. The Spaniards never hesitated to exploit the Indians, and they exploited them implacably, but they never denied them their humanity. As in the society from which they had come, they accepted the consequences of behaving harshly, for being oppressors of other men, and they did not excuse themselves on the grounds that they were exploiting inferior beings.

All this gave the subjugation of the indigenous masses some very peculiar facets, because it established contradictory relationships between the Indians and the Spaniards. The priest, who was spreading the Gospel, teaching, and befriending the Indian, was a "Spaniard" rather than a "white man," and no one ever spoke or thought in terms of skin color; actually many Andalusians were very dark. Fr. Bartolomé de las Casas, a former soldier who took holy orders and became the most aggressive defender of the Indians against the authorities of Mexico and Spain alike, was all Spaniard in his tireless and obsessive campaigning, which led him finally to propose that Indian labor should be eased by importing Negro slaves. He hoped that the crown in so doing would manumit the indigenous people, yet do no harm to the Spaniards who needed their labor. Equally Spanish was the *encomendero*, who was granted a certain number of Indians as a labor force to work his lands, who quickly forgot that these people were "commended" to him, as the law put it, for his protection and their instruction, and who worked them like slaves and treated them as such. Spanish, too, was the artisan who was never able to rise above mediocrity, who almost always lived surrounded by Indians and with an Indian woman by whom he had children. And Spanish the great lord who bitterly opposed the New Ordinances promulgated by the Spanish king in 1542–43 to safeguard the Indians, who refused to apply them, and who used instead a formula which later served colonialists all over the world: "We respect it, but we don't comply."

The Spaniard, then, was father to many people in the literal meaning of the word and to almost everyone in the figurative sense. At the same time he was the enemy, the oppressor, the stranger. This ambivalent role lasted many years. Independence was won to the cry of "Out with the Gachupines!" (meaning the Spaniards), but the Gachupines were still living in the country a century later, owning lands and dominating commerce, with no one to say them nay.

The Church was another Janus to the Indian. One side of it destroyed his temples, persecuted his priests, and imposed new creeds; the other defended him against the rapacity of the *encomendero*, taught him to read and write, recognized him as a spiritual equal (though not a social one), and even salvaged whatever now remains of his culture. One of its most distinguished priests, Fr. Bernardino de Sahagún, only a few years after the conquest dedicated his time to copying codices and to reconstructing pre-Cortesian history, thus defying an interdict from Spain forbidding such work, which was considered subversive.

Spain passed on to the colony her administrative forms, her well-staffed bureaucracy, crown control of commerce, the use of iron and other metals, the wheel, domestic animals, and the plow. In return, New Spain gave the motherland enough gold and silver to make her wealthy. In the eighteenth century, a third of all the silver in the world came from the workings in Guanajuato. One man, Count de Regla, took out of his mines in Pachuca 500 million pesos; he was rich enough to be able to offer Charles III two warships and a credit of 1 million pesos that was never repaid. José de la Borda acquired an enormous fortune from his mines in Taxco, where he built the cathedral at the same time that he laid out extensive and very beautiful gardens in Cuernavaca for his own enjoyment. From 1537 to 1914, Mexican mines exported 90,000 tons of silver.

Yet the gold and silver from the Indies did little for Spain except to weigh down the country. By the end of the Austrian dynasty (1504–1700) and during the entire rule of the Bourbons (1700–1931), except for the short period of enlightened despotism under Charles III—the country's only enlightened monarch— Spanish decadence could be traced to the flood of precious metals from America. Abundant gold and silver enabled the court to finance one war after another in Europe, and it taught the *hidalgos* to scorn manual labor. In the final reckoning, Spain lost by her conquest of America and, simultaneously, by the loss of her best minds with the expulsion of the Jews and the Moors by the Catholic monarchs.

Momentarily, however, Spain gained, particularly from the efforts of those who went to the Indies to hold office or to get rich. As time went by, many who had planned to stay only a few years settled in New Spain. They built cities, established businesses, founded universities. The University of Mexico, opened in 1551, is the oldest institution of higher learning on the continent.

No one can strike a balar ـe between what one country brings to another and what it receives in return. To be sure, wealth can be computed, but its consequences, not always good, and its ultimate price cannot be weighed. One thing is certain: Rome and Spain alone in Western history acted as true agents of civilization. They are not the only empires to give a culture, to teach techniques, to bring progress, but they are the only ones that integrated their colonies into a system that included the mother country to some degree. The Spanish and Roman empires spread their own culture, religion, and language throughout the colonies and, at the time of their withdrawal, left them with the same social organization, the same problems, and at the same stage of culture and advancement as the mother country. Thus the barbarians who invaded Rome, or Gaul, or Iberia, found everywhere the same institutions and organizations. When Spanish rule was broken in the Indies, her colonies were marked by a social and administrative structure and a way of life not fundamentally different from what prevailed in Spain. Indeed, the poor Creoles (Spaniards born in America) and Indians who fought for their independence were not very different from the Spanish peasants and artisans who drove Napoleon from the peninsula; the wealthy Creole leaders of the Mexican armies of independence differed in no way from the Spanish aristocrats and bourgeosie who commanded the armies of the Junta de Cádiz, which for two years held out against the French siege of 1810. This is not to imply, however, that the society of New Spain was ideal—far, far from it. Exploitation, tyranny, and injustice reigned there, more or less of the same kind and to the same degree as in Spain.

In fact, the people of the Indies enjoyed certain guarantees which the Spaniards lacked, for example, the legislation promulgated in Seville at the behest of the Council of the Indies subjected the colonies to a commercial monopoly, but it also embodied a complicated system for safeguarding the Indians— seldom applied, to be sure. Furthermore, before the Spanish functionaries in the Indies could leave office, they had to submit to a *juicio de residencia* (formal review) in the course of which complaints, charges, and denunciations concerning their term in office were heard. The trial was neither a matter of form nor a parody. On several occasions a captain general, a justice, even a viceroy ended his days in prison as a result of the evidence presented in the formal review.

Authorities in New Spain and throughout Spanish America could never be unaware that they were on a short rein held by the people. Popular rebellions were not at all uncommon. An official never knew at what moment Spaniards might gather in front of the viceroyal palace to vent their anger at some attempt to limit the power of the *encomiendas*—the institution that assigned specific native towns to colonists, who then extracted tribute and service from the inhabitants—by legislation protecting the Indians. Conversely, the Indians and poor Creoles often mutinied in protest against food scarcities and high prices. The Indians who were forced to work in the mines rebelled too, against maltreatment and miserable conditions. The Negroes on the coast, the only place in Mexico where they were numerous, escaped from their masters, fled to the mountains, and attempted to form an independent kingdom. A group of distinguished Creoles conspired to proclaim the colony's independence. The ferment of nonconformity was always at work. Spanish rule was often flouted. Even the few Jews defied Spain, though they were in Mexico more or less on sufferance as New Christians, for the immigration of Jews as Jews was forbidden. A few families of New Christians settled in Monterrey, the city that is the most important steel center in the country today, and from Monterrey they branched out. One of the group, Luis Carvajal, believed himself especially enlightened in religious matters and defied the Inquisition. He was a mystic who claimed to be a prophet; his religious harangues frequently contained warnings against the ill-treatment of the Indians. He was found guilty of heresy and was burned at the stake in front of the Cathedral of Mexico City.

Later, in the second half of the eighteenth century, the French Encyclopedists strongly influenced the people of New Spain, particularly the young clergy, who constituted the most cultivated portion of the society. But the French *philosophes* inspired their followers to establish an enlightened society, rather than to free the Indians.

Rebellion was an old tradition in New Spain, beginning with the conqueror Cortés himself, who disobeyed his governor. Later, Cortés had to quell rebellion among his own men: first, after the mutiny of Cristóbal de Olid in Central America; and then, when his few subjects in the capital hanged the governor he had left in charge while he pursued his conquests in Honduras. After the death of Cortés, his son, Martín Cortés, a great landholder in Oaxaca with the title of the Marquis del Valle, conspired with other aristocrats to expel the viceroy who was attempting to enforce the New Ordinances protecting the Indians. Martín Cortés was arrested and imprisoned. Indian uprisings, often abortive, inspired Fr. Bartolomé de Las Casas to champion their cause. Two later viceroys, Marquis de Mancera and Fr. Payo Henriquez de Rivera, forbade corporal punishment of the Indians and Negroes who had taken part in local mutinies. As a rule, the Indians were considered submissive and resigned. This was true after independence, but in the colonial period Indians protested frequently, perhaps because they felt then that they had been given some guarantees and that there was someone to whom they could turn in search of justice, either the king or his representatives. (After independence, however, the president of the republic proved to be more distant and indifferent than the monarch had been in far-off Valladolid or Madrid.) The first important Indian insurrection, as far as we know, was that of the Tepic miners, in 1598. Again, in 1680, the Indians of Tehuantepec rebelled and for eight years controlled a large part of the lands in the Isthmus. And in 1692, when the Spaniards mutinied after a poor harvest had brought famine to the capital, one Indian lost his life in the fighting, and Indians burned the city hall when their efforts to bring the guilty man to justice were rejected. In 1761, the descendants of the Maya in Yucatán, led by Jacinto Cano, rose in armed rebellion against excessive tributes. They also demanded that their owners be denied the right to flog them. The protest was crushed, and in reprisal eight Indians were drawn and quartered. As late as 1801, the Indians of Tepic again rebelled, under the leadership of Mariano.

If the Indian mutinied against taxes and ill-treatment rather than against his condition of servitude, the Negro rose up against his condition as slave. Unlike the Indians, the Negroes could not hope for the king's protection. They felt they had to protect themselves against a return to slavery by organizing a kingdom of their own and making a bid for power. The best-known Negro uprising occurred during the eighteenth century, near Orizaba. It was led by Yangas with such success that the rebels were given their freedom and were permitted to found a village called San Lorenzo de los Negros, under their own rule.

The Creoles were not the sort to be controlled easily either. Their fathers had brought with them from Spain the custom of governing their own municipalities through town councils. In seventeenth-century Spanish America, the people voiced their protests through the *comunero* (common man) movements. The *comuneros* deposed viceroys, altered laws, and even advanced the doctrine of popular sovereignty, as formulated by Fernando

Mompo (or Mompox) in Asunción, Paraguay. "The power of the common man is greater than that of the king himself," he said. This idea was echoed during a demonstration against an unwelcome governor just arrived from Spain. "What does 'Vox populi, vox Dei' mean? Your Mercy may answer whatever way he wishes, but he must know that it means the common man." In 1624, the people in Mexico City mutinied with the intent to put a forcible end to the monopoly on grains held by a friend of the viceroy, which had raised the cost of living to a very high level. A quarter of a century later, Creole resentment against the authorities reached a high pitch, and the state of unrest offered Guillen Lombart, a Frenchman, a chance to turn the popular anger to his advantage. In 1659, he forged documents appointing himself viceroy and attempted to proclaim the independence of New Spain, but the Creoles themselves deserted him as soon as they learned of his deceit, and he was executed soon afterward.

Spain's feat of colonization in America is amazing, in spite of all its shortcomings, in spite of the brutality of the *encomienda* and *repartimiento* systems, which held the natives in virtual serfdom and granted great power to a very few men. The Spaniards started at the bottom, laying out roads (for the Indians, lacking the wheel, also lacked vehicles and needed only footpaths for travel), building bridges, constructing convents and churches, and with every new discovery of gold and silver, opened new mines. The Spaniards plunged into the jungles of the south and founded cities there. They explored the pestilential coasts and founded cities. They penetrated the deserts in the north as far as present-day San Francisco and founded cities along the way. In all these new settlements, one or two families of Spaniards lived surrounded by dozens or hundreds of families of Indians. A handful of monks—four or five—would call the Indians together to learn the catechism and to help them build a fortress-like convent and work the land around it. While the first colonists were doing all these things, they were learning the native languages, teaching Spanish, familiarizing the Indians with Spanish clothing and life in the Spanish manner, partly through sheer dominance, partly through missionary zeal. They established courts and registries that complicated life with all the Byzantine convolutions of Spanish bureaucracy, made the necessary preparations for shipping goods and letters to Spain, penned protests to the Council of the Indies or the Casa de Contratación (Board of Trade). Some even found time to copy codices or write memoirs, like Bernal Díaz del Castillo. This modest soldier compiled his astonishing *True History of the Conquest* in his old age, when he was ailing and filled with nostalgia for his youth; he left a record of his comrades and his leader, Cortés, that has never lost its freshness. Scholars managed to compile grammars in Nahuatl and to draw maps of the country. The name New Spain was no misnomer. The conquistadors and the colonists made every effort to shape their new land into a replica of the one they had left across the sea. They created a New Spain.

But Mexico had her will of the newcomers in the end, for the Spaniards were transformed into Mexicans. To be sure, the change was not immediately visible, for Mexican cities resembled Spanish cities. Even today Taxco, Morelia, and Puebla look like any number of Andalusian or Castilian cities. But other phases of life were different, although household manners and customs, the square, the church, the salons of the viceroyal palaces were like their counterparts in Spain. Strange fruits from strange trees were eaten; priests added native acts and symbols to the mass, to help the Indians identify themselves with the new religion. Private life, too, developed odd touches. Although many Spaniards married Indian women, while others brought their brides from Spain or chose from Creole maidens, in either case, the men responded to the seductions of the girls of the new country, and many a Spaniard headed a secret family in a "little house," as such homes away from home are called in Mexico where the custom still survives.

Work in rural regions was performed by Indians aided by the few animals that had been imported. Naturally, many of the Indians' inherited methods and techniques of farming were retained. Spain is a terraced land, but whether the Spaniards were too impatient for a harvest, or whether the Indians resisted, no successful effort was made to terrace a terrain with few levels of its own. Consequently, the soil suffered erosion and impoverishment at the same time that the number of agricultural workers decreased and those going into the mines increased. Of course, the mines were a general obsession; they yielded the silver and gold which were transported to Veracruz in long mule trains and loaded there for shipment to Seville. (If corsairs should capture the galleon, the cargo would go into the holds of pirate ships.) Along the way, the mule trains lengthened as they were joined by others from Acapulco carrying spices and silks from the Philippines to be shipped from Veracruz to Spain with the gold and silver.

As mines were opened, new cities sprang up. The life of the mining towns was intense, hard, glittering, even magnificent. To-day, many of those communities are ghost towns; they remain as if fixed in the eighteenth century, each with its baroque church, its *nouveau riche* palaces, its narrow winding streets laid out for protection against the sun. Some of the houses have been torn down to retrieve the bits of silver ore that might be found in their brick walls.

In the sixteenth century, Bartolomé de Medina discovered the patio process for removing waste material from silver ore by amalgamating the metal with mercury. This process brought the Mexican mines to a fantastic pitch of productivity because it saved money at the final smelting stage. The method was tried out first in Pachuca in 1557, and five years later, thirty-five reduction plants were in operation. By 1571, a Mexican miner had introduced the process to Peru. The metal was cast almost in the doorway of the smelter, and pesos went to Spain to defray the expenses of the wars in Flanders and Germany. During the eighteenth and nineteenth centuries, a great many circulated in the Orient, where the peso became the common coin of countries and colonies with no coinage of their own.

When Alexander von Humboldt visited New Spain in 1803, he found that the methods used to work the mines were in many ways very advanced, but he saw, too, that many miners clung to obsolete customs, such as using mules to turn the bucket wheels that drained the water from the tunnels.

In the end, however, mining had only a small influence on the economy of New Spain, for most of the silver went straight from the mines to Seville. Except for the thousands of Indians employed in extracting it, no one had much contact with it. Nothing to compare with the colony's contact with bureaucracy—a very Spanish institution. Spain has been always a country with a plethora of laws. Actually, Spain needed the administrative organization because the kind of feudalism that was typical of France and England never took hold in the Iberian Peninsula. Bureaucracy took the place of the administrative ramifications of the fief and the feudal lord. No sooner were the Indies discovered than administrative institutions to deal with their conditions were created: the Council of the Indies, and the Casa de Contratación, which controlled the trade with them. The conquistadors brought their scribes with them; many of the scribes emerged as chroniclers; the missionaries became mayors, notaries, or historians, according to the needs of the moment. And when the royal administration was installed and superimposed on that of the conquistadors, the bureaucracy quickly grew.

The state, the viceroy, the captain general, and the justice of the appellate court had a hand in everything, or so it seemed to the people of Mexico. The economy was controlled in all its fundamental aspects. Tariffs were many and complicated; laws covered a multitude of matters—from treatment to be accorded Indians to ceremonial titles, protocol, and the order or precedence among the various categories of government employees. Regulations even went so far as to forbid Negroes to carry umbrellas.

Even today, Mexico has not abandoned two inheritances from colonial days: one is the dominance of a ubiquitous bureaucratic middle class—in addition to that of the lawyers, teachers, artisans, physicians, pharmacists, and so on—generally educated in the University of Mexico or trained in Spain; the other is the habit of this middle class and of all society, for that matter, of accepting as natural the intervention of the state in the economy and many other aspects of life.

Another characteristic inherited from colonial times, especially from its later years, was a steadfast desire for reform. Charles III, the only Bourbon monarch who might be called an enlightened despot, adopted the suggestion of his premier, the Count de Aranda, to make the American colonies into a commonwealth. The plan, which was never put into effect, was to give each of the

Spanish princes a colony to rule over as king, each kingdom being a member of a greater Spanish federation. But the plan also contained a project for reform—prepared by a *visitador* (inspector) for the crown named Jose de Gálvez, who served in the colonies between 1765 and 1771—and this was carried out. Gálvez created a tobacco monopoly to secure revenue, executed the royal order expelling the Jesuits, and established a system of intendancies to simplify the administration. Later, Viceroy Revillagigedo retained and broadened these reforms. And to compensate for the closing of the schools resulting from the expulsion of the Jesuits, new institutions were established, such as the Academy of Fine Arts, the School of Mines, and the Botanical Gardens. Coincidentally, Revillagigedo entrusted the missionary work in California to a group of Franciscans headed by Fr. Junipero Serra.

As long as the colony lasted, the struggle between the viceroys and the archbishops was a never-failing source of gossip on the promenades and in the salons. The Church used its control of the Indian masses to expand its influence, and its real-estate wealth grew in both the cities and the countryside. The viceroys, on the other hand, in duty bound to follow the crown's policies of protecting Indian lands, preserved them as well as they could, setting aside communal pastures and woodlands called *ejidos* for the Indians. This conflict came to a head when the Jesuits were expelled from Spain and her colonies in 1767. Refugee Mexican Jesuits discovered in Rome an idea they had never found in New Spain— a consciousness of the Mexican fatherland. Archaeologists had established the distinction between the history of Mexico and that of Spain, and from there it was but a step to affirming the existence of a Mexican nation. Men like the priest J. F. Clavijero were able to take that step, but it was not so easy for others to move from books to the street. Several decades had to pass first.

A trifling event that occurred about that time ultimately served as a coalescing influence. This was the decision to conscript the inhabitants of the colonies into the Spanish army, which until then had been made up of Spanish volunteers. This change in Spanish policy was made partly to cut down expenses, partly because the number of eligible men was diminishing. And several times during the closing years of the eighteenth century and the beginning years of the nineteenth, the viceroys had to call up armies of draftees to put down rebellions or to pacify restive Indian tribes. Each time, some of the officeholders grew rich by supplying the armies. Thus the Mexicans, men born in New Spain, were allowed to bear arms for the first time since the arrival of the conquistadors. More than a century and a half would pass before they would lay them down.

To sum up, then, Mexico was founded and grew up under several forms of servitude before she acquired her own name and national personality. In matters of law, Mexicans had to submit to the colonial juridical system; their society was subjected to a system of landholding that made the Indians virtual serfs; the people were dominated by the cultural and psychological servitude emerging from crossbreeding during the long and inevitable period of transition. Independence liberated the country from the first type of servitude. A century later, the revolution freed it from the second. It is struggling still to free itself from the third.

Each kind of servitude has weighed heavily on the country. Every time Mexico goes through an upheaval, the people try to win complete emancipation from all servitude, but every time, the different social groups have sought different objectives. During the struggle for independence, the Creoles wanted only to separate from Spain, because the mother country seemed to them too liberal. The then embryonic middle class and the Indian masses wanted to emancipate the country from juridical and social servitude to the big landowners. During the periods of reform in the middle of the nineteenth century and during the Revolution at the start of this century, reformers and revolutionaries alike worked to attain objectives either exclusively political or nationalistic. Others wanted the same, but also strove for revolutionary measures of a social nature.

3 · Mexico's Several Independences

MANUAL ABAD Y QUEIPO (1775–1823), Bishop of Michoacán, described New Spain at the beginning of the nineteenth century as follows:

> It is composed . . . of 4 million inhabitants who may be divided into three classes: Spanish, Indian, and half-caste (Negroes and mestizos). The Spaniards comprise a tenth of the total population, and they alone hold almost all the property and wealth of the realm. The other two classes, who make up the other nine-tenths, may be subdivided into thirds: two of mixed breeds and one pure-blooded Indians. The Indians and mixed breeds take care of domestic service, agricultural labor, and ordinary offices of trade, arts, and crafts. That is, they are servants, menials, or day laborers for the first class.

The bishop went on to say that in Mexico there are no shades of difference between the two chief classes: "they are all either rich men or paupers, noblemen or villeins," and this system gives birth to "envy, thievery, poor service on the part of the latter; contempt, usury, hardheartedness on the part of the former." He concluded that an agrarian law was needed to enable the Indians, Negroes, and mestizos to acquire property which would encourage them to take an interest in the laws and government. His proposal was to give them the idle, uncultivated lands of the great landholders, and he added that they should not be burdened with tributes; that they should be permitted to hold civil office; that they should have the choice of living wherever they might wish; and that cotton and woolen mills be established.

The critical picture drawn by the bishop notwithstanding, the situation of New Spain was better at the turn of the nineteenth century than it had ever been. Perhaps for this reason, the need for reform was felt all the more keenly. Because some degree of well-being had been achieved, there was leisure for reading and taking to heart the works of the Encyclopedists, Jeremy Bentham, and Benjamin Constant, and the speeches of the new leaders of the fledgling United States.

Only very small groups were affected by the new ideas, however. When Napoleon's armies were threatening Spain, New Spain was represented in the Cortes in Madrid by instructed delegates who made almost no mention of social problems. They did, however, offer a petition that "the natives and original peoples of America, Spanish and Indian alike," be granted the same rights as Spaniards in Spain, and that half the public offices be given to American appointees. Miguel Ramos Arizpe (1775–1843) went further; he asked for recognition of the Negroes as citizens with the right to positions and honors, since the Negroes and mestizos paid almost all the taxes and filled almost all the ranks in the army.

On September 16, 1810, a Creole priest in Michoacán, Miguel Hidalgo (1753–1811), proclaimed the independence of New Spain to the cries of: "Long live Mexico!" and "Death to the Gachupines!"; "Long live Ferdinand VII!"; and "Death to bad government!" Hidalgo was not a man of doctrine, although he had read the Encyclopedists, and the Indians who followed him (four Indians were among his first followers, and others soon joined them) understood nothing of such matters. But they did under-

stand the Guadalajara Manifesto (December 6, 1810), which proclaimed the abolition of taxes and tributes imposed on the
Negroes and mestizos and ordered the emancipation of the slaves
and the surrender of lands to Indians and Negroes. Hidalgo was
defeated, captured, tried by the Inquisition, sentenced to death,
and executed in 1811. According to the viceroy's propaganda, he
was an enemy of property, not a champion of independence. But
the social conscience of the man who carried on his work, José
María Morelos (1765–1815), was even stronger than his. For
Morelos, who continued the struggle until his death four years
later, adopted such revolutionary measures as nullifying internal
tariffs, dividing up the land, burning official archives, proclaiming
the abolition of slavery, and convoking a congress. The congress
met in September, 1813, in Chilpancingo, near the Pacific coast,
proclaimed Mexico's independence for the second time, and made
Morelos head of the independent government. (Like Hidalgo,
Morelos was later taken prisoner, tried, and executed.) Meanwhile, Mexican delegates to the Cortes of Cádiz (1810–12)
pressed for autonomy, and conservative Spaniards in Mexico deposed their viceroy for being too liberal, replacing him with
another, more reactionary one.

A man of action beneath his priestly garb and also more open
to ideas than Hidalgo, Morelos drew up several plans for organizing Mexico and sketched out some political programs, or "plans."
(Thus, he may have originated the Mexican custom of marking
off historical periods according to the plans drawn up during
them, each of which carries the name of the town where it was
proclaimed.) There is no doubt that Morelos was more perceptive
than the lawyers and merchants who made up the congress that
ratified Mexico's first constitution on October 22, 1814. This
Constitution of Apatzingán, inspired by the liberal Spanish Constitution of Cádiz (1812), did little more than to declare the
regime of the craft guilds null and void and demand that property
be respected always. The rebels wanted to make changes and
to create a new society, but they lacked a clear idea of how to
go about it or what it ought to be.

Soon the liberal spirit of Cádiz was to be shattered by Ferdinand VII, the young king whom Napoleon had forced to abdicate

(along with his father, Charles IV) and had kept sequestered in Bayonne. For a time, though, it gave courage and hope to the Spanish guerrilla fighters against the French army, and, with the help of the English, the Spaniards forced the French to withdraw from the Peninsula. Meanwhile, the Spaniards in Mexico began to think of separating from Spain—that is, from the liberalism of Cádiz. They did nothing, however, for fear of advancing the cause of Morelos' liberal followers. (One Spaniard, however, Francisco Javier Mina (1789–1817), who had won fame as a guerrilla fighter against Napoleon, came to Mexico following the war in Spain to take his stand beside the rebels. Unfortunately for Mina, there were few bands of active fighters then, and he was taken prisoner and shot.)

After the restoration of Ferdinand VII, in 1814, loyalty reigned once more in Spain and Mexico, for the king was a reactionary. Mexico City, which had been faithful to the crown, was the scene of many Creole conspiracies, most of which were uncovered and crushed without difficulty. The struggle for independence went on, sporadically and diffusely, in remote regions. The army was ineffective because for some time Spain had not been able to send any soldiers to the colonies; hence, the troops were mainly Indians and mestizos, though the officers were Spaniards and Creoles.

These by and large unfocused struggles constituted a real but disguised civil war. Society was divided between liberals and conservatives. In Spain, an army mobilized to be sent to the "Indies" mutinied in 1820. One of the captains, Rafael de Riego, seized command and set up a government which lasted three years, and which restored the Cádiz Constitution of 1812. Thereupon, the reactionaries of Mexico suddenly discovered that they were great Mexican patriots and that they, too, wanted independence. What changed their minds was a suggestion sent by the Spanish king to Viceroy Juan Ruíz de Apodaca suggesting the proclamation of Mexican independence: behind this generosity, apparently, was the intention of making Mexico his own kingdom if he should fail to oust the liberals in the Spanish government. Whether or not this was true, there was a reactionary independence plot that involved the viceroy himself and a clever, cruel, and rapacious soldier named Agustín de Iturbide (1783–1824). The viceroy sent Iturbide to defeat Vicente Guerrero, the last of the rebels of 1810, who continued his resistance from a refuge in the southern mountains. Iturbide opened a parley with Guerrero; they signed a plan (the Iguala Plan) and proclaimed independence on February 24, 1821. The Iguala Plan offered guarantees to everyone—the insurgents, because they had fought for independence; the reactionaries, because their plan offered the Spanish monarchs and infantes the throne of Mexico; the Church, because it proclaimed Catholicism as the state religion. An army was assembled, called the *Trigarante* (roughly, Three-Guarantee), with that Mexican passion for injecting into the language complicated words that would later become accepted usage. A flag with three stripes—green, white, and red—was adopted. The officials sent from Spain deposed the viceroy, but many Creole officials went over to the insurgents.

A new viceroy arrived from Spain. Iturbide went to receive him at Córdoba, conferred with him, and convinced him that he should adopt the Iguala Plan. The Three-Guarantee troops occupied Mexico City. But King Ferdinand refused to ratify the Córdoba agreements. A congress was elected to decide the country's destiny. Iturbide, supported by the Spaniards, succeeded in dominating the congress, which had at first favored a republic, and had himself proclaimed Emperor Agustín I. He made many mistakes and committed many violent deeds, dissolved the congress, and finally abdicated in 1823 when the republicans mutinied. A year later he came back, was captured in the north, and executed at Tamaulipas. His nine-month empire had included Texas and California in the north and territories as far south as Nicaragua, which had voluntarily joined the empire. Later, the countries of Central America withdrew peacefully; those in the north were occupied by the United States at various times and by various means.

Mexico's independence, then, was the achievement of two opposed sectors, each working toward a different immediate objective. One side wanted to separate from a liberal Spain and continue the system without the motherland. The other side wanted separation from Spain too, but it wanted to wipe out the colony and establish a new order—especially a new political order. The Iguala Plan, the base of the transitory alliance of these contradictory elements, declared that "All the inhabitants of New Spain, without any distinction whatsoever between Europeans, Africans, or Indians, are citizens of this monarchy, with the option of choosing any employment which accords with their merits and virtues." To Iturbide, this meant that the status of the Europeans must be guaranteed; to the liberals (the ideologists of independence, the readers of Rousseau), it meant the abolition of slavery—which, in fact, was legally forbidden in 1824, after the downfall of Iturbide—and a consecration of the principle of the equality of all men before the law. In Mexico, however, this was to relegate the Indians to a position of inferiority and leave them without any special protection. Thus the plan as construed favored the *latifundio*, as we shall see later, and inadvertently nourished those things that came to a head in the Revolution of 1910. In this sense, independence carried within it the seeds of revolution to come.

Immediately after the proclamation of the republic, which came soon after Iturbide's downfall, the Mexicans split into two main wings, which were to endure, under other names perhaps, until the Revolution. These were the centralists and the federalists. The centralists of 1824 became the conservatives of a later day; the federalists became the liberals. The centralists wanted to industrialize the country, and they looked toward Europe rather than the United States, which they distrusted. For the most part, they were strong Catholics who relied on the Church and army to provide foundations for the new nation; they won support in Mexico City and the industrial and mining cities surrounding it. One author has compared them to the Hamiltonians of the young United States. If so, the Jeffersonians were the federalists and liberals, the people in the provinces who looked to the United States and distrusted Europe, especially Spain, were opposed to a powerful central government, and favored instead stronger provincial authorities. They hoped to abolish the special jurisdictions and privileges of the Church and the army, whose members were exempted from civil trial. (Priests were tried by ecclesiastical tribunals only, regardless of the civil or criminal charges against them, and the military only by courts-martial.) The liberals were against any type of corporative structure, too; they opposed the guilds, collective property, and, particularly, Church ownership of land. On principle, they were also opposed to the indigenous communes, the *ejidos,* a position that was to bring a train of complications and unfortunate consequences.

During the following quarter-century, the struggle between centralists and federalists over the organization of the state was the hub around which Mexican history revolved. The conflict between conservatives and liberals over the direction in which society ought to move was almost as crucial. Incident and drama attended the conflict: wars, uprisings, dictatorships on the one hand, and study, sacrifice, idealism, and the establishment of industries on the other. Such events seem picturesque now, but they were starkly real to those who lived through them. Here and there distinguished figures stepped forth, some of great stature, others somewhat grotesque.

Mexico was divided into many large segments. In the center was Mexico City, with an agglomeration of wealth around it: Puebla, with its textile mills founded a few years after independence; Guanajuato, Pachuca, and Taxco, with their mines. In the north was the rich Bajío region of fertile lands and dignified cities, rich in architecture and liberalism; along the Gulf, Nuevo León and Monterrey, industrious and orderly; and Veracruz, the port in which the traveler preferred not to linger for fear of the yellow fever. All of forgotten Mexico was compressed into the narrow end of the horn of plenty: the ancient Maya of Yucatán, where the Indians still lived in a state of virtual slavery, despite several rebellions combining social protest and local pride. There the middle class were separatist because it felt that the politicians in Mexico City had abandoned it. The distant coastlands of the Pacific were still in the grip of local petty chieftains. The enormous semidesert of the north was actually controlled by the missions, for Mexico had never succeeded in populating it. In later years, farmers from the eastern United States settled there. As for the virtually independent regions of Sonora, Nayarit, and Chihuahua, where some Indians lived on a subsistence level, no one bothered about them.

During that era of few roads, the geography of the country helped to shape its political institutions. Most communities, whether city or hamlet, were isolated. They had few contacts with the rest of the country; they purchased little and sold little; they were ruled by the *caciques,* the local strong men. More often than not, the *cacique* was a man who had fought for independence with Morelos or one of the lesser *caudillos,* and who kept the spirit of independence alive with the people's help, given largely because he was from their own locality.

The capital and the wealthy cities formed a world apart; they *were* the state; their leading figures were men who had fought against independence for eleven years and accepted it only to appropriate it. Mexico City dealt with the world, that world about which the provinces knew nothing. The people outside this urban enclave identified themselves with their *caciques* because he was a local fellow, and they regarded him as a bulwark against the central government, though in fact he not infrequently played into the hands of the government in order to maintain his control. But the entity that truly constituted an autarky to those who dwelt within it was the hacienda, with its enormous tracts of land, its central cluster of buildings with rampartlike walls, its chapel, its dozens, hundreds, even thousands of families dependent on it. To their owners, who sold the abundant surplus harvests in the cities or the export markets, the haciendas were a part of the market economy. But the peons had nothing to do with this rationale of the hacienda.

On the other hand, the hacienda as an institution set the tone of Mexico's everyday culture and way of life. Even in the cities, relationships between master and servant tended to preserve its style, and the houses of the very rich were organized like the hacienda household. But on the hacienda, control was tighter. The people had to buy in the hacienda store; they were paid in scrip, and they could not leave the grounds as long as they were in debt to the store, which meant all their lives. The local community was strong and authoritative; the Mexican felt that he was a part of the community—his hacienda, his village, his small city, or his quarter of a big city. As a nation, the Mexicans remained in the hands of an exiguous minority of politicians, intellectuals, and cultured people.

From the time of independence on, the social question was the crucial one. Ultimately, all the political and religious disputes were disguises for the question of how Mexican society was to be organized. The anticlericalism of many rebels such as Fr. Servando Teresa de Mier (1765–1827) and José Joaquín Fernández de Lizardi (1776–1827), a writer and journalist, was but an outward expression of a deep social unrest. Mier constantly demanded freedom of religion and a Church poor in worldly goods. Lizardi was the first man in his country to pin the label of mortmain on the clergy's property, which he said was prejudicial to the nation's progress as long as it lay stagnant and sequestered in the power of the Church. In his opinion, the opposition of the Church to independence could be traced back not to the whim of the bishops or to simple fealty to the crown, but to the fear that the economic privileges of the clergy would vanish in an independent country.

Concern about social issues failed, however, to inspire anything much beyond a certain paternalism in these men. Fr. Servando said, in 1822, as he was addressing the congress: "The great number of feast days must be decreased, for they are extremely harmful to the poor who are forbidden on such days to do the work so necessary to their subsistence." In his outline for a constitution, Mier recognized that "no man has a right over another man, *unless he himself has granted it. . . .*" With those words, he justified the foundation of the hacienda system. In truth, no one dared to probe the problem to its depths.

With independence came a degree of interest in the Mexican economy. In 1823, several deputies proposed the establishment of two weekly university classes in economics, adding a suggestion that "the jargon of scholasticism be dispensed with." No great knowledge of economics was needed, however, to see that hunger for land was keen. Juan Francisco de Azcárate (1790–1831) drew up plans for land settlement in 1822; the following year, the congress ordered a division of the lands in Puebla; in 1827, Lorenzo de Zavala (1788–1836) distributed the land of forty villages; and in 1829, Francisco García (1786–1841), governor of Zacatecas, founded a bank that was instructed to buy land and divide it among those peasants who had none, in a perpetual leasehold. Settlement was encouraged. Practical offers were made, such as those for dividing the lands of the Isthmus of Tehuantepec, where tracts were broken up into three parts: one to be distributed among retired military men and bureaucrats; another to be sold to foreign and national capitalists; and the third to be distributed among the people without land who lived in the region. A few years later, the government offered the farmer who had received land enough credit to pay for moving, tools, and equipment, plus maintenance for a year. The law forbade the accumulation of great tracts of land by a single owner and prohibited the resale to the clergy of lands distributed under it.

During Mexico's long advance toward independence, the country passed through two clearly marked stages. At first, proponents of independence did not deny their colonial past; instead they used it as the basis of their plea for separation from Spain—then without a king, for this was at the time that Charles IV and his son Ferdinand VII had abdicated and were sequestered by Napoleon during the Peninsular War. This left the colonies without the traditional tie that bound them to the monarch's person, and the independence group considered that the absence of a ruler in Madrid nullified the pact between the motherland and the colonies. In the second stage, all things Spanish were abjured and the colonial past along with them. Fr. Servando de Mier in his memoirs accused Spain and all of Europe of feeding off America. But even as the colonials denied the past, they felt a certain nostalgia for their origins, which was sharply accentuated in those who were aware of their status as mestizos. Fr. Servando offered a twofold remedy: an "American constitution" for Mexico and the defense of the Indians. And Morelos proclaimed to the peripatetic congress of the first days of independence: "The twelfth day of August, 1521 [the day when Tenochtitlán surrendered to the Spaniards], was followed by the eighth day of September, 1813 [the day when Congress was convened]." Later he announced: "We are going to re-establish the Mexican Empire." By this he meant the Aztec empire, for the word Mexico derives from *Mexica*, the name given to the Aztecs. Patriots went so far as to propose that an emperor of Indian origin should rule them, their candidate for the throne being a descendant of Moctezuma who belonged to the Spanish aristocracy. Aztec legend was made graphic on the great shield, showing the eagle and the serpent. Thus did the liberals look back on ancient days.

The conservatives did not care for these manifestations of nostalgia; they wanted Mexico to be a continuation of the colony and its institutions. And the small sector of the people concerned with politics, who formed public opinion, favored a union of conservatives and liberals in a common effort to reject their Spanish origin.

In the public mind, then, Mexico was seen as a possibility, but the differences among the political leaders were deep and divisive. Until the Revolution of 1910, the country's political history was a record of the struggle between two concepts: one, that Mexico was still in the making; and the other, that it was whole and complete. The landowning classes, very small in number, were of the first opinion; the bureaucratic and business middle class of the second. Not infrequently, attitudes that seemed proper to one side were adopted by the other. Industrialization, for example, became an obsession with certain conservative politicians, whereas the liberals paid little heed to it. Conversely, a good many cultured landowners dedicated their leisure to study of pre-Cortesian antiquities, while many middle-class intellectuals studied economics. (Throughout the eighteenth century in Spanish America, a scientific movement had been warmly encouraged by Charles III for the purpose of learning more about the geography, botany, topography, and natural resources of the viceroyalties. And many distinguished men of science were studying the Americas when the struggle for independence interrupted their activities.)

Consequently, most of the politicians who emerged with independence were forced to improvise, for their only training had been under the viceroys, where politics did not exist, but only the administration. The influence of the French *Encyclopédie*, Thomas Paine, and the institutions and debates in Philadelphia

and Paris lingered vividly in the memory. But each gleanfing had
to be sifted through a great mass of people with deep religious
convictions. Lorenzo de Zavala, a Mexican historian and bold
adventurer in politics, described this situation confronting the
first politicians in independent Mexico:

> There is a constant clash between the doctrines professed, the in-
> stitutions adopted, the principles being established and the abuses
> already sanctified, the customs that prevail, and the semifeudal
> rights that are respected; between national sovereignty, equality of
> political rights, freedom of the press, popular government and the
> intervention of armed forces, privileged status, religious intolerance,
> and the owners of immense territories.

The Iguala Plan, the alliance between the colonialist soldier
Iturbide and the rebels who believed they could resuscitate
Cuauhtémoc, consecrated Mexico's formal independence. Iturbide's fall established its political independence. But a long road
stretched ahead, which had to be traveled before economic and
social independence could be reached, until the country could
enjoy its wealth, and the voice of the masses could be heard.

4 · Reforms

DURING THE CENTURY following its achievement of independence, Mexico groped for a form of organization. In the beginning, people were classified according to Masonic rites as either York or Scottish,* later, as centralists or federalists, and still later as liberal or conservative, positivist or idealist. Beneath these formal designations, which basically reflected the various opinions on how to construct the state, flowed a common underlying concern to re-form society, with conservatives such as Alamán and the Emperor Maximilian wanting it to be done one way, demagogues like Santa Anna another, and liberals like Juárez or social revolutionaries like Flores Magón and his brothers in still others.

Outwardly, the history of Mexico became a kind of nineteenth-century novel of absurd adventure. Presidents, generals, bishops, *coups d'état*, expropriations, exiles, executions followed hard one

* The reasons why are discussed below, pp. 53–54.

upon another. Concurrently, Mexico fought wars with the United States, Spain, and France. But this wealth of event touched only very small groups, only a minute portion of the country's surface: the capital and a few other cities, mostly in the north; Veracruz, where the exiles shipped for Europe or New Orleans (then the refuge of Mexican political emigrés). The great mass of the Mexican people turned their backs on politics and refused to be aroused except when they themselves were in danger of being drafted into the army. The majority remained submerged in their haciendas or villages, living in virtual servitude, except for a small fraction who worked in the factories that were being built in Puebla, Mexico City, Monterrey, and Guadalajara, or else in the mines. Another fraction was busily filling out a slowly but constantly growing stack of papers in government offices, writing and reading newspapers, teaching in the universities, caring for the sick, presiding in the courts, or arguing in the cafés.

To anyone looking at only the surface of Mexican history, it may seem incredible that there could be any progress, any thought in the midst of so much public disorder. But there was progress: companies were founded; ships were bought; loans were negotiated (generally in London, at a high rate of interest and at a fantastic discount of up to 55 per cent); factories, especially textile mills, were built; and as four presidents came and went in the capital, the first telegraph line was strung and opened in 1853. Nor was that all. Mexico's press was ample in both the capital and the provinces; mediocre novelists and pompous poets were emerging alongside historians and political thinkers of great stature—Alamán, Zavala, and Mora, to mention a few. People were dying for political causes, too, as often and as easily as the foremen would flog the peons on the haciendas.

Much of the visible history of the first thirty years of the republic revolved around the picturesque figure of General Antonio López de Santa Anna (1795–1876). Santa Anna, only a youth when independence was declared, was a partisan of Guerrero and a patron of Zavala—in short, a friend of the extreme liberals—at the outset of his military career. Later, he was elected president as a conservative; he was exiled and returned to office as a liberal. He was defeated in the war over Texas (which gave the United States an excuse to acquire an enormous amount of territory, although by invading Mexico in 1847, the American government committed the first of its many blunders in Latin America), was forced to go into exile again, came back to claim the title of Most Serene Highness, and in the end was expelled by the liberals. He was pompous, ineffectual, corrupt, brilliant, and fond of grandiose ceremonies and glittering uniforms. For still incomprehensible reasons, the people followed him, yet no one drained the country as dry as did this inglorious general. Today, the name of Santa Anna is equated with national shame. But in his lifetime, he aroused great admiration, along with a hatred so deep that even as he was engaged in war with the United States, the liberals unhesitatingly rose up against him. After losing a leg in battle, he ordered the extremity to be interred publicly with due solemnity; afterward he used his wooden leg as a kind of political persuader.

As the general was leaving for his final exile, he took with him some resin from the chicle tree. He liked to chew its gum. A businessman in Boston with a flair for novelty watched Santa Anna and conceived the idea of chewing-gum, which brought money into Mexico for many years. It was Santa Anna's sole contribution to his country. But in another sense he was indirectly useful to Mexico in lending his ridiculous prestige alternately to the liberals and the conservatives, thus giving each group the opportunity to apply its policies.

Behind the ups and downs of congress, the elections, the presidents, and Santa Anna's intermittent rises to power, the political life of Mexico was unfolding congruently. Three figures of that time stand out. One, Lorenzo de Zavala (1788–1836), a liberal and a historian, was more preoccupied with the well-being and progress of his country than with principles. As governor of the State of Mexico, he distributed lands and forced the clergy to abide by the law. Later, he emigrated to Texas. The second man of distinction was Lucas Alamán (1792–1853), a businessman, a conservative politician, and a historian of insight, who devoted his life to the encouragement of industry and to organizing credit banking—two activities that were revolutionary in the Mexico of his day. Finally, there were José María Luis Mora (1794–1850) and Valentín Gómez Farías (1781–1858), two men who might be regarded as one, for Mora was the liberals' theorist and Gómez Farías the executor of their programs, first in alliance with Santa Anna and later in opposition to him.

A reading and comparison of Zavala's *Ensayo Histórico de las Revoluciones de México* and Alamán's *Historia de México* provide an interesting adventure. Two contrasting minds meet—the classic and the romantic. Two truths, each equally supported by fact, appear to clash, but the purpose of the authors is the same. They are searching for ways and means of turning the country into a nation, of making a congruent whole of a formless mass of humanity clustered around a few chaotic cities. In Alamán's view, this fundamental aim must be achieved via organization and economic evolution: by creating industries, banks, improving the education of the workers, by imposing from the center of power a certain general direction and order. Zavala believed the same end could be reached by arousing the people in the villages from their inertia, by giving them land, and by summoning them to participate in government, thus freeing them from the tutelage of the clergy. A reading of Zavala's history makes it understandable why in the end he went to Texas out of frustration with the obstacles confronting him in Mexico, believing that he had found among the Protestant immigrants of Texas a community where his ideals could be realized.

All these outstanding men spent their lives in government offices, writing for the press, and delivering speeches before congress and at election rallies. (Particularly the làst, for elections were held frequently, although only a small minority of the country's inhabitants could vote. In the provinces, the *caciques*, the local strong men, decided the winners. This meant that what electoral power there was, was restricted to the enfranchised urban voters; Mexico City was virtually the only place where elections were more or less free and open.) These influential men were constantly on the move, traveling in uncomfortable carriages along roads dusty in summer and muddy in winter, descending from the cold of the high plateau to the humid heat of the coast. They spent hours dressing in their French-style clothes in preparation for festivals and soirées. At home, they acted as patresfamilias to large households, with servants and children in every nook and cranny of huge, patriarchal mansions. At night they passed through poorly paved, evil-smelling streets in the capital to attend secret meetings where they wove plots and laid plans for uprisings. They knew that every time anyone raised his voice for or against them, every time they signed their names to some plan for an uprising, their lives were in jeopardy. Yet, in spite of everything, they found time to delve into archives, to rummage through uncataloged documents, to order books from New York and London, and to write histories that could run to eight volumes in abridged editions. That they managed to do so much during a period when ghost-writers were nonexistent seems as incredible as the climb made by Cortés from Veracruz to Tenochtitlán.

In a sense, Mexican history of the nineteenth century is the record of the adaptation of the *continuistas* (conservatives) to the necessities for reform. In taking stands that seemed to have nothing to do with the social question—finance in Alamán's case, anticlericalism in Gómez Farías', industrialism in Porfirio Díaz'—they were all trying to modernize the country. And more often than not, this modernization was accomplished by the efforts of strong personalities rather than by political parties. Only small, well-to-do minorities, in contact with what was going on abroad, were concerned enough about politics to form political centers or clubs. The so-called parties indicated little more than scattered tendencies, spontaneous movements, not real political organizations. Civil struggles were the work of intellectuals, the military, the bureaucrats. Mexico's first political rally took place in 1847 during the invasion by the U.S. Army.

The Masonic lodges imported from Spain and welcomed with enthusiasm into Mexico were the first organizations to focus politics in any particular direction. Lodges of the Scottish rite were established in 1818; most members were Spaniards who wanted representative government and reform of the clergy. A split within the lodge occurred in 1821, and many Mexicans changed their membership to the lodges headed by Nicolás Bravo (1787–1854). The lodges of the Scottish rite contributed greatly to Iturbide's overthrow. Lodges of the York rite, centered around

Guadalupe Victoria (1789–1843), the first president of the republic and a hero of the war for independence, were founded in 1826. In 1828, the two opposing rites collided: the liberals, who chose the York rite, supported Vicente Guerrero (1783–1831) for president, while those in the Scottish rite backed Manuel Gómez Pedraza (1789–1851), a conservative. Pedraza won, but the congress refused to recognize his victory and named Guerrero instead, with Zavala as his adviser and Santa Anna as his protector. Guerrero soon thereafter became a "national hero" by winning a battle near Tampico against the followers of General Isidro Barradas, a fantastic Spaniard who had come to Mexico in the absurd hope of reconquering the country. But a few months later, toward the end of 1829, Vice-President Carlos María Bustamante (1774–1848) rebelled, and the very same congress that had given Guerrero the presidency took it away from him and handed it over to Bustamante, who remained in power until 1832. The hero, for whom the State of Guerrero is named, retired to his lands. Two years later, he was assassinated.

Bustamante, who followed the conservative Scottish rite, had rebelled because he was alarmed by Guerrero's proposal to expel Spaniards and "level out the classes." Furthermore, Guerrero had invited Robert Owen to found a socialistic colony in Mexico (probably at the suggestion of Zavala, who was more familiar with European experimental movements). Nothing ever came of the proposal, but in 1830, a book by a canonical lawyer named Francisco Severo Maldonado (?–1832), *The Triumph of the Human Species*, appeared in which it was argued that society is supported by the "adversity of the proletariat" ("proletariat" was the term he used) and that the first step toward the goal of transforming society was the organization of industry, agriculture, and commerce. The problem, then, was to establish a controlled utopia; this was the first such suggestion in Mexico.

These various ideologies, which become more and more finely spun out, are not easily described. The liberals believed that freedom, won through education and industry, would lead to progress and order. The conservatives believed that industry, a technical and moral education, and order would lead to progress and freedom. Basically, both wanted reform. The spirit of con-

servative reform was manifest in Lucas Alamán, a great gentleman, cultivated and refined, who served under Santa Anna through
several administrations. Even though he despised the pompous
little man, he remained with him because Santa Anna permitted
him to do things. Alamán took part in many of the conservative
maneuvers, but he acted not so much out of conviction as out of
loyalty to the Church. On the whole, his policies were progressive,
although they were not couched in the liberal rhetoric. He favored the distribution of land to rural workers and founded a
credit bank to give loans to the new owners and to people who
wished to start new industries. Alamán believed that property is
the guarantee of public morality; and he also established a savings
bank for workers to enable them to acquire the wherewithal to
become owners. He encouraged immigration and settlement and
was prepared to accept foreign investments, especially from
Europe, that might counterbalance the potential threat of Spain
and the United States. He knew that the rich would never give
anything away unless forced to, yet he distrusted revolution because the violence it entailed ultimately weakened all authority.
He favored a revolution from above, however, a protective or
tutelary revolution. As a historian, he held a cyclical theory of
history: a period of peace and prosperity is followed by one of
revolution, he believed, because the people tire of tranquility, just
as they soon tire of the disorder and swing back to calm and order.

Many of Alamán's thoughts could not be expressed openly because of his political position, but he had a friend, Esteban de
Antuñano (1792–1847), who could speak for him. Antuñano,
who founded the textile industry in Puebla and created the General Administration of Industry in 1833, was a critic of the mine
owners for their failure to use their wealth, derived from the
mines, to better the condition of their workers. And he had other
radical ideas: to send the army to border areas ánd keep it there;
to close the "Latinist" schools to make room for technical education; to do away with religious communities and reduce the
number of priests; to use Church property to foster immigration
from Europe, to establish credit banks, and to build roads. On the
whole, Alamán and Antuñano were more advanced than the lib-

erals, but they did not dare to apply their ideas, or were not able to.

For the liberals, France was the beacon light. The French Revolution demonstrated a way of wiping out the colonial past they detested. They saw in French liberalism the means of erasing political oppression; in the republic, the instrument for doing away with the empire; in free trade, the cure for national poverty; in Jacobinism, the strategy to accomplish their ends. To many Mexicans, living in a society that was changing very slowly, liberalism was more than an ideology, it was a way of life. To the young, it offered the chance for spontaneous protest against the older generation, who, it seemed, had closed all doors to them—and Mexican society was essentially young, for death came to the average man at the age of forty or fifty as a result of violence, illness, war, or destitution. To moderate liberals, confiscation of Church property and abolition of mortmain were means to fight Church influence in politics and the economy. To the radical liberals, confiscation was one step only toward the social reorganization of the country. These "pure liberals," as the radicals called themselves, were firmly dogmatic, whereas the more flexible moderates preferred to come to an "understanding" with the Church.

Perhaps the liberal attitude was most evident in the war over Texas. Liberals criticized the Texans who wanted independence on the ground that they "wanted to open a new theater for the execrable systems of Negro slavery." After Mexico lost Texas, the Mexican Government pressed the U.S. Commissioner, Nicholas Philip Trist, to "promise not to consent to slavery in that portion of Mexican territory which might be definitely acquired."

The Mexican philosopher Leopoldo Zea has said that at heart the liberal is a man with a personality which he does not consider his own and which he does not like; he is searching for one that will fit him. He is a man in transition—hence the current reality of the country influences him, even in his dogmatism. For example, his liberalism almost never derives from economic theories, for he has only a relative concept of property. To the liberal, then, the Mexican war for independence was an attack on prop-

erty rights; this was the reason for his allegiance to it, a view that
marks his separation from the conservative.

Be that as it may, the liberals were not of the people but a part
of the oligarchy. (The people, in fact, were on the fringe of
politics.) Justo Sierra (1848–1912), the historian of the period of
Porfirio Díaz (in whose cabinet he served), described them as
follows:

> The petty bourgeoisie who hated the Spaniards; the young lawyers
> and men of science, most of the greedy politicians; and at the head
> of this intellectual phalanx, thirsting for equality and recruited
> mainly from the state capitals, a group of patriotic thinkers, per-
> haps in advance of their time and certainly ahead of the social
> environment which surrounded them—these were the elements
> composing that fraction of the oligarchy which called itself re-
> formist.

These men were reformers because they believed that Mexican
society must be transformed. They came into power with Gómez
Farías in 1833, with a program that embraced freedom of expression, suppression of the special legal privileges accorded to the
clergy and the army, abolition of the death sentence for political
crimes, colonization of open lands, destruction "of the clergy's
monopoly on public education," and "measures to increase the
number of landholdings . . . and to facilitate means for advancing
the needy classes, without offending the rights of private indi-
viduals or touching them in any way." They favored the establishment of a revenue system, for almost no taxes were being
levied and the state was supported on income from customs. They
also favored the abolition of interior tariffs and of the system of
forced recruitment into the army, which fell most heavily upon
rural and industrial workers.

The liberals failed to face up to the question of the indigenous
people. They proved dogmatic, and this had tragic consequences.
In the case of the Indian, equality before the law translated into
flagrant social inequality. For once an Indian became a citizen,
he lost his status as a protégé, and, while he was granted rights,
he did not have the means to use them in his own defense. He
was exempted from special tributes but had to pay sales taxes and

was forced to serve in the army, which took him away from his people and flung him into an alien world. He remained, in fact, outside the law, for it no longer protected him.

The liberal program remained unchanged for many years, and each time the liberals came into office they strove to apply it: in 1833; during the Reform of 1854; and later under Díaz—all of which indicates that while the country adjusted its economy to changing times, it did not adapt its social structure. Basically, the liberal program differed from the conservative in few fundamentals—the main difference being on the issue of who must bear the cost of applying it. The liberals believed the rich must pay, especially the rich clergy; the conservatives and, later, Porfirio Díaz believed that the people and foreign capital must pay.

Mexican liberals enjoyed three periods in power. In each of them, there were a theorist and a man of action. In 1833, Mora was the theorist while Gómez Farías exercised power; in 1854 and the years immediately following, Ocampo was the theorist and Juárez the power; and in the Díaz period, a group of positivists (extreme liberals, practicing a kind of Jacobinism of the rich) took charge of the theory and General Díaz wielded the power. Alternating with these three periods of attempted liberal reform were two great efforts to achieve conservative reform: Alamán's efforts to industrialize and Emperor Maximilian's program to "protect" the people. While the liberals had the support of their partisans and a portion of the army to help them carry out their reforms, the conservatives, Alamán and Maximilian particularly, were opposed in their reform efforts by their partisans, whom another part of the army supported.

The Rousseau of the Mexican liberals was José María Luis Mora, a reformer, not a revolutionary. According to Mora, persuasion must shape opinion so that progress can be achieved without bloodshed. He said this would call for "great skill in identifying the common interest with one's own"; that is, the nascent middle class and bourgeoisie must represent the interests of the entire society. He believed that the country needed the clergy and the army, though not as monopolists of power, and that whenever both groups united, they tended inevitably to establish a monopoly. For this, independence was partly to blame, for it increased ecclesiastical and military power and "created the habit of considering brute force and the aspirations of the clergy the only powers." Only one remedy could be effective against this: the education of the middle class.

Mora saw that latifundism was one cause of the country's poverty, and he advocated dividing the land by selling it. But in temperament, Mora was a conservative, and not on the agrarian question alone, in that he favored keeping the best of the past. Yet Mexico was a country where there was almost nothing to conserve, and consequently he had no choice but to be a reformer, for only through reform could wealth, institutions, and interests worth conserving be created. "The best form of government," he declared, "is that one which is already established, provided that it is not despotic." Man must be ruled, but the ruling hand should not be obvious. Man aspires to democratic forms of government and wants to control the means that provide comfort, which he expects the political system to ensure for him; since only the propertyowners are trained to govern, the task of reform falls on them. The changes they make must be rapid but gradual, and must be irreversible; their aim must be not to subjugate the citizen to authority, but to protect him against it. To Mora, the most important thing was not independence; it was freedom, yet "very much and very little freedom are equally uncomfortable for nations."

Clearly, then, Mora had certain touches of skepticism, combined with a dogmatic approach to principles that would be considered very moderate today—indeed, they were moderate enough in his day for Europe or the United States—but for the Mexico of the early nineteenth century, they struck a revolutionary note.

In practical matters, Mora sponsored a continuing study of the economy by establishing a chair of political economics in 1823. He hoped to see Church property replaced by small landholdings, and though he never intervened directly in politics, he inspired the reforms of the Gómez Farías government in 1833 that called for the seizure of mission property and its division into parcels large enough to feed a family and pay off a mortgage at a fixed interest rate of 5 per cent per year. The interest would be set aside for agricultural development schemes in the municipalities in which the money was raised. These reforms were passed by congress and applied while the ubiquitous Santa Anna was president and Gómez Farías vice-president.

Then, in 1834, in a sudden shift, Santa Anna became allied with the conservatives, who got rid of Gómez Farías and restored conservative policies. A centralist constitution was proclaimed in 1836, and Santa Anna and Carlos Bustamante alternately served as chief executive. Neither of them concentrated his or the nation's efforts on development, to use a present-day term; in fact, they more or less abandoned the regions in the north—Texas, California, and New Mexico—because they needed all their available resources to smother the constant liberal uprisings. The vacuum they left in the north was filled by colonists from the eastern United States. Eventually, this led to the incorporation of those territories into the United States by treaty, purchase, and absorption.

No one saw these things more clearly than Lorenzo de Zavala, a liberal in speech and a radical in politics. For Zavala, the system under which Mexico was still living was similar to that imposed by the Spanish monarchy. He believed that men of wealth and intelligence had to govern for the common good. He tried to put his political beliefs into practice while he was governor of the State of Mexico, then the richest state in the country, but the vicissitudes of politics thwarted him, and he left for Texas, where he believed he could create a society in which every man would be a landowner. He joined the Texas federalists, not realizing that they wanted to secede from Mexico, entrusting his hopes to them and believing that he could carry out his work in Texas. He died in 1836, considered a traitor to his own country.

At the time of the Louisiana Purchase in 1803, Texas was a part of the Mexican state of Coahuila. With the acquisition of such a great part of the central portion of the continent, the United States needed Texas to protect New Orleans and the Mississippi Valley. Many settlers from the slave-owning states moved into Coahuila and established slavery there. Soon, these American settlers were demanding trial by jury, free foreign trade, and government under English common law. Naturally, Spain would not accede to such demands. But after Mexico won her independence, she granted lands in Texas to sixteen colonizers in 1821. One of them was Stephen Austin. The colonizers paid a minuscule price for the land and became Mexican citizens, without relinquishing their real desire, which was to make Texas part of the United States. In fact, General Long had attempted to occupy Texas by armed force, but he was defeated and executed. In 1826, other Americans, Austin among them, made an abortive attempt to proclaim Texas the "Republic of Fredonia." Then, a few years later, when Guerrero was president of Mexico, he decided to abolish slavery in Texas, and later, Alamán levied customs duties and closed the doors to new colonists. In 1834, Santa Anna, as president, received a delegation of Texans that included Austin and Zavala, but when he replaced the federal system with a centralist regime in 1835, the Texans revolted and soon afterward declared their independence. Santa Anna had neither troops nor money, but he gathered an army as best he could, marched to Texas, and won the victory of the Alamo. The American settlers were ready to withdraw, but Sam Houston, their leader, won a surprise victory over Santa Anna in the battle of San Jacinto and captured him as he was attempting to escape in disguise. Houston induced Santa Anna to sign a document promising Mexican recognition of Texas as an independent republic. In return, Houston gave Santa Anna his freedom and sent him to Washington for an interview with President Andrew Jackson.

In 1845, the United States Congress voted to annex Texas. Meanwhile, settlers were penetrating New Mexico and California—a migration the impetus for which came from the southern states and which was opposed by the northern ones, which did not want slavery spread into new territories—and this stimulated an old desire to acquire California lest France or England take it first. The annexation of Texas, the friction over Mexico's delay in settling long-standing American claims, plus the surge westward all combined to bring about a rupture of United States–Mexican relations and the outbreak of war between the two countries in 1846.

The Mexican Army (commanded again by Santa Anna) was poorly armed and badly led. It lost one battle after another until

the American "gringos" entered Veracruz and Mexico City.*
Gómez Farías, who had returned to office as vice-president, tried
to organize the defense of the capital and to force the clergy and
great landowners to pay special levies for the support of the war,
but he had no time to accomplish anything. It was evidence of the
weakness of the bonds holding Mexico together that Yucatán proclaimed neutrality in the war, and the wealthy men in that state
assembled an army by enlisting the Indians and issuing them arms.
When peace was restored, the Indians rebelled and were slaugh-
tered in the ensuing struggle.

By the treaty of Guadalupe Hidalgo (1848), Mexico ceded all
her territory north of the Rio Bravo in return for $15 million
from the United States. (This money helped Santa Anna to restore some of his prestige, tarnished so badly in his Texas defeats.)
Mexico had lost more than 918 million square miles of territory,
over half the nation's entire area. Later, in 1853, the Mexican
Government, then conservative, sold the Valley of the Mesilla
(now southern Arizona) for $10 million to the United States in
order to raise money to pay its troops.

But Mexico had not learned the lesson of Texas. Zavala saw
that the disaster in the north could have been averted by a policy .
of massive immigration and colonization of the semidesert. If
Mexican settlers had been living there, the United States could not
have made such serious incursions, nor would the secession idea
ever have caught on. The government of Mexico had been remiss
in not sponsoring large-scale settlement, in devoting its attention
for more than half a century on the center of the country, leaving the north to the great landowners, many of them foreigners

* The presence of U.S. troops in their capital had deeply wounded the
Mexicans' national pride, and it left a residue of hatred that is still felt.
Many conservatives later supported Maximilian not so much for ideological
reasons as because they looked to the European powers for any opportunity to strike back at the United States and believed Juárez was too
friendly to what was already called the colossus of the north—a Protestant
colossus to boot. This reaction overlooked the fact that sixteen members
of the U.S. House of Representatives had protested against the Mexican
War. (One such opponent was Abraham Lincoln.) And of course the
Whigs (out of which the Republican Party grew) opposed President Polk
on the issue; Henry Clay and John Quincy Adams condemned the war on
the ground that it was needless and unconstitutional.

from the United States and, especially, from Spain. Exploitation of the tropical south was also foreclosed, owing to the widespread subdivision of land among the *ejidos* there. Somewhat later, wealthy German settlers set out to conquer the southern tropics, establishing coffee plantations that formed the basis for a new type of latifundism and gave the south certain unique qualities. What the planters wanted above all was the cheap labor available in the villages. (The Mexican labor supply was always being reduced by the draft, for after the war over Texas, Mexico entered upon a period during which the army became much more than an instrument for bringing off *coups d'état*. It became an active element in the life of the country during thirty years of constant civil war.) Southern politicians with national aspirations sought electoral support by calling up the men of the local villages to fight for them. And local politicians, with the tacit approval of officials in Mexico City, served the coffee-planters as agents.

The first thirty years of independence, then, overshadowed by Santa Anna and the struggle between federalists and centralists, was followed by another strife-torn thirty years dominated by Juárez and marked by the conflict between liberals and conservatives and between Mexicans and French. This period was succeeded by a new stage, also of thirty years, in which Porfirio Díaz held power. That, in turn, would lead to thirty years of revolution and its sequel.

The loss of the north disturbed Mexican political society for some time. Presidents came and went: Manuel de la Peña y Peña, José Joaquín de Herrera, and General Mariano Arista. Conservative rebellions and Indian uprisings followed one upon another. Industry was paralyzed; a shortage of funds hindered attempts to attend to the needs of education. After Arista, the inevitable Santa Anna returned to power in 1853; this time in a kind of delirium of splendor. He established a "perpetual" hereditary dictatorship, persecuted the press, sold new blocs of national territory to the United States, and insisted upon being addressed as "Your Serene Highness." The liberals coalesced and prepared a coup in 1854, which they announced, as usual, in a plan—the Ayutla Plan—and bitter civil war ensued. Until that time, coups had been short-lived: either they never reached the battle stage or the battles were few. Now, however, a series of skirmishes went on for years all across the countryside of Mexico, especially on the northern plateau, once the geographical center of the country but then a frontier region.

By 1857, the liberals had momentarily triumphed, but in many regions the conservatives refused to lay down their arms and they never ceased to plot. The liberals realized that this chaotic situation could not be corrected without basic reform of the political structure. Some of them, strongly influenced by Proudhon, went so far as to advocate reform of the social structure. In 1857 they tried to bring about such reforms legally through a new constitution—the panacea of the Latin American—a true declaration of principles. They were young intellectuals, self-educated or trained in the more modern provincial institutes set up by Gómez Farías, instead of in the old universities, from which came the conservative intellectuals. Melchor Ocampo (1814–61) was the social theorist of this group; Benito Juárez (1806–72) was its statesman; Ignacio Ramírez (1818–79), who wrote under the pseudonym of the "Necromancer," fired some punishing salvos at the Church and religion; and Ignacio M. Altamirano (1834–93) and Guillermo Prieto (1818–97) were its poets. This generation of romantics, many of whom often risked their lives and one of whom, Melchor Ocampo, was murdered by soldiers, refused to be defeated by rebellions or to be dazzled by university scholars. General Ignacio Comonfort (1812–63) had headed these liberal followers of the Ayutla Plan. When he became president, however, he came to an agreement with his enemies, the embattled conservatives, in order to restore peace after three years of fighting. But one man never lost his faith in the liberal cause: Benito Juárez (1806–72), then president of the Supreme Court, who was the constitutional successor in the event of the absence or death of the president. When, in 1858, Comonfort went into exile, the republic found itself with two presidents: Felix Zuloaga, backed by the conservatives and the army in the capital, and Juárez, the legal successor. Juárez and his partisans, the most exalted liberals, the most romantic provincial intellectuals, refused to yield. They rounded up small armies, packed the whole government into carriages, the administration into several wagons, and wandered over the countryside behind their troops. They were beaten at Salamanca, were almost captured and executed at Guadalajara, sought sanctuary in Veracruz, which Juárez reached after taking ship in Manzanillo on the Pacific Coast and crossing the Isthmus of Panama against the rip tide of immigrants heading for California.

In Veracruz, Juárez put some political content into his government by issuing the laws that became known as the Reform. Thus he completed in 1859 the work begun by Gómez Farías in 1833 and continued by a few laws passed in 1856 and by the constitution of 1857. Primarily, Juárez was trying to affirm the supremacy of the state over the Church. The new laws secularized the life of the country, nationalized the property of the clergy, and separated Church and state.

By the summer of 1861, although earlier their generals had been defeated, the liberals had reorganized and returned to the fight; in the end, they conquered almost without having won a battle.

The essence of the Reform is embodied in two laws: the first was the so-called Ley Juárez, which abolished the jurisdiction of the ecclesiastical courts over members of the Church in civil cases. (Juárez was particularly concerned with establishing the equality of all Mexicans before the law.) The second was the Ley Lerdo, drawn up by Miguel Lerdo de Tejada (1812–61) and passed in June, 1856. This outlawed corporations, religious or otherwise, from owning property other than that indispensable to their immediate needs, such as church buildings. At that time, the Church owned lands valued at some $300 million. The law ruled that this property must be sold at public auction unless previously bought by renters. Lerdo believed that a class of small and medium landholders would be created by this legislation, in cities and rural regions alike, and that their taxes would augment the national income. Clearly, the law was inspired by the auctions held during the French Revolution and by the dissolution of the property of the Church decreed in Spain by Prime Minister Mendizábal some thirty years earlier. Lerdo hoped, too, that the lands so acquired would serve as security for loans which he felt confident he could float in the United States. The law made no explicit mention of the importance of diminishing the economic and political power of the Church, for the liberals preferred to present their measure as being exclusively an economic one. But on those grounds, during debate on the bill, only Ignacio Ramírez, the aforementioned "Necromancer," foresaw that, instead of creating new landowners the legislation would increase the holdings of the *latifundistas* and, far from impoverishing the Church, would make it the "banker for the nation," with funds from the sale of its properties. And that is what happened.

The Church, however, was not yet aware that it would, and besides, it did not wish to appear defeated. When the measure became law, the Archbishop of Mexico refused confession and burial in consecrated ground to anyone who bought ecclesiastical properties, and he excommunicated those who refused to resign their positions in the government (which required an oath of support of the law). More moderate lay Catholics argued that some of the Church's wealth was being used to succor the poor and that the Ley Lerdo would cut off this charity.

All in all, urban estates worth 10 million pesos and rural estates worth 2 million were expropriated from the Church. The wealth of the clergy was so great that it worried even a conservative like Alamán, who had pointed out years earlier that the clergy had grown rich not only from the ecclesiastical lands, but more especially from mortgages on the property of the faithful that the Church held. (These were not touched by the Reform laws.)

A war between the liberals and the conservatives, instigated by the Church, went on for three years. The Ley Lerdo, vigorously applied and reinforced by other legislation, gave the liberals the means to carry on the conflict. But the ultimate effects of the law were not those envisaged by its author. The Reform laws contained a threefold negation, as Octavio Paz has said: they denied the Spanish heritage, the indigenous past, and Catholicism, which had served to reconcile both heritages. In addition, the Reform tried to create in Mexico what the French Revolution had created in France—a class of small landowners, especially in the rural regions. In France, however, not only was the property of the Church released from mortmain but that of the nobility too, but in Mexico, non-Church property was left untouched. The juridical base of the Reform was the liberal conviction that the soil and subsoil are property of the nation, granted for use by the state as a concession, with the state retaining the option of expropriating it in the national interest. The Reform laws did not propose to change the social structure by any measure as radical as those advanced in revolutionary France; rather, they simply aimed to alter the political structure by taking away the economic power wielded by the Church and hoped to encourage industry and small landownership.

Yet the dogmatic liberals did not confine themselves to expropriating Church property. They also declared the *ejidos*, the public lands, the property of the whole nation. These communes of the Indians, in existence since the colonial era, were now to be distributed among the Indians who had been cultivating them. The result was that the Indian, who had never known private ownership, soon found himself faced with ruin, handicapped by debts, isolated from the old *ejido* institutions that had once protected him, and forced to sell the land he had acquired—after which he had to work it for the benefit of a new master. For the same people, many of them Spaniards, who had bought Church lands now bought the lands that the Indians had been granted but did not know how to cultivate on their own. In this fashion, as Ramírez had predicted, the dogmatism of the liberals—their blind faith in the concept that the Indians were the equals of all other citizens, needing no special protection or teaching—reinforced latifundism. For naturally the *latifundistas* were easily able to expand their holdings at the expense of the Indians, and as late as the Díaz regime the Ley Lerdo was used to destroy existing *ejidos* and accumulate land. Before the passage of the law, there had been three large groups of landowners: the Church, the ranchers and *hacendados*, and the Indians and mestizos on the *ejidos*. After the law, only the hacienda owners and ranchers remained. By the time of the Revolution of 1910, the number of haciendas had doubled from 6,000 to 12,000 and the big ranches from 15,000 to 30,000, until 97 per cent of the cultivated land in the country was in the hands of 1 per cent of the people.

The Ley Lerdo thus became a tragic example of how dogmatism—in this case, the application of liberal dogma that envisaged equality between the Indians and hacienda owners—can be so twisted from its original purpose of helping the poor as to benefit the rich at the poor's expense. And thus was independent Mexico's fundamental problem—Church-state relations—transformed into an agrarian problem after the Reform. Thousands of property owners were able to enlarge their holdings and turn them into haciendas. These huge estates became enormous, self-contained, autarkic production units. On the other hand, the people on the *ejidos*, which had previously been juridical entities with some influence, lost that status; the Indian found that he was abandoned, and he became a *de facto* serf of these new *latifundistas*. Later, the lesson of this development was taken to heart, and it helped to free the Mexican Revolution from the dogmatism that made the liberals of 1857 unwitting accomplices of the most regressive of great landowners.

In spite of their blunders, however, the liberals had not forgotten the Indians completely. The constitution of 1857 provided that no Indian would be obliged to lend his personal services without just recompense or without his full consent. In no case could the law authorize contracts resulting in loss of freedom—whether in fulfillment of a religious vow, in serving an apprenticeship, or in labor. "Free labor and free industry" was the liberal slogan.

The liberals had a left wing of their own, who saw the need "not to destroy, but to generalize property." Ponciano Arriaga (1811–65) was the exponent of this view. Others, influenced by utopian socialists, favored dividing property and establishing a rural middle class. Esteban Ávila, governor of Aguascalientes, promulgated a law in 1861 that levied a tax on large landholdings in order to force the *latifundistas* to sell land to small farmers. But the law never worked effectively.

In the course of the three-year civil war that followed the Reform of 1857, the Mexican mentality underwent a change that would prove to be lasting. For one thing, both camps were led by young generals and politicians; the graybeards did not predominate. For another, because the liberals needed money to pay their troops and support their government, Juárez, impelled as much by this need as by loyalty to liberal principles, responded to pressure from his generals by speeding up and generalizing the expropriation of Church property. Even before the expropriation law was made public, the liberals had seized the wealth of the churches in many cities and villages. In the heat of the battle, they had also executed the armed priests encountered in conservative ranks. And as a consequence, the Mexican lost his superstitious reverence for the clergy and learned that he could fight against the Church and survive.

None of the liberal leaders amassed fortunes for themselves, but they could not prevent many of their followers from doing so. This created a new middle class of war profiteers, ready to support the liberals out of self-interest. Indeed, this wealthy middle class managed to remain in power until the Revolution. For their part, the conservatives found that the clergy were turning their moveable wealth over to the faithful for safekeeping. But when the war ended, the faithful joined the liberal side in great numbers to avoid having to return the wealth entrusted to them, and they made common cause with those liberals who had grown wealthy from the property of the clergy.

In the final analysis, the interests of both parties overrode the national interest. To raise money, Miguel Miramón (1832–67), the clever and audacious general who led the conservatives, sold national bonds at an infinitesimal price to a Swiss broker named Jenker, who began at once to make Mexico's business his business. On the liberal side, Ocampo signed a treaty (the McLane-Ocampo agreement) that permitted passage of people from the United States across the Isthmus of Tehuantepec in perpetuity, hoping by this means to stave off American intervention, which was being hinted at; in return, the government in Washington promised to pay $2 million and agreed to indemnify citizens who had suffered damage in the Mexican War. The U.S. Senate refused to ratify the treaty because the Northerners believed it would favor the South.

At long last the war ended. The liberal generals entered Mexico City amid loud cheering and the proffers of laurel crowns. Juárez arrived a few days later, minus the brass bands, dressed in black, and riding in his black berlin, which had traveled over half of the country. For the first time, Mexico had a president dressed in mufti. But of all her presidents, he was the one who had been most involved in war.

Indeed, the conflict had no sooner ended than the conservatives began to prepare for a new thrust. They hoped that this time it would be definitive.

In time, the Reform laws might have profoundly affected Mexico's structure, as Ocampo had hoped. In his view, the laws were not drawn up to diminish the authority of the Church so much as to create new landholders and prevent the rise of economic forces stronger than the state. But time was not on Ocampo's side. As soon as the Reform laws were applied, they provoked a strong reaction from the unseated but not vanquished Church and from the conservatives. This reaction was to reach its apex with the establishment of a Mexican Empire ruled by an emperor imported from Europe. That, in turn, ignited a new civil war, and the Reform laws could be applied in a normal way only at the end of that long conflict. Even then, a dictatorship was needed to apply them, using the laws to keep the Church neutral rather than as an instrument for transforming the country.

Mexico's treasury was empty. Proceeds from the sale of Church property, instead of being used to build schools and roads, had been diverted to finance a civil war. Many liberals were demanding a dictatorship, but Juárez, who had fought to defend the constitution, intended to be a democratic executive. He called an election and was returned to office, only to be beset by criticism from a congress made up of impatient young men.

Juárez granted amnesty to the conservatives under sentence of death. But, in the north, bands of guerrilla priests still scoured the land. In 1861, they captured and executed three of the strongest leaders in the liberal camp: Ocampo, General Santos Degollado, and General Leandro Valle. Meanwhile, Spain, France, and Great Britain were demanding indemnities and apologies for the damage done to the property of their nationals during the civil war. With the coffers empty, Juárez was forced to decree a two-year suspension of payments on foreign debts. At that very moment, civil war broke out in the United States. Juárez realized then that he was standing alone against the possibility of foreign intervention.

The possibility was strong indeed, and it was provoked by the conservatives. Juárez proposed an accord with England and, to prove that the nation was without funds, offered the British an opportunity to supervise customs, but the Mexican congress rejected the agreement. Meanwhile, Spain, France, and England had agreed to "teach Mexico a lesson" and by the Treaty of London undertook to intervene to protect their interests. In January, 1862, the first detachments landed at Veracruz—Spaniards under the command of General Juan Prim (who, years later, was to depose Isabel II and die at the hands of an assassin). To justify their presence in Mexico, the three powers issued a manifesto declaring that their expeditionary forces had been sent "to preside over . . . the country's regeneration." To the Spaniards and English, regeneration meant paying the debts owed them. But to the French under Napoleon III, it meant effecting a plan concocted by a group of Mexican exiles and implanted in the Emperor's and the Empress Eugenie's heads to establish a vast Catholic empire, stretching from Texas to Panama, facing the Protestant Anglo-Saxon republicans to the north. This idea had been fathered by Archbishop Labastida of Puebla and General Juan N. Almonte (1803–69), who had turned to Paris for help. Their patron was the Duc de Morny, an associate of the Swiss banker Jenker, who by now held $15 million in Mexican bonds.

The plan, reported to Juárez, offered him a stratagem. He sent his foreign secretary to General Prim to inform the general of France's secret designs, and soon afterward, in April, the English and Spanish troops withdrew, while a new French army landed at Veracruz. General Almonte, arriving with it, had hardly set foot ashore before he acted out an old dream by proclaiming himself president. The Mexican exiles in Paris had felt confident that the people would welcome the French invaders and support them with arms. Trustingly, therefore, the French advanced toward Puebla, halfway between Veracruz and the capital. There, an army of seasoned guerrilla fighters met and defeated them with fieldpieces bought in Europe forty years before, after Waterloo.

Napoleon III was shorn of his illusions, but he did not care to lose his prestige. He dispatched 30,000 more troops.

Juárez levied new taxes and ordered a general mobilization. The results were not encouraging. The country was exhausted. A new attack on Puebla settled into a two-month siege, which ended with the surrender of the Mexican defenders of the city—almost the whole of the regular army. Troops were taken prisoner and sent to France. One of their officers, Porfirio Díaz (1830–1915), eluded capture and remained in the country. Only 14,000 men were left to Juárez, and not a single trustworthy general. Knowing that he could not defend his capital, Juárez moved the government northward to San Luis Potosí. The French entered Mexico City on June 7, 1863, where they were welcomed cordially by the clergy and the old conservatives.

The Mexicans had made a fool of Napoleon in the beginning; now he intended to make fools of the Mexican conservatives, just as he had deceived the Spaniards and the English. General Forey, commander of the invading army, decreed that ecclesiastical properties were not to be handed back to the Church, since he had discovered that many Frenchmen were the buyers of those properties.

All in all, the French turned out to be far too radical for the conservatives' taste. In order to checkmate them, a group of conservative notables hastened to offer the crown of Mexico to a European prince, the Archduke Maximilian of Austria (1832–67). Maximilian was a vacillating man, but he was also a man of good will, better than those who invited him. He insisted on a plebiscite to demonstrate whether or not the Mexican people wanted him as their monarch. Bazaine, the new French general, received instructions from Paris to organize the plebiscite.

Meanwhile, Juárez was traveling from city to city, trying to recruit soldiers, rally support, and raise money. In the north he stood almost alone; in the south, Porfirio Díaz held Oaxaca, and the old general Juan Alvarez (1790–1867) was in command of Guerrero. The rest of the country was in the hands of the conservatives, who were busy jailing and executing liberals. Maximilian, persuaded that the favorable plebiscite was genuine, sailed for Mexico with his wife, Carlotta. In preparation for their arrival, peons from the haciendas built a stone bridge called the Emperor's Bridge (still in use) along the road from Puebla, so that the imperial cortege would not need to ford a river.

In a sense, this moment—when Juárez and the liberals seemed to be conquered, abandoned, and without prospects—marked the beginning of the Mexican's grasp of his nationality. No longer was it a question of battles between parties, of ideological rivalries, or of factions—though to be sure all those things were still operative. Above and beyond everything else was the fact that the country was occupied by foreign forces, that an alien monarch was to govern it, and that the people, worn out by three years of civil war, seemed resigned to this. Yet out of that discouraging and defeating situation, the people emerged on their own, with no outside help, to no great fanfare, with a stubborn will to resist, choosing their own officers and leaders from their ranks, in the midst of intrigue, heroism, cowardice, maneuvering, ambition, bungling, firmness—all the acts and attitudes that cluster around moments of great historical tension. The revolt against the Empire was the first episode in Mexico's history of which Mexicans felt proud. Possibly it was the first moment when many, very many, Mexicans really felt that they were Mexicans.

All illusions were shattered. The conservatives lost theirs in the discovery that Maximilian was not a firm monarch but a dreamer and a liberal; Maximilian's vanished when he realized that he had not been called by the people and that it would be difficult to reign as an enlightened and progressive sovereign. He managed to persuade Napoleon to station troops in Mexico until 1867, even though the cost of their upkeep tripled the country's foreign debt. He tried to establish a reform government composed of moderates; he refused to return clerical property; and he even attempted to impose religious freedom. The Church began to favor attacks against Maximilian, and it was declared from the pulpit that the emperor was syphilitic, which was why Carlotta had borne him no children. Meanwhile, Maximilian concentrated on drafting laws—seven volumes in all—in the belief that he could solve his problems by legislation.

By about 1865, Maximilian had overcome almost all opposition. Even the liberals were applying for posts in the bureaucracy, the only source of income for the middle class. Just then the Civil War in the United States ended, and the government in Washington (which had never recognized Maximilian) began to aid Juárez. The Juarists were able to collect large supplies of munitions at the frontier; General Bazaine showed his brutality by executing them; and the people blamed his acts on Maximilian, although the true source was Napoleon, who wanted to finish Juárez off as quickly as possible so that he could withdraw his own forces. The number of guerrilla fighters multiplied, and the Juárez armies were reborn. Victor Hugo wrote to Juárez from his home on the Isle of Guernsey that he was fighting *à coups de montagne.* Carlotta sailed for Europe to ask for help and went mad there when her pleas were denied.

Maximilian was prepared to abdicate, but the conservatives organized so many demonstrations of loyalty that they persuaded him to remain. He was alone, for at last the French had sailed for home. Finally, the conservative army met defeat at Querétaro; the emperor was taken prisoner and executed with his generals. For the second time, Juárez entered the capital, as always riding in his black, dust-covered berlin. The wandering government had come to rest.

From top to toe, the Empire had been an artificial creation, put together to destroy liberalism. The religious newspaper *La Sociedad* had written: "The European political world must prevent America from becoming democratic in every sense and from submitting to the single and dangerous influence of Washington." Yet Maximilian had wanted to rule as a liberal, and even his general, Miguel Miramón, recognized when he took command of the imperial government in its last days that "no government has ever consolidated its hold on the country, because none has taken care to adapt the individual well-being to that of the public." In 1865, Maximilian had manumitted the serfs on the haciendas by decree, but the landowners refused to comply with his law. His plan to protect the Indians, the only people who welcomed him with some enthusiasm (perhaps because he was blond or a new incarnation of the old pre-Cortesian myth of Quetzalcoatl), proved abortive, too. Maximilian had fixed the working day at ten hours, shorter than was common then; he had forbidden strikes, but he had also abolished the hated company stores. These regulations were fixed by fiat, like the order that every hacienda with twenty or more families of peons and every factory with 100 operators must establish a school. They were never obeyed.

Maximilian started with many ingredients for success: a good army, the support of the Church and of France, and the war-weariness of the people. But aligned in opposition were a stubborn and dedicated group and the disadvantages of his own weak character, burdened with good intentions. He alienated the Church by failing to return its property. His Mexican generals found they had to play second fiddle to incompetent French officers, and, to add insult to injury, they had to support them because France controlled the revenues. Maximilian also made a number of mistakes: he granted high government posts, such as director of colonization and head of the land office, to Confederate generals and politicians who sought sanctuary in Mexico after the American Civil War and sold them land cheaply so that they could establish themselves in Cordova and Coahuila. They went down with the Empire. (Of course, the Mexicans hated the Confederate immigrants, because they feared that if their influence grew strong, they would try to establish slavery.) Another of Maximilian's mistakes was to negotiate with Juárez—to no avail—instead of taking the logical course of capturing him at any cost. In the end, the conservatives respected Maximilian's memory less than the liberals, whom he had impressed by his refusal to escape after defeat and by his yielding of the position of honor before the firing squad to a Mexican, his own general Miramón.

None of these events had succeeded in dividing the people. The Empire had made liberalism identical with national independence in their eyes. When Juárez returned to power, he found his country devastated, but united. For the first time, it would be possible really to govern the country. In fact, Juárez made every effort to create not only a government but an administration as well. He understood that he could not leave the Indians without safeguards, and, accordingly, he tried to keep the *ejidos* operating, even at the cost of not applying that part of the Reform laws which decreed the distribution of communal lands. In 1867, Juárez was re-elected president and immediately encountered opposition from his own partisans, who before long branded him a dictator.

During the regime of the conservatives, most of the *caciques* were liberals. But now that the liberals were in power, bossism was slated for extinction, for, as someone said, a central *cacique* was about to take the place of the local *caciques*. Matías Romero (1837–99), secretary of the treasury, succeeded in imposing on the country a degree of austerity and in combating administrative corruption. Industry and commerce began to recover, thanks in great part to the disappearance of the guild system, which had survived in various forms after independence. British engineers resumed their work of building a railroad from Veracruz to Mexico City, which was started in 1837 and opened, finally, in 1873.

Juárez had said that he would welcome Protestant ministers to his country because they would teach the Indians to read instead of demanding money from them for the saints. Now he made a vigorous effort to organize a school system. He appointed Gabino Barreda (1818–81) to do the job. Barreda had recently returned from Paris where he had been a disciple of Auguste Comte. Seven years later Mexico had 8,000 schools with some 350,000 pupils out of a school-age population of 2 million.

The army that won the victory for Juárez had numbered 90,000 men. He discharged 60,000 without pensions, provoking many mutinies and executions of insubordinates. Juárez wanted to have done with militarism, but he never achieved his wish. Porfirio Díaz, a very popular general whom Juárez distrusted, saw his chance in the discontent of the army and the *caciques*. He ran against Juárez in the next election and was defeated. In 1871, Juárez decided to run again. Sebastián Lerdo de Tejada (1820–89), a trusted friend, also ran against him, thus, with Díaz, splitting the liberal party into three factions. As none of the three candidates received a clear majority, congress chose Juárez as president. Lerdo became president of the Supreme Court (which meant he was vice-president). Díaz rebelled, was defeated, and went into hiding. Then, just as the country seemed about to enter upon a period of order, Juárez died of a heart attack. Lerdo succeeded him and was later elected president.

The new president's first act was to grant an amnesty to the Díaz rebels. But though he was highly intelligent and a fine orator, Lerdo was a complete failure as chief executive. Arrogant and vacillating, he alienated all his supporters. When Lerdo ran for re-election in 1876, Díaz proclaimed the so-called Tuxtepec Plan and the slogan "Effective Suffrage and No Re-election" (a motto that his adversaries were to use against him thirty years later). Support for Díaz came from the United States, where businessmen looked mistrustfully upon Lerdo because he refused American railroads permission to continue into the Mexican interior, declaring "Between the powerful and the strong, the desert." In November, Lerdo resigned and left the country. Díaz entered the capital, put down the small force that supported the president of the Supreme Court, and proclaimed himself president. His inauguration marked the beginning of a period of contradictions—dictatorship with material progress and civil retrogression. Historians have named this period the Porfiriate.

Under Díaz, the life of the country moved toward uniformity. Positivism became the intellectuals' straitjacket. All the Jacobin leanings still lingering in the liberal mind—or in the conservative, for that matter—coalesced in Mexican positivism. Side by side with this, the strength of the labor movement was growing—almost clandestinely—as it adapted utopian socialist doctrines, imported from Europe, to Mexican needs.

The men of the Reform had hoped that with the release of ecclesiastical property from mortmain a strong middle class would emerge. The middle class did grow, but latifundism grew faster. The positivists also hoped that they could construct by what they called their "mental revolution" a Mexican bourgeoisie, indispensable to the stability of society. In fact, the still feeble Mexican bourgeoisie did increase under Díaz, but it never threatened to dominate or dared to risk its privileges by opposing latifundism and destroying it. On the contrary, latifundism prevented bourgeois control. All in all, then, positivism was reduced to a "scientific" justification for the privileges of the bourgeoisie. Its motto was "fewer freedoms and more order and peace."

The Porfiriate did establish a degree of social peace, which lasted a decade. But two more decades passed during which the government wrestled with various symptoms of illness: the first strikes, Indian uprisings, agrarian revolts. Díaz ruled by repression through the local *caciques*, hired bandits as rural policemen, and made generals governors. But his was not simply a government of soldiers. He tried sincerely to find solutions to the country's problems; he brought progress; and he attracted intellectuals and businessmen, especially foreign capitalists. And he understood the importance of the agrarian problem. Díaz had no desire to change the *latifundista* society which confronted him, only to regulate it, and the haciendas served him as instruments for control. He was willing to try to distribute the *ejido* lands provided they would not pass ultimately into the hands of the big landholders, but his attempt failed. And, like many another dictator, the older he grew, the more he hardened himself against social reform. In 1908, in the last days of his regime, Díaz summed up his administration by telling James Creelman, the American correspondent for *Parson's Magazine*,

We have kept the republican and democratic form of government. We have, however, adopted a patriarchal policy in the present administration of the nation's business, by guiding and restraining popular movements, in the complete confidence that an enforced peace will permit education, industry, and commerce to develop elements of stability and unity among the people, who are intelligent and sensible by nature.

Then, because he knew his country well, he added:

The rich are too preoccupied with their wealth and their privileges to be of much use in advancing the general welfare. Their children don't make any great effort to improve their education or their character. On the other hand, the needy class, as a general rule, is too ignorant to become powerful. Democracy must depend for its development on the efforts of an active, hard-working middle class, desirous of advancement. That class derives, for the most part, from the needy class and to a lesser degree from the wealthy class; it is the middle class that is concerned with politics and that promotes the general advancement. . . . In days gone by, we had no middle class in Mexico, because the people's intelligence and energies were completely absorbed in politics and warfare.

This middle class, which Díaz considered a product of his regime, was what finished him.

5 · Modernizations

THE MACHINE AGE reached Mexico thirty or forty years late. New Spain had had almost no industry, owing mainly to the control which the mother country exercised over the colony and the trade monopoly she established. (And Spain herself was very backward in manufacturing.) In Texcoco, built around the lagoon that was once the site of Tenochtitlán, there were some textile mills; Guadalajara had some soap factories; and Puebla had a few cotton mills and some potteries.

Independent Mexico inherited the Spanish traditions of government monopoly and economic control. A few weeks after independence, the new government undertook to encourage home production by banning the importation of certain goods. In 1828, two Englishmen petitioned to lift the import ban on cotton for seven years, offering in return to establish 1,000 looms in Puebla; but the adverse reaction of the congress and Mexico's few industrialists ended that proposal.

In the absence of investment, production depended upon manpower—hence the extreme poverty of craftsmen and early factory workers. José Antonio Alzate (1729–90), a priest and scholar, constructed a cotton gin in Mexico twenty years before Eli Whitney did, with an output fifty times greater than that of one man, but it was never put to use because fifty peons would work for less than the cost of the machine. Mining alone—Mexico's chief source of income—made progress, thanks to the founding of the School of Mines in Mexico City in the seventeenth century. But the industry was generally backward even after 1801, when a "hydraulic machine built by Monsiu Lachaussé, an artisan native to Brabant" was installed in a mine. The machinery was always old and the labor supply inadequate. The series of civil wars that marked the second third of the nineteenth century aggravated this backwardness and thwarted any efforts made to overcome it.

The Church and the big landowners refused to invest in Mexican industry. Consequently, there was no ready Mexican capital. A Mexican named Godoy tried to establish industries in cooperation with foreigners, but ultimately he failed, for he realized that the people must be given education and land if they were to prosper, and as soon as he began to say this publicly, everyone turned on him.

Industry could find no market inside the country. Very little was exported, and most of the exports were products that should have been consumed at home, on the high plateau of the interior where rural poverty was widespread. Alamán saw that the paucity of workers and consumers was an obstacle to progress and wanted to encourage immigration—even from Asia, he said. He was not content to be a theorist, and, in addition, from 1830 on, he set up textile mills, potteries, glass factories, and a foundry. (He also proposed to open savings banks to forestall an increase in inequality as industrialization spread.) At the same time, he tried to attract British capital to Mexico in order to thwart schemes of the United States and Spain. But not until Porfirio Díaz came to power could genuine industrialization be reconsidered and means sought to accelerate it.

Ironically, Porfirio Díaz sowed the seeds of his own destruction by giving a new impulse to industrialization.* The United States, for example, was interested in developing a railroad network in Mexico as an extension of the lines then being laid in the West. But before that step could be taken, Mexico's feudal agrarian system would have to go, for railways could not prosper where there was no freedom of movement and no ready markets for the merchandise to be transported by rail. The wealth of available foreign capital and the neglect of the nation's resources created discontent that found expression in a strong nationalism, exacerbated by memories of the war over Texas. Andrés Molina Enríquez (1868–1940), a Mexican sociologist with almost prophetic vision, wrote: "The dynamite of the railroads lighted the fuse which later exploded in the Revolution."

The Mexican of that period justified not investing in national industries by saying that a Mexican, meaning an Indian, is basically incapable of handling machines—which was manifestly untrue, since Mexicans had operated mining machinery throughout the colonial period and after. And once the Revolution had ended and industrialization of the country resumed, they demonstrated that they were excellent mechanics and industrial workers.

Statistics on the subject are scarce and dubious. But we know that in 1823, after independence, there were 44,800 mine workers and 2,800 textile operators. A man could earn about 18 centavos for a 14-hour day in the mines, or 30 centavos for an 18-hour day in the textile mills; women and children received only 12 centavos for the same unending work. By 1854, the number of textile workers had grown to 12,000, with an average daily wage of 37 centavos. In 1873, 43,000 industrial workers (of whom 32,000 in the textile industry) worked a 12½-hour day in the summer, 12 hours in the winter, to earn 3.19 pesos a week. Thus, in twenty years, the pay had risen one peso a week and the length of the

---

* During·Alamán's last years in office, 2 textile mills were operating by steam; 34 by hydraulic motor; 14 by animal treadwheels, and 9 by human treadwheels—59 all told. In 1880, shortly after Díaz came to power, 54 factories were run by steam and water power; 36 by water power alone, and 9 by steam alone—in all, 99.

By the time the Porfiriate fell in 1910, investments in industry and mining were distributed as follows: United States interests, 499 million pesos; British, 87 million; French, 10 million; Mexican, 29 million.

work-week had been cut by six hours. The great number of strikes that occurred after Maximilian's downfall had accomplished this much. (In 1867, the strikers on "La Fama Montañesa" of Tlalpam, a suburb of Mexico City, had demanded a 12-hour working day for women in order that they could "attend to their duties of the hearth.")

In 1880, the number of workers, apart from 70,000 miners, had risen to 80,000. The newly industrialized workers had come from the countryside to the factories to make money. On the haciendas, married peons earned 6.50 pesos a month (bachelors, 4), and these wages were spent almost exclusively in stores operated by the landowners who, by offering minute amounts of credit which, trifling as they were, the peons would never pay off, bound them ever more tightly to the hacienda.

For a time, the liberals acted as interpreters of the needs and aspirations of the workers. But before long the gap between the nascent proletariat and the liberal middle class widened. Groups of workers immigrated from France and Spain, bringing with them the ideas of Charles Fourier, the utopian socialist, or of the anarchist-syndicalists, or of the Marxists. These newcomers were better able than the Mexican liberals to perceive the incompatibility of the interests of the middle and working classes in that early period of industrialization.

Some mutual-benefit societies for artisans had been set up, but they could do nothing for their members beyond providing for them in case of illness and for their widows and orphans in case of death. Little by little, as the artisan class identified itself with the proletariat, the mutual-benefit societies became trade unions, although they did not use that name. During an election campaign, trade unions always supported some candidate; indeed, Porfirio Díaz counted on them during his early campaigns. On the whole, however, they were nonpolitical, and antipolitical when they were headed by anarchist-syndicalists. Later, all the unions began to organize on the national level and formulate programs for social change and improvement.

The idea of mutual-benefit societies was taken up by the artisans. The Colegio Artístico and the Junta de Fomento de Artesanos (Association for the Encouragement of Craftsmen) had already been founded in 1843, under Santa Anna, both with the Virgin of Guadalupe as patroness and dedicated to the protection of apprentices. The two institutions circulated a document that pledged the signers to use only products made in Mexico. Eventually, many craftsmen were converted to the cooperative movement before the proletariat absorbed them. Their cooperative organizations had proposed to protect them especially from such absorption, but inevitably failed to do so.

In the workingman's literature of that period, certain concepts imported from Europe were constantly repeated. But in every case, they sounded with the characteristic voice of a different reality, a Mexican reality, even though the writers might be men born outside Mexico. Numerous workers' newspapers were established, but they were short-lived. In 1874–75, for example, *La Comuna (The Commune)* appeared with some radical proposals, not only defending the right to strike, but also championing an idea that was exotic for its time—women's rights. Guillermo Prieto, a poet who was also a professor of political economy who attacked socialism in his courses, was one of many liberals who wrote for *El Socialista,* published irregularly between 1871 and 1888. But the journal with the greatest influence was *El Hijo del Trabajo (The Son of Toil),* edited between 1876 and 1886 by José María González, a tailor. González believed that mutual-benefit societies would solve the social problem, and he denounced specific cases of exploitation which, he said, could have been prevented by them. González often showed concern for the Indians and their condition, an unusual preoccupation for anyone in the labor movement, and re-published the texts of French writers: Lamennais, Proudhon, Victor Hugo, Babeuf, and Eugène Sue.

Curiously enough, not many utopians emerged in this environment, as they had in Europe; in fact, the Mexican scene was marked by a certain respectful and modest despair. The only man to suggest a model for a new society was Juan Nepomuceno Adorno (1807–87), a prolific inventor and an employee of the tobacco monopoly. In the manner of Proudhon, he asserted in *Los Males de México (The Ills of Mexico)* and *La armonia del Universo (The Harmony of the Universe)* that money must represent labor and serve humanity as a means to enable mankind to return to primitive simplicity and to a federative organization based on love of one's fellow-man.

There was nothing utopian about Polonius C. Rhodakanaty, however, a Greek tailor (tailors appeared to play the role of initiators in the Mexican labor movement that typographers filled in other countries) who tried in vain to found a Fourierist phalanstery and later dedicated himself to the education of the workers. In 1866, Rhodakanaty founded a school called the Escuela Moderna y Libre, in the State of Mexico, which graduated several labor leaders; two of its impassioned young students organized socialist clubs and printed newspapers that were constantly moribund or being resuscitated. A disciple of this school, Julio Chávez, organized a peasants' rebellion in 1869, which spread through Puebla and Veracruz until Chávez was captured and shot in the patio of the school where he had learned his theories.

Another Fourierist, Alberto Santa Fe, became the father of a short-lived Communist Party in 1878, and wrote in prison a "Law for the People" which, when published, was excuse enough for the authorities to suspend the newspaper that printed such incendiary doctrine. And there were some young poets who indulged in a kind of lachrymose socialism. But neither Marxism nor Bakuninism, then dominant in the European labor movement, ever seized Mexico. Mexicans were more inclined to fight for immediate objectives than for theories that would presumably transform society.

In 1870, a group of Rhodakanaty's disciples founded the Gran Círculo de Obreros de México (Great Council of Mexican Workers), which was loyal to the First International. The Gran Círculo platform demanded equality in military service, free elections, the appointment of labor counsels (government defenders of workers' interests, similar to the *procuradores de indios* appointed by the Spanish crown to protect the Indians), and wages adjusted to the cost of living. The Gran Círculo, which lasted for ten years and whose membership reached 8,000, sponsored the publication for the first time in Mexico of the works of Marx, Bakunin, and others.

During the same period, the railroad and textile workers were organized, under the influence of some anarcho-syndicalist workers from the United States who came to Mexico to lend their professional skills to their colleagues. Nicasio Idar, who had lived in the United States, set up a Supreme Order of Railroad Workers in 1888. The title obviously is modeled on the names then commonly used in the United States.

Numerous other attempts were made to create organizations of workers on a national scale. In 1876, the Gran Círculo convened the First Permanent Workers' Congress with the motto "My Freedom and My Right." In 1880, the Second Workers' Congress met, presided over by a woman named Carmen Huerta.

With all this going on, a movement to organize farm workers got under way for the first time in the country's history. In 1877, the first Farm Labor Congress met to form a Central Communal Committee and establish local agrarian leagues. In 1879, delegates from fifteen of these leagues in the rich Bajío region signed a plan for an insurrection that would install a "socialist or municipal" government. In 1880, General Tiburcio Montiel founded the Mexican Agrarian League with which he worked actively until he was accused of being a "Communist" and exiled to Baja California, where he died in 1885.

The Church in Mexico had always been an entity of decisive importance and always an overt defender of the social order. But under the Porfiriate, the pressure to better the condition of the people and the first pricklings of a social conscience aroused the interest of some priests. In 1896, Monsignor Francisco Banegas, Bishop of Querétaro, wrote:

It is a fact that slavery exists [in Mexico] more horrifying than the ancient slavery, because it is veiled by an appearance of liberty. . . . It is not necessary to travel far to find it; in a few hours the railroad will bring us to where it is. We come to a country estate. Here we find the laborer: he is worn out by work, his life has been sacrificed, and even his conscience has been immolated. He guides the plow from morn to night; from morn to night he digs and delves; hour after hour he tills the soil, waters it, cuts the wood, gathers the harvest; and in exchange for this horribly fatiguing toil, he receives only eighteen to twenty-five centavos a day, which is given him partly in seed and partly in legal tender, and even this amount seems excessive to the landowners, who find ingenious ways to reduce it. The worker needs other things to feed and clothe himself; the owners will give them to him. Here is the store in which he can provide himself with everything. Behold the consequences: the peon gives his labor and in return he receives only bad food and worse clothing.

The bishop went on to warn the masters of the peons:

Rich men, you have no choice: either you open your hearts to charity . . . and alleviate [the workers'] 'sufferings by decreasing the hours of work and increasing the day's pay, in line with the charitable thinking of Leo XIII, or you shall pile up hatred and resentment, and when the socialist wind blows through Mexico—and perhaps it will blow soon—it will increase the turbulence of those seas which you yourselves have stirred up, until your wealth and your lives will be swept away in their rude and powerful thrust.

Men in authority from liberal and anticlerical backgrounds viewed the vague gestures Catholics made toward the social question with some mistrust. The aristocrats, all very Catholic, criticized the priests for concerning themselves with it. But Catholic congresses, seminaries, and journals began to come to grips with the theme, especially in the first decade of the present century. One very aggressive journalist, Trinidad Sánchez Santos (1859–1912), distinguished himself in this effort by fighting hard for the protection of the Indian and the extension of small landholdings. Several Catholic trade unions sprang up but were not successful. Later, in the midst of the Revolution, a Jesuit priest, Fr. Alfredo Méndez Medina, established the Catholic Social Secretariat and even founded an ephemeral Catholic Party in 1913–14.*

Businessmen were few in number. The so-called upper class was composed mainly of the owners of haciendas, many of whom were politicians and generals. The industrialists' by and large never deviated from the conventional currents of opinion and left it to the lawyers to find solutions for the country's problems.

* Documentation for all references in this chapter will be found in Chapters IV and XII of Víctor Alba, *Las ideas sociales contemporáneas en México* (Mexico City, 1960).

Their general indifference toward social questions is revealed by the experience of one industrialist called Carlos Ariste, whose name has come down in Mexican history not because he was a millionaire or for his deeds of charity, but because in 1877, when overproduction was a widely discussed problem, he recommended reducing the hours of the working day as a solution, and of course no one would listen to such heresy. It never occurred to anyone that "overproduction" in a country like Mexico, with a backward and feeble industry, was a clear indication that industry needed more markets, and that expansion could occur only in the rural regions and the poor quarters of the cities, since the wealthy were already buying all they needed. But the mere thought of giving peasants and workers the means to turn them into consumers and customers was completely foreign to the governing class and the businessmen, even to the politicians who were oriented culturally to Europe. At that time, European culture ruled the salons in the capital, the gloomy ministerial offices, and the haunts of the theorists and scientists.

In the days of Juárez, a young Mexican teacher, Gabino Barreda, had gone to Paris, where he sat at the feet of Auguste Comte, and had come home to reorganize the educational system. Like others in the Reform movement, Barreda hoped by corrective legislation to help to create a strong bourgeoisie that would unify his war-torn country. Porfirio Díaz sought to achieve the same unity from the seat of power.

The men educated under Barreda's system, which was established in the final years of the Reform and the first years of the Porfiriate, were positivists. Concurrently, positivism was spreading through Latin America as an ideology of progress. Even today, in Brazil, it is possible to find churches of the positivist religion. In Chile and Argentina, it affected the labor movement. In Mexico, it was essentially the doctrine of those who hoped that Porfirism would serve as a springboard to the creation of a new and modern bourgeoisie.

Half a century earlier, Mora had spoken of the need for bringing about a "mental revolution." The positivists wanted that, too. But they soon ran into a basic contradiction. The Mexican bourgeoisie was small, feeble, living in the shadow of the government and latifundism. Political order depended on the regional *caciques*. If the bourgeoisie was to flourish, it had to destroy latifundism and democratize Mexican political life. But it was too weak to attempt either, and knew it. Instead, it tried to accommodate to the situation and to prosper without changing. Naturally, the result was failure, and the field was left open to the lower middle class and working class, who felt wholly estranged from oligarchic latifundist society. Someone once said that in Europe positivism served to soothe the bad conscience of the rising bourgeoisie. In Mexico, it acted to soothe the feelings of impotence aroused in a bourgeoisie that wielded some influence but could not dominate.

Adherents of positivism argued that it had made England the greatest nation in the world and that it could do the same for Mexico. Telésforo García (1844–1919), one of its theorists, claimed so openly. But, said the positivists, for the time being and as a first step, they must form a conservative party (Díaz still called himself a liberal) to bring together the elements of order in Mexican life, relinquishing part of their freedom in exchange for greater order and peace. As Barreda argued, in the third stage of Mexican history (the first was the theological [colonial]; the second was the metaphysical [independence]; and the third was positive [Reform and after]), the state is the guardian of the material order, in which the rights of each individual are limited by the rights of others. Wealth is "a public force that society has placed in the hands of the rich for the common good and for progress."

All these positions were finally expressed in political terms when, in 1892, the positivists—who were nicknamed "scientists," in the sarcastic Mexican way—organized their political party, called the Liberal Union. One "scientist" stated in his newspaper, *La Libertad:* "On the day when we can say that our basic charter has produced a million settlers for us, we shall have found the constitution that suits us best. Then it will be no longer a phrase on the lips: it will be a plow in the hands, a locomotive on the railways, and money everywhere." The Liberal Union judged that the moment had come to grant greater commercial and eco-

nomic freedom to make money. They even went so far as to oppose the laws prohibiting usury.

The positivists were true Jacobins, insofar as "the deepest root
of Jacobinism is dogmatic reasoning," as Comte had written. If
they failed, they considered that it was Mexico's fault, not theirs.
In Mexico, the Comtian slogan of "Love, Order, and Progress"
was changed to "Freedom, Order, and Progress." (In Brazil, the
people dispensed with love *and* freedom and left only "Order and
Progress" on the great shield of their country.) Catholics and
liberals attacked them on the ground that they were concerned
only with material goods, but, said Barreda, if the wealthy were
to share their goods, "perhaps they would go to heaven, but the
rest of mankind would languish in a real hell." All that was
needed, he thought, was to imbue the rich with a realization of
their social function.

Positivists were not content with books; they had to act. Positivist devotees founded the Sociedad Metodofila in 1877 with the
aim of achieving "self-sacrifice by superiors for inferiors; respect
and veneration by inferiors toward superiors." In Mexico—where
the souls of the prehistoric, of the conquistadors, of medieval
society, and of the nineteenth century met and mingled—the only
force that could unify so much diversity was science, that is,
science as interpreted by the positivists, of course.

These paternalistic Jacobins were concerned about who could
succeed Díaz, grown old in office. They would have liked to find
not so much a person, as a law, good or bad, which everyone
would obey. The material progress of the country was bound to
continue creating the habits of order necessary to the enjoyment
of freedom and the real exercise of suffrage, they thought, but
until capital became abundant, there must be no talk of bettering
the lot of the proletariat; that would be sheer demagoguery. José
Yves Limantour, one of the most prominent "scientists," who
served under Díaz as secretary of the treasury, wrote in 1901 that
freedom was the privilege of the elite and that it was not an end,
but a means. Others, however, positivist-trained but less dogmatic,
realized that the public must be given a voice, albeit gradually
and with many precautions taken. Sierra, for one, believing that
Mexico's great problem was to achieve nationhood and that in

order to do so, it must pass through a stage of "administrative power" (that is, dictatorship), said that before it could emerge from this phase, the indifferent masses must be "disentailed," "to make them live the life of present-day humanity."

This was not exactly what the Porfiriate was doing, although without realizing it, it was creating the necessary conditions. No one of the period talked of the agrarian problem, except for a few scholars, whose words were later echoed on the eve of the Revolution. The price of land had continued to rise, for all the tracts granted to the Indians by the Reform had been acquired by others, and there was no more cleared land available. On some of the haciendas, modern agricultural methods began to be used, but the owners' treatment of the workers was far from modern. When Díaz established a land registry and decreed that no one could own land unless he could show title to it, the hacienda-owners, knowing that only rarely could an Indian produce documentary proof of ownership, rushed to seize the *ejidos* and public lands that had somehow survived the Reform laws. Enormous tracts in the virtually unpopulated lands of the north were distributed to them and to surveying companies. In this fashion, 90 million acres were turned over to seventeen enterprises. On the eve of the Revolution, 3,000 families owned half of Mexico; of the 10 million persons who worked on the land, 9.5 million owned none of it. In the regions where the Indians could live semi-independently, several rebellions broke out in protest against this despoilment but were harshly crushed.

At the same time that he was disposing of open land, Díaz encouraged industry. During his consecutive terms of office, the production of metals quadrupled; the Valley of Mexico was drained as a health measure; bridges and port facilities were constructed; telephone lines were strung; textile mills and sugar refineries were opened. Mexican bonds sold at high prices on the foreign market. By the early twentieth century, the foreign debt had been reduced to its lowest point in the history of the country. But the wealth thus created was controlled by foreigners and by a very small group of Mexicans. Of the sixty-six important firms that figured in the report of the Mexican Central Bank in 1908, thirty-six shared the same thirty men on their boards of directors.

Díaz had encouraged the building of railways with foreign capital, especially from the United States and Britain. Consequently, new population centers emerged, not at production points (the haciendas), but at distribution points. (This situation increased the freight rates and raised living costs.) Mexicans continued to invest in land instead of industries, and, for the most part, new plants were foreign-owned. Frenchmen, who had settled in Mexico in considerable numbers, especially Frenchmen from Barcelonnette, a region in the Alps, were owners of clothing boutiques, fabric shops, and, later, large department stores. Spaniards owned land, but they also went into the grocery and baking businesses and, because they were most visible, became a favorite target of caricaturists. Germans settled in the south, in Chiapas, where they established coffee plantations. Still later, English and Americans focused on the oil industry in the northeast near Tampico. North Americans also had mining interests, the most famous of which was the Cananea, and acquired important tracts of land, many of them as hunting preserves.

A measure of social peace prevailed for a decade, but as soon as industries began to develop new conflicts arose and social pressures increased. The government and the positivists attributed the unrest to the manipulations of "outside agitators," their own blind spots depriving them of any real awareness of the situation everywhere at the beginning of the new century.

Thinking that cooperatives might serve as a sop, Díaz attempted, by decree, to unite all the labor organizations into a single mutual-benefit system under government control. Two governors (but never the federal government) tried to initiate some social legislation, though they confined their efforts to regulating the employers' obligation to care for men accidentally injured on the job. In 1877, the workers of Tlalpan petitioned the secretary of the interior to rule on labor conditions in the factories, but the secretary refused to do so because "it is not within the scope of the administrative authority to impose conditions on proprietors and workers."

Díaz and his advisers thought of the country's problems in economic rather than political or social terms. They hoped to maintain order through the *caciques*, by the brute force of the rural police, by the motto of "little politics and much admin- istration," and by the tactics expressed in two of the dictator's phrases: "bread and the stick" and "shed a little bad blood to save the good."

This indifference to the social situation prevailed even into the last days of the Porfiriate, when the need to organize parties to succeed Díaz was felt. None of the political parties formed at that time had a social program, though all of them avowed that edu- cation was indispensable to the attainment of liberty. Only a few scattered persons talked about social problems. The Revolution, hovering over them, came as a surprise to everyone, even to those who were working to bring it about.

6 · Rebellions

THE FIRST TO BE SURPRISED by the Revolution was Díaz, because
he believed he had brought prosperity to the country, especially
to the middle class, and because he did not know that periods of
prosperity are the very times when those who believe they are
bearing the burden of the national economy begin to desire power
for themselves. And the middle classes were surprised because
neither among their ranks nor among those who held power was
there any consciousness of the other face of Mexican society—of
the peasants made serfs (sometimes slaves, as in the case of the
people forcibly transported to Yucatán to work on the haciendas). It took J. K. Turner, an American member of the IWW,
to write the classic indictment of the Díaz regime from the social
point of view.[*]

The people in the cities, the only people who "counted," had

* *Barbarous Mexico*, belatedly published in 1911.

turned their backs on the countryside, but not everyone in the nation was uninformed as to the condition of the rural areas. Those who were aware of it, who warned in vain, were the true precursors of the Mexican Revolution, even before they dared to espouse it and before they could predict that it would come.

Ricardo Flores Magón (1873–1922) and Andrés Molina Henríquez (1868–1940) were the theorists of this ideological current that was to lead to the Revolution. Others, too, in philosophical and juridical studies, cast aside the positivist straitjacket and laid the intellectual groundwork for consideration of revolution as a possibility. Antonio Caso (1883–1946), in philosophy, and Winstano Luis Orozco (1857–1927), in jurisprudence, were the most outstanding figures in this area.

José Covarrubias (d. 1936), a lawyer in the final years of the Porfiriate and a friend of the few intellectuals and men of affairs who were thinking about social change, described their common aspiration as follows: "The remedy for the situation in which the country's politics is directed by a bureaucratic group that does not amount to 20 per cent of the total population is to see to it that the rural proletariat is incorporated into the political mass. There is no other way to achieve this purpose than to provide it with economic independence, that is, to make its members landowners." At a time of guerrilla fighting and mutinies, Covarrubias pointed out, "the fact that two-thirds of the inhabitants envy the life of the rebel in arms, because he is free, explains the constant upheavals in the history of Mexico." In the nineteenth century, he said, people wrongly believed that progress meant an increase in wealth, not a better distribution of it; only political remedies (laws) had been applied to social ills, and they remedied nothing.

A movement with a more precise social ideology was created by Ricardo Flores Magón and his brothers Jesús (1871–1930) and Enrique (1877–1955). They started with a political party called the Partido Liberal Mexicano, which kept that name to the end, although its ideology changed rapidly in response to events. The Flores Magón brothers had allied themselves with the IWW during their several exiles in the United States, and this gave the anarchists reason to consider them their own, but in reality their position, aside from a general tone of active protest, was tinged with characteristically Mexican ambiguity and pragmatism. They founded the newspaper *Regeneración* in 1900 but soon were forced to publish it in San Antonio, Texas, and St. Louis, Missouri, in order to escape government persecution. They organized liberal clubs, conventions, even uprisings—often by mail, which proved that the people were ready for them. Often they saw the insides of jails; Ricardo died, blind, in the U.S. prison at Leavenworth. As we shall see, they had no faith in politicians; indeed, when the Revolution was in full swing, they opposed Madero and tried to join up with Zapata. Ultimately, with the aid of some members of the IWW, they established a Socialist Republic in Baja California to bring pressure to bear on the moderate center of the country in the hopes of radicalizing it.

But the importance of the Liberal Party lay in what it did before the fall of Díaz when, without consciously setting out to do so, it prepared the way for injecting social aspirations into political opposition.

In 1900, Jesús Flores Magón was a fledgling lawyer; Ricardo had already started to practice law. The first numbers of *Regeneración* concentrated on exposing cases of venality in the courts. The memories of the village in Oaxaca where they were born, their study of the Reform and the social consequences of its laws, and contact with the IWW—all had a powerful influence on the Flores Magón brothers. In 1901, they still believed that a revolution could be averted by granting freedom and ensuring administrative integrity, and they established liberal clubs to support a candidate from the "producer class" to follow the ailing Díaz. But in 1906, when they and other like-minded leaders issued the manifesto for the new Liberal Party,* its revolutionary character was evident. For they understood that there was no possible hope of change within the Díaz system. They distrusted all government, demanded such important reforms as abolition of obligatory military service, establishment of a national guard, naturalization of all foreigners who acquired property in Mexico, a ban on Chinese immigration (then considerable) in order to shut off competition from cheap labor, nationalization of Church property,

---

* They were in St. Louis, Missouri, at the time, in exile.

closing religious schools, an eight-hour day, and a minimum wage of 1 peso a day. In the view of these new liberals, all these measures were bound to create conditions that would permit the workers to fight freely for their goal, which was to change society. They espoused labor laws that would guarantee Sunday as a day of rest (something unknown at the time), that would prohibit child labor and company stores, and that would set up a system of compensation for accidents, layoffs, or discharge, and a pension system. They advocated the return of communal lands to the villages and the granting of land to farm workers, the legal seizure of unworked lands, and a farm bank to offer credit to the small landowners. The Liberal Party viewed the social question even more broadly. For example, it demanded that legitimate and natural children be regarded as equals; that penitentiaries be turned into labor colonies; that education be provided for the Indians. It even advocated a guarantee of the integrity of the Latin American countries by some form of union. The slogan of the Liberal Party was "Land and Liberty"; the Revolution adopted it a few years later.

During this period, many Catalan weavers came to Mexico to work in the mills of Puebla and Orizaba—all of them anarchists. At about the same time, Ricardo Flores Magón had concluded that the Díaz dictatorship could not be terminated by simple political means. The people would be forced to resort to armed action against "that three-headed monster: the government, the clergy, and capital." Whether Díaz could be re-elected or must give way to another candidate, a problem which the urban middle class was passionately considering, did not interest him. "The Anti-Re-election Party seeks only political liberty," he wrote, "leaving the great land monopolists to keep their vast holdings, the workers to continue being the same beasts of burden, and the monks to continue to stupefy the masses. . . . The Anti-Re-election Party is [in fact] the conservative party."

The Magonist liberals worked tirelessly. They organized groups of field workers, headed trade unions, prepared the ground for rebellions into which they would try to draw the city and farm workers and the more radical elements of the middle class. The agitation and uprisings that marked the last years of the Díaz

regime were their work, for they knew how to take advantage of
the discontent that rose to the surface as soon as the country's
material progress permitted some sectors of the proletariat and the
peasantry to live a somewhat less brutalized life. Soon the Magonist forces heard their doctrines echoed among the schoolteachers.

In June, 1906, a Great Council of Free Workers, affiliated with
the Liberal Party, was organized in the factory town of Rio
Blanco in Veracruz. A few months later, eighty more such clubs
(they would be called plant cells today) were scattered across
the country, particularly in the textile mills, asking for a minimum
wage of 75 centavos as an immediate concession. Newspapers
with somewhat muddled socialist and anarchist leanings multiplied in the provinces. New political figures emerged around
them, whom the politicians in the capital refused to take seriously, but soon they were to organize the squadrons of the
Revolution.

The liberals took a radical stand on the country's problems only
because they were driven to radicalism by the conviction that the
Porfiriate would neither change from within nor commit suicide
by calling a legal election. But they understood fully that their
achievements could only be modest. They also understood a basic
contradiction which the middle class and bourgeoisie were not
wise enough to see: namely, that industrial progress could be at-
tained only if labor were trained and free and if a broad rural
market existed; they realized that these two conditions would
never come about as long as latifundism prevailed. But in order to
destroy latifundism, Mexico would have to temporarily renounce
the kind of peace that the *latifundistas* guaranteed and that the
capitalists wanted and desired above everything (most of them
being foreigners, hungry for immediate profits and not concerned
about future prospects). The only people who would bother
about such things were those who had nothing to do with the
capitalists and who could see the contradiction. In a sense, the
Revolution came to fill the vacuum created by the timidity, the
lack of imagination, and the faulty understanding of their own
interests which prevailed among the nascent Mexican and foreign
capitalists.

The first step to take in resolving that contradiction—although the liberals did not recognize it as their immediate aim—was to demonstrate that the Díaz regime could no longer insure public order.

The countryside was restive. Latifundism was in full sway. There were more than 300 haciendas, none covering an expanse of less than 24,000 acres; 116 embracing about 50,000 acres; 51 nearly 70,000; 11 as much as 240,000; and 7 stretching over 500,-000 acres or more. Many of the proprietors of these haciendas were Spanish. The field workers—who lived like serfs, bound to the land by might if not right, liable to be transported across the country under the pretext of a military draft to work lands recently opened to cultivation—were Indians or mestizos whose way of thinking and way of life were very like those of the Indians. Porfirio Díaz had sent his troops to subdue the tribes that had thus far succeeded in remaining unconquered—the Yaquis in Sonora and the Maya of Yucatán—and, through terror and brutality, managed to subjugate them. Subsequently, these Indians' lands passed into the hands of generals and politicians, and national lands were also distributed with a prodigal hand to Mexicans and foreigners who put them under cultivation and went off to spend the wealth earned from them outside the country, generally in Paris. Fifty-seven thousand villages became enclaves on the big haciendas. The buying power of the peons shrank to a scant quarter of what it had been at the end of the colonial period. A rural guard, made up of men trusted by hacienda owners—some were pardoned outlaws—maintained peace in the country.

It is not surprising, then, that in spite of the hazards that political work in the rural areas entailed, the Magonist liberals found the ground more fertile in the somnolent provincial towns, and among the *Indiada*, as the gentlemen of the haciendas contemptuously labeled the peons, than in the cities. This rural tension easily accounted for the long series of agrarian uprisings in the last years of the Porfiriate, the strongest and bloodiest of which occurred in Tenochic in 1892, in Papantla in the vanilla-growing region in 1895, in Acayucan in 1906, and in Viesca in 1908. The liberals played no part in the first two, but they used the experience gained in early local rebellions to organize those which followed.

Magonist propaganda was also heeded by miners and industrial workers. News of the St. Louis Manifesto, proclaimed by the Flores Magón brothers from exile, came to Mexico City simultaneously with the first news of what had happened in the mining city of Cananea, in Sonora State, where liberals had organized the Liberal Brotherhood Union. In May, 1906, miners affiliated with the union asked for wages and treatment on a par with those granted to foreign workers (who were earning three times as much as Mexicans and had access to a hospital exclusively for them) and struck when their plea for equality was rejected. The 8,000 strikers marching through the streets were first attacked with hoses, then fired on by officials of the mining company. When the government learned of this, it sent in troops to "save order and civilization." Inasmuch as Cananea was close to the U.S. border, William Green, the major shareholder in the mining company, and 300 U.S. soldiers crossed into Mexican territory, with the permission of the Díaz government, to fight the strikers. The casualties were heavy; the dead were estimated at the time to number more than 200 men.

The textile industry was also ailing. After the establishment of a Magonist organization that could channel and direct the workers' unrest, strikes occurred frequently. Díaz decreed that after January 1, 1907, all strikes must cease and that thenceforth the workers would be issued certificates of good conduct (a reverse method of drawing up a black list). On January 7, a rebellion broke out in Rio Blanco in protest against the government order. Troops arrived to quell the revolt and their commander promised that the workers' demands would be met, but after the workers had accepted his pledge and returned to the mills, the troops began to slaughter them.

In the heat of this turmoil, liberal groups rose up in arms at various points across the country. They were crushed by the army and had to seek refuge in the mountains, where they stayed until the Díaz regime ended.

The restlessness bred in the cities by Díaz' endless stay in power, the growing influence of foreigners in the national economy, the frustrations of the middle class, which was not gaining real participation in power, the workers' mutinies, the farmers' rebellions, and the liberals' guerrilla warfare—all this added up to nothing more than a state of mind. It would have to be transformed into a conscious will before there could be any political results—and that would never happen so long as the dogmas and the mental habits created by more than three decades of positivist teaching prevailed. The young intellectuals of the day, later known in Mexico's cultural history as the "Generation of the Athenaeum," took it upon themselves to destroy these paralyzing dogmas.

On March 20, 1908, Justo Sierra delivered a speech that—he did not realize it—marked the beginning of a new epoch. "What great fundamental scientific truth," he asked, "has not been debated or is not being debated at this moment?" If science is doubted, the "scientific" doctrine of positivism must also be doubted. Bergson's theory of creative evolution, first introduced to Mexico by Antonio Caso (1883–1946) and later espoused by José Vasconcelos (1882–1959), demonstrated that nothing is immutable, least of all a political regime. In affirming that man is capable of acting disinterestedly, Caso justified in advance the redemptive theories.

In 1908, the young men who took Caso's teachings to heart established the Ateneo de la Juventud (Youth Athenaeum). Its members brought literature and ideas from Europe, breathed new life into the cultural atmosphere, opened doors and windows to the winds of the world. From the Athenaeum's rostrum, Caso voiced the rebellion against positivism, thereby re-creating a sort of intellectual virginity among the new generation. Vasconcelos, together with Alfonso Reyes (1889–1959), the humanist and poet Enrique González Martínez (1871–1952), Julio Torri (b.1889), and others, definitely changed the country's culture. Vasconcelos was to say later that "our very desperation, our silent grief at contemplating life without nobility or hope, brought us this new feeling." These young intellectuals who knew Europe better than Mexico now tried to get close to the people and in 1912 founded the Universidad Popular (People's University), which lasted with some interruptions until 1922. It was there that Caso gave Mexico's first course on dialectical materialism—which he opposed—and declared that the political constitution must adapt itself to the reality of the country and, once having done so, must continue to reflect reality. Mexico needed three cardinal virtues to become a strong nation: wealth, justice, and enlightenment. The objective of Mexico's younger generation must be the attainment, not of commercial or industrial prosperity, but of social progress.

Caso said there were five forces in Mexico, four of which must be integrated in the future constitution: the army, the rich, the proletariat, and the Church. The fifth was the influence of the United States, which the constitution must always reject lest Mexico cease to be an independent nation. Finally, Caso warned, the country must stop imitating others: "Our poverty today, our inveterate habit of revolution, our tragic bitterness are the sour fruits of unreflecting imitation. Let us be democrats, socialists, or fascists, but always in the Mexican manner." The two races, which he called archaeological (the Indians) and historical (the mestizos and Creoles), had not succeeded in forming a people, a nation. In order to achieve this, "we must turn our eyes . . . to what we really are."

Some political thinkers had already tried to do this, but they were voices crying in the wilderness to which positivism had relegated them. After the Athenaeum, however, they began to make themselves heard. Andrés Molina Enríquez was the principal one of these, and a major influence in Mexico, for his work gave the middle class a concept of themselves with which they could shape the nationality that Caso complained was lacking. Molina's basic book, published in 1908, was *Los grandes problemas nacionales* (*The Great National Problems*), in which he foretold the end of the Porfiriate and outlined a program for the regime that would succeed it. After the outbreak of the Revolution, he suggested a plan with an unmistakable social content—the Texcoco Plan.

Molina believed that progress in the country would be achieved only through the action of the mestizo. He was concerned because he could not see Mexico as having a nationality. The nation is built on property, he said, and the mestizos should be the foundation of nationhood. This crossbreed of the Creole and the Indian must be encouraged to create unity and to govern. But before the mestizo could become a landowner, or the Indian a consumer, the *latifundios,* basically anti-economic, must be broken up. At the same time small property ownership should be fostered. As long as none of this was done, there would be no industrialization, however much foreign capital might be brought in. Only when both national and foreign capital could create 30 million actual landowners would foreign capital cease to be a threat to the nation. But rural feudalism would not disappear by evolution; it must be removed by revolution.

The legal structure of Molina's concept of property as a social function, a concept adopted later by the Revolution, was formulated by Winstano Luis Orozco, a jurist from Guadalajara. In a country steeped in law, where every politician is a lawyer and where the legalistic monomania inherited from Spain pervades the cities, this juridical argument turned out to be as important as the philosophical case for revolution outlined by Caso and the youth of the Athenaeum.

To break up ownership of the land, Orozco said, was to increase its productivity. Being a landowner in colonial times had been tantamount to being a conqueror; property had been synonymous with violence and remained so after independence; if this situation was not ended, democracy in Mexico would never be possible. Industry, rather than governmental action, should be the agent to enforce distribution of the land, with the government confining itself to selling the public lands, to buying haciendas, breaking them up, and selling them. Only in this way could "Mexico's feudalism, without brilliance and without blazons, which . . . constitutes a true oligarchy," be obliterated.

Both Molina Enríquez and Orozco, then, pointed to a problem that the government and its supporters would have liked to ignore. The cartoonists (among others) showed, in high relief, another problem that was alive in the public mind but ignored by the politicians: foreign investment.

In 1884, not long after Díaz rose to power, a mining code was drawn up. The old Spanish law had ruled that all minerals were the property of the crown, and after independence, this decree was ignored but not abolished. Now Díaz openly placed Mexico's mineral wealth at the disposal of private parties: under the new code, coal, petroleum, and metals belonged to the owner of the land on which it was found. Accordingly, whenever the state granted or sold public land, it might unwittingly be turning over abundant mineral deposits with it. U.S. capital began pouring into Mexico, and the governmental income increased; simultaneously, the administrative corruption tolerated by Díaz among his supporters became general.

When Díaz relinquished his high office to General Manuel González to avoid having to offer himself as a candidate for re-election, the new puppet president began to subsidize the railroads being built at the time by foreign companies, and subsidy and corruption soon emptied the treasury. To combat the threat of bankruptcy, the government borrowed at a high interest rate from the Bank of Mexico (an institution recently established with French capital) and also acknowledged its debt to England of 91 million pesos, consistently rejected ever since the Juárez government. General González' administration was so corrupt that the people were only too glad to have Díaz in office again—precisely the outcome Díaz had planned on when placing his former comrade-in-arms in the presidency from 1880 to 1884.

Soon, a new policy toward the Church was initiated. Archbishop Labastida, the prelate who had summoned Maximilian to Mexico, agreed to let Díaz approve the priests designated for ecclesiastical positions, in exchange for which Díaz would cease to implement the Reform laws. The Church, acting through intermediaries, started immediately to accumulate land again. It supported the dictatorship and again became identified with despotic rule, as in the colonial period and under Maximilian.

Foreign investors believed that the regime was solid, and so it was to all appearances; accordingly, they increased their investments. By the end of the century, 9,000 miles of railways had been laid; the yield from the mines had risen from 30 million to 90 million pesos a year since 1880. New deposits of copper and

REBELLIONS · *105*

lead were discovered and exploited, and new plantations of coffee, sugar cane, sisal hemp, and cotton were operating. Blast furnaces were built in Monterrey, which became a major industrial center. The export trade increased from 50 million to 200 million pesos in the last twenty years of the century. The budget was balanced. Díaz had himself elected again and again, and, convinced that opposition would vanish with prosperity, he even considered "liberalizing" his regime. The "Scientists" lent a certain moral tone and a degree of efficiency to his administration. They dispensed with internal tariffs, encouraged the establishment of banks, consolidated the internal and foreign debt, put the peso on the gold standard, increased the number of public works, modernized Mexico City, and made an effort to wipe out illiteracy in the cities—all of which made Mexico still more attractive to foreign capital.

Early in the railroad era, everyone thought that a rail network would have the same influence on Mexico as it had had in the American West. But they forgot that in the western United States the rails ran through endless stretches of open land, whereas in Mexico the right of way crossed expanses that were part of the haciendas. The landholders refused to lend their peons for building the lines so that temporary labor had to be imported from Jamaica. In the United States, the railroads built the West, thanks to the Homestead Act; but in Mexico they built nothing, because of the haciendas. To some degree, the railroads served as a link between Mexico City and some of the provincial cities, which they helped to modernize, but they had almost no effect on rural life. As a consequence, the railroad companies lived a precarious existence and were unable to keep their equipment in repair or to modernize it. On the other hand, the railroads became an important tactical element in the Revolution.

Some capitalists in the United States, alarmed by the policies of Theodore Roosevelt, were saying that what Washington needed was a Díaz—that even though Díaz was dark, his soul was white. Like the positivists, these foreign capitalists could not see that the characteristic Mexican entity was the hacienda (notwithstanding the enormous cattle ranches in the northern states, the cotton plantations in the east, the sugar plantations in the center, the coffee and sisal hemp plantations in the south, all operated on capitalistic lines) and that not even capitalism could get a firm foothold as long as it existed, nor could the people emerge from poverty. Mexico's few capitalists were indignant at the privileges granted to foreigners, and the people echoed them. Three-quarters of Mexico's mineral wealth was held by companies run by Americans: Hearst, Guggenheim, U.S. Steel, Anaconda, Standard Oil, McCormick, Doheny, and others. All along the border, Americans owned huge cattle ranches. In 1910, U.S. investments amounted to more than $2 billion, more than all the capital in the hands of Mexicans. British capital was active in petroleum—half of the oil-bearing lands were British owned, the other half belonged to U.S. interests—and the same was more or less true of public utilities and the mines. The French owned the textile industry. The Spaniards controlled the food industry, many haciendas, and the terrible tobacco fields in the dread National Valley, where workers lived and toiled in virtual slavery. Foreigners living in the country kept to themselves, despised the Mexicans, and refused to become Mexican citizens. And the government did nothing to enable the country to profit from the financial and technical expertise that the very presence of foreign enterprise might have made available. (For example, the government permitted railroad builders from the United States to lay out their routes at will, with the result that several lines connected Mexico City to the United States, but not a single line ran south from the capital.)

The Díaz policy with regard to oil ultimately had serious consequences. In 1900, Edward L. Doheny, an American investor, began to buy up oil-yielding tracts in Tampico for an insignificant sum (barely $1 an acre), and in time the Rockefeller enterprises and the English firm of Pearson and Son followed suit. Some of the oil wells produced as much as 50,000 barrels a day and did not require pumping. Yet the oil industry paid no Mexican taxes except for a very small amount levied as a stamp tax; it was permitted to export without hindrance and was not even required to sell oil cheaply within Mexico, for the domestic selling price, without taxes, was the same as the price in the United States, where the industry paid high taxes.

No serious study was given to this situation. The people did not dare to speak out against foreign capital for fear of reprisals by the investors, but a flood of resentment was cresting. This was reflected in a number of cartoons in various newspapers, which were quickly suppressed, cartoons directed not so much at foreign capital as at the Mexicans who submitted to it.

Yet Díaz and the positivists did want to modernize the country. Their efforts, like the earlier serfdom, the independence movement, and the Reform, had as many facets as Mexico itself. Technical modernization came with the government's protection of foreign capital. Intellectual modernization came among urban youth in spite of the government. Modernization of the social conscience of the workers and their fighting tactics came too. But the Díaz regime thwarted itself and all these movements as well by clinging to the most anachronistic of all landholding systems. The essential step in modernizing the country would have been to lift from the rural masses the crushing weight of the hacienda, which was mortgaging all efforts made in all other phases of national life.

Everything the future was to bring was already foreshadowed: a frustrated middle class, indignant at the arrogance of foreign capital; an urban youth longing for freedom of thought and expression; a proletariat in constant protest; a stultified and downtrodden peasantry, which sent off occasional sparks of rebellion; a certain number of theorists of change, which all the other groups confusedly hungered for; and a few organized and militant groups with programs for action.

But the weight of the dictatorship and urban prosperity were so great that all this discontent went underground; the surface showed no signs of eruption.

The Revolution came without so much as one dress rehearsal.

7 · Revolutions

PERHAPS NO ONE in Mexico had read Lenin in 1910. Had anyone done so, he would have contended that the three conditions basic to every revolution were absent in Mexico. The ruling class did not believe that the situation could not be maintained; the oppressed classes did not consider a change possible; and no organization existed capable of directing the pressure for change; even the influence of the Magonists, who were very active, was not strong enough. Yet revolution came.

In the final analysis, the modern history of Mexico is one of revolution. Although there were several kinds of independence (of the Creoles, the mestizos, the peasants, and the traders) and several reforms (those of the liberals, the radicals, even Maximilian), the movement that crowned this whole process consisted of several overlapping revolutions: the political, with Madero and Carranza; the agrarian, led by Zapata and Villa; and the nationalist, which embodied elements of each of the others. The predominance of one type over the other gave each period its particular tone: politics from 1910 to 1913; agrarianism from 1913 to 1917; a transitional stage with the constituent assembly of 1917; after which different governments applied revolutionary principles, each in their own manner, according to the personality and politics of the president, or according to the interpretation of these principles given by the leaders of the group that happened to be most influential at the moment.

One of the things most surprising to historians is that revolutionary objectives were very vague in the minds of the Mexicans who did the actual fighting. Only a few politicians and intellectuals in the cities knew what they were fighting for. Proof of this fact is that almost no political text can be found in all the folklore of the time. All the guerrilla fighters sang the famous song "Adelita," yet it contains only one political line—"Nevermore let a tyrant rule."

The revolution surprised everyone, a fact that bears repeating. José Vasconcelos said:

> Writers and educators of the old scientific type often expressed the opinion that our people, particularly the Indians and the workers, constituted a caste that could not be redeemed. . . . The revolution and life itself made a mockery of the positivistic doctrine that progress brings forth a fortunate class which represents the selection of species because it possesses greater gifts and, therefore, has the sacred right to exploit the inept and subject them to its domination.

The surprise, amounting to fear among those of that "fortunate class," was a revelation to Mexico's youth, as Gómez Morín, then a young revolutionary, today a rightist thinker, tells us: "With optimistic stupefaction we became aware of some unsuspected truths. Mexico did exist, Mexico as a country with its own capabilities and aspirations, its own life and problems. . . . Mexico and the Mexicans did exist. The colonial policy of Porfirism had made us forget this elementary truth."

Still, there was little political and economic preparation for revolution; Porfirism had created no demand for it. For decades, people had been thinking more about producing than about distributing wealth. So there is nothing strange in the fact that the active revolution ended before any effort had been made to initiate basic reforms on the national level. Of necessity, what reforms there were had to respect certain foreign and domestic interests; they often had to be partial, fragmentary, and gradual, often contradictory; they had to reconcile opposing interests. But in any case, the revolution destroyed the obstacles that had impeded the realization of even the most minor reform until then.

The aim was to create a simple government *for* the people, that is to say, a government created in the name of the people and for their benefit. All Mexican liberal political literature was an effort to open the way for this idea and to make it triumph. The formation of a small group of men imbued with this idea was the one means by which Mexican democracy could advance. . . .

In spite of almost incredible improvisation, the generals finally physically overpowered the enemy, thus achieving the first of two victories. The second was won by the civilians, a group of the most brilliant, the most tenacious, and the most disinterested ideologists Mexico has ever known. A third group contributed to both victories, and in the end its contribution was the greatest and the most decisive, precisely because it had the strength of numbers: the Mexican people, who contributed as soldiers to the triumph of arms and as political partisans to the triumph of ideas.*

These words were written by a historian of the Reform, but they can be applied to the 1910–17 revolutions. The same causes that motivated the Reform motivated the Revolution. Without the Reform, with its immediate triumph and eventual failure, the Revolution would have been neither necessary nor possible.

The Political Revolution

About 1890, supporters of Díaz began to talk about who would succeed him, and in order to deflect their energies, the dictator permitted the organization of the positivists' Liberal Union. Later, friends of General Bernardo Reyes, the governor of Nuevo León,

---

* Daniel Cosio Villegas, *Historia moderna de México. La republica restaurada* (Mexico City, 1955), I, 52; 66.

organized their own party to bring Reyes into power as a successor to Díaz. Reyes already had shown his capabilities by converting Monterrey into an industrial center, and, even though he came down hard on strikers, he had promulgated the first workmen's compensation law.

In 1904, Díaz saw to it that the presidential term of office was extended to six years from four. He provided for the election of a vice-president and chose Ramón Corral, the governor of Sonora, who had grown rich from selling the Yaqui Indians as slaves for haciendas in the south. At the same time, Díaz used against foreign investors his familiar tactic of supporting first one faction, then another, for the purpose of inciting rivalries that would then necessitate his services as arbitrator. Seeing that U.S. capital had grown too influential, he began granting petroleum concessions to a British firm and offered sanctuary to a president of Nicaragua who had been deposed and exiled after a rebellion fostered by American interests. He authorized a visit by the Japanese Navy. Washington began to lose confidence in Díaz and for the first time permitted exiles who opposed the dictatorship to move about freely in the United States.

In 1908, as Mexico was feeling the effects of a poor harvest and the repercussions from the preceding year's crisis on Wall Street, Díaz granted an interview to the American journalist James Creelman, in which he told him that the grand plan of his dictatorship had been to guide the country toward democracy and that the Mexicans were now prepared to govern themselves democratically. Naturally, as soon as the interview became known in Mexico, his words gave wings to the opposition. Apparently, however, Díaz had said what he did to placate Washington, not to be taken seriously in his own country.

But there was no holding the opposition. A group of young lawyers, together with Filomeno Mata, a journalist who had been imprisoned thirty-four separate times, formed a new Democratic Party. Díaz exiled Governor Reyes, whom he had always feared, and announced that he would stand for re-election with Corral again as the vice-presidential candidate. No one imagined that he could be stopped.

At that time, a book entitled *La Sucesión Presidencial de 1910*

(*The Presidential Succession of 1910*) became very popular. Its author, Francisco I. Madero (1873–1913), was an abstemious and vegetarian spiritualist who had been educated in France and the United States. He came from a Porfirist family who had some industrial holdings and owned a hacienda in Coahuila but who were troubled by the preponderance of foreign capital in Mexico. In his book, Madero did not discuss Mexico's social problems; he confined himself to political questions and took a very moderate stand. Yet the national climate was so charged that the book caused a sensation. Madero began to give lectures and then founded a newspaper and, with a group of friends, organized anti-re-election clubs. In April, 1910, an anti-re-election congress met. Its members chose Madero as their presidential candidate and Reyes' friend Francisco Vásquez Gómez (1864–1926) as his running mate. Madero and Díaz met face to face, but the dictator refused to take seriously this gesticulating little man with a goatee and the eyes of a dreamer. Then, as the masses flocked to Madero's meetings, Díaz decided he had better have him arrested. Madero was interned in San Luis Potosí in June, 1910, accused of planning an insurrection. In September, the centenary of Mexican independence was celebrated, and delegates attended from all over the world. Two weeks later, the elections were held. The eighty-year-old Díaz won, with Corral as vice-president. Officially, Madero garnered 196 votes.

The public was most indignant about this result for Madero. Thanks to his influential family, Madero was released on bail and left for the United States, whence he declared that the elections had been fraudulent and that he was the rightful president of the republic; at the same time, he called upon the Mexican people to rebel on November 20. His brother Gustavo Madero, the only member of the family who supported him, and Vázquez Gómez went to Washington to solicit the support of the United States. On November 20, Madero crossed the border and entered Coahuila, where some friends had promised they would have an armed guerrilla band waiting. But when he found that the band numbered only twenty-five, Madero returned to Texas, feeling deceived. (In Puebla, meanwhile, Aquiles Serdán, a labor leader who had taken to heart the call to rebellion, had been besieged in his home by soldiers and died. Several other local uprisings were crushed.)

While Madero was staying in New Orleans, discouraged, waiting for passage on a ship to Europe, he received word that events had taken a serious turn in Chihuahua, the enormous cattle-raising state in the north, where farmers and peons lived like serfs to a family with enormous landholdings, the Terrazas, a hard and touchy breed. A storekeeper named Pascual Orozco (1882–1915) and Doroteo Arango, a peon who had taken to the mountains and who was later known as Pancho Villa (1877–1923), had rebelled and defeated the federal troops there and cut the lines of communication between Mexico City and the border. When Madero seized the moment to return, he found himself in friendly territory.

The government could not smother news of the success in Chihuahua. The peons in Morelos, at the doorstep of the capital, rose in arms under the command of an Indian peasant, Emiliano Zapata (1873–1919), and simultaneously attacked the municipal authorities and the haciendas. By April, guerrilla bands were roaming the whole north and center of the country, and even in Yucatán and in Díaz' own state, Oaxaca. The army was commanded by old generals, and the United States, growing alarmed, stationed 20,000 soldiers on the border. Limantour rushed back from Europe, changed the personnel, exiled the most hated politicians, and in April, 1911, reached an agreement with the rebels for a cease-fire and the start of negotiations.

Vázquez Gómez was the spokesman for the Maderists, who feared that Madero himself would be too accommodating. They demanded the resignation of Díaz and the abolition of government by the "Scientists." Limantour refused. While negotiations were still going on, an armed struggle between guerrillas and the army flared up in Ciudad Juárez, just south of the U.S.-Mexico border; Pancho Villa and Orozco seized the city without waiting for orders from anyone. Two days later, Zapata took possession of Cuautla. Guerrilla forces descended on the state capitals, and the masses mutinied. On May 21, an accord was reached in Ciudad Juárez: Díaz and Limantour were to resign and Francisco de la

Barra, then ambassador to Washington, was to be provisional president until new elections could be held.

But Díaz, ill in Mexico City, refused to resign. His troops fired into a crowd of people milling around in a tropical spring rain, killing 200. Eventually, Díaz's terrified friends convinced him that he must yield. He signed a statement of resignation, took a train for Veracruz, and sailed for Europe on the German ship *Ipiranga*. He died in Paris in 1915, convinced that his way of government had been the appropriate one. He never realized that the upheaval was not a simple factional struggle, but an out-and-out revolution, the first of the twentieth century.

The first act of the de la Barra government was to send forces to crush the rebels. General Victoriano Huerta (1845–1916)—an alcoholic and a drug addict, but still a clever general with a certain charisma who had subdued the Maya in Yucatán—was ordered to crush Zapata's forces, but he failed. Meanwhile, in the north, many guerrillas laid down their arms or disbanded, believing they had won. The Revolution lost its first impetus. Madero entered Mexico City, a little man on horseback, welcomed by the masses; he became, as one Porfirist put it, a rival of the Virgin of Guadalupe.

Francisco Vázquez Gómez and his brother, Emilio, who had entered the government as representative of the revolutionary forces, had little faith in Madero's political sense, and they made use of their new position to distribute arms to new groups, intending to have forces of their own ready and able to cope with any possible military coup. This move divided the revolutionaries. A convention chose Madero as a candidate for the presidency, as was to be expected, but chose José María Pino Suárez (1869–1913), a journalist from Yucatán, for the vice-presidency, instead of Vázquez Gómez. The newly formed Catholic Party put up de la Barra as its own vice-presidential candidate, although it supported Madero with no enthusiasm. In October, Madero and Pino won in a genuinely free election.

Madero had no understanding of social problems. He took steps to limit the influence of foreign capital, but he did nothing to return the land to the Indians as he had promised in his campaign he would, and he continued to send troops against Zapata. Madero was temperamentally so soft that he was unable to contain even momentarily the reactionary ambitions of the Díaz military men and the landholding oligarchy, and he lost popularity very rapidly. It remained to be seen whether popular disillusion would manifest itself in a return to indifference or in a new revolutionary drive. The masses wanted what the Magonists had proclaimed in their slogan "Land and Freedom." Madero said the people wanted freedom more than bread, and he favored a political revolution. But the people wanted a social revolution. The few intellectuals who took the populist side favored a nationalist revolution, like Madero, but with social aims, in order to complete the work that independence and the Reform had started.

But at least there was freedom. The small labor organizations formed the Casa del Obrero Mundial (World Workers' House). Zapata, who had not laid down his arms, returned from a quiescent period to action and launched the Ayala Plan. This plan demanded that the land taken from the people by the big landholders be returned and, in addition, that a third of each hacienda be distributed to the people. Zapata applied the plan by blood and fire—particularly fire, for his bands almost always burned the buildings of haciendas before giving the land to the peons. In congress, a group of deputies led by Luis Cabrera (1876–1952) called loudly for social action by the government.

Meanwhile, General Reyes, who had returned from Europe, entered Mexico from Texas, declared himself a rebel, found no following, and surrendered to the authorities, who incarcerated him. In February, 1912, Orozco (whom Madero had made a general) turned on Madero in the north, accusing him of betraying the Revolution. (Even today, it is impossible to judge whether Orozco acted in good faith or whether, as was asserted at the time, he had been egged on by the Terrazas, the powerful landowning family who ran Chihuahua.) Madero sent Victoriano Huerta against him, and he was defeated and forced into exile. The victorious Huerta, however, on his return to the capital, was unable to render an account of the money he had spent and was stripped of his command. In October, Félix Díaz, a nephew of the old dictator, led an uprising in Veracruz and was defeated, too,

almost without a struggle; he was condemned to death, but
Madero pardoned him.

The big landholders, the generals, and the U.S. Government
all wanted to see an end to this situation. President Taft had
watched the new regime with sympathy at first, but when he
discovered that it was hostile to Americans, he turned against it.
Henry Lane Wilson, his ambassador to Mexico, closely allied to
the Guggenheims, advised reinforcing the border garrisons. By
February, 1912, 100,000 U.S. troops looked across into Mexico.
Munitions were stored in the American Embassy in Mexico City
as if to stand off a siege, and Ambassador Wilson warned American citizens to leave the country. He also sent a note to the
Mexican Government, protesting the death of thirteen U.S. citizens—a charge that was never proved—and the Mexican Government replied with a list of eight Mexicans lynched in the United
States. All these moves created tension and panic.

Meanwhile, Félix Díaz and General Reyes, in jail together, concocted a plot against Madero. Madero refused to believe that he
was in danger, in spite of the warnings of his brother Gustavo,
but on February 9, 1913, troops poured into the streets; cadets
joined them, freed Reyes and Díaz, and tried to seize the National Palace. The soldiers guarding the palace fired on them,
killing Reyes, and the rebels fortified themselves in the Ciudadela
barracks. Madero ordered Huerta, who had sworn to defend the
regime, to bring them to heel.

For ten days cannon thundered back and forth from the National Palace to Ciudadela and from Ciudadela to the National
Palace. Huerta somehow let his loyal troops be decimated, however, and also managed to exasperate the public. Ambassador
Wilson, too, objected to the firing of government batteries because the noise bothered him.

Wilson was, in fact, playing an undercover role, trying to
mediate between Huerta and Díaz. On January 18, Huerta invited
Gustavo Madero, who had organized the Palace resistance to
Reyes, to dine with him in the hope of alienating him from his
brother. Meanwhile, another general named Blanquet seized the
National Palace and arrested Madero and Pino Suárez. When the
news of this coup was confirmed, Huerta arrested his guest, Gus-

tavo Madero, and turned him over to the rebels in Ciudadela, who tortured and then murdered him. That night, Huerta, Díaz, and Ambassador Wilson celebrated in the U.S. Embassy and arrived at an agreement: Huerta would be president; Díaz would succeed him as soon as elections could be held. Wilson called together the other ambassadors and asked them to recognize the new regime. A cable to Washington announced that "a wicked despotism has fallen."

Next, envoys from Huerta convinced Madero and Pino that they should resign; in exchange, Huerta promised to respect the lives of their supporters. Pedro Lascurain, secretary of state and constitutionally next in line, became president, formed a short-lived government in which Huerta served as secretary of state, then resigned, leaving the presidency to Huerta. It was all very legal. A disconcerted and intimidated Congress accepted Huerta as president with few dissenting voices.

Before Lascurain resigned, he exacted from Huerta a sworn promise to permit Madero and Pino a safe-conduct to leave the country. But Madero and Pino remained under arrest. Several diplomats asked Ambassador Wilson to intercede with Huerta, but Wilson now explained that he could not intervene in Mexico's internal affairs. On February 22, Madero and Pino were taken from the National Palace and, on the way to the penitentiary, were forced out of the car and killed in front of the prison walls. It was officially announced that an armed gang had tried to rescue the prisoners, who had been killed during the shooting. Ambassador Wilson telegraphed Washington that he considered this version the true one.

Madero and Pino had proved, at the cost of their lives, that a political revolution was not possible in Mexico without a social revolution. For, although Huerta was responsible for the murders, the instigators were the landholding oligarchy, the "Scientists," and the foreign interests.

Huerta governed from the saloons, in a constant state of drunkenness. One by one his cabinet resigned. When Senator Belisario Domínguez denounced the situation in a speech, he was assassinated shortly after. And when congressmen protested the crime,

Huerta ordered 110 of them hustled off to jail and appointed a new congress composed almost entirely of army officers. He disposed of the likely candidacy of Félix Díaz in forthcoming elections by sending him to Japan.

Huerta made the same mistake as Díaz had: he did not attach sufficient importance to his enemies. These, meanwhile, were concentrating their forces in the north, where the governor of Coahuila, the Maderos' own state, Venustiano Carranza (1859–1920), had refused to recognize Huerta. Carranza had been a senator under Díaz, later a supporter of General Reyes and, finally, of Madero. He was a conservative, but a man with political sense, and he had at his disposal a small body of troops under the command of General Pablo González. In March, Carranza met with some army officers and northern politicians and launched the Guadalupe Plan (named for the ranch where the meeting was held). He was granted the title of commander in chief of the Constitutionalist Army. Carranza believed that he could not wage a successful political fight against Huerta; only arms would serve his purpose. But his general, González, was always a loser.

Meanwhile, in Sonora, when the local legislature refused to accept Díaz, the governor asked to be relieved of his office and went into exile, and a young rancher named Alvaro Obregón (1880–1928) took command of all the troops in the state. With the aid of brilliant improvising officers—including Plutarco Elías Calles (1877–1945), Francisco Serrano, and Salvador Alvarado (1880–1924)—he won a series of victories. Carranza, at the same time, had established his government in Nogales, on the U.S. border.

Pancho Villa, who had been imprisoned by Huerta but escaped to the United States, now returned to his country with eight comrades. Within a few days, Villa had gathered around him a veritable army, which seized Ciudad Juárez, the city of Chihuahua, and the entire state. Carranza did not trust Villa but, since he needed him, accepted him as a Constitutionalist commander, in spite of the guerrilla leader's highly unorthodox methods. The city of Chihuahua was a stronghold of Madero politicians, and young intellectuals, who had fled the capital, were trying to indoctrinate the masses of peons and farmers who plunged into the fight more for the pleasure of it or because of some obscure longing for revenge than in defense of a program. When Villa's forces took over a city, they killed the Huerta officials, leftovers from Porfirio Díaz, sacked the city, and shared the booty. That was the time when the "finger generals" emerged, their nickname coming from the practice of appointing officers by pointing a finger at a man and saying: "You, be colonel; you, general; you, governor. . . ."

Obregón and Calles were perhaps the only major figures with any clear idea of objectives, beyond that of re-establishing the constitution. Both men turned out to be able military commanders and daring politicians. Both believed that Carranza would cause the revolution to fail politically because of his conservative ideas. Carranza was proud, honorable, and fond of negotiation, but he was also egotistical and domineering. Many became discouraged by the atmosphere around him and went over to Villa, who was cruel and frenetic but open and courageous: in Chihuahua, he had given land to the peons and between battles put his guerrilla army to work building schools or cleaning the streets. (He also issued fantastic amounts of paper money.) General Felipe Angeles, a professional officer with aristocratic poise, marched out on Carranza, whom he did not like, to become Villa's military brain; Martín Luis Guzmán, who later told the story of Villa in several novels, was already serving as his secretary.

But Huerta had an enemy closer to him: the "emancipating army" of the south, commanded by Zapata, which had already conquered Morelos, Puebla, and Guerrero, burning haciendas as it went, killing the managers and turning the land over to the peons. Zapata's troops did not constitute an army in the literal sense of the word, for they spent more time cultivating the land than fighting, a dual role conforming more nearly to the old revolutionary concept of a people in arms. Antonio Díaz Soto y Gama (1874–1967), a gifted orator with vague socialistic leanings, joined Zapata. But the intellectuals as a group took alarm at Zapata's well-directed brutality, for he was systematically eliminating the enemies of the Indians, and were concerned because the Zapatists valued the Indian so highly. (On the other hand, the intellectuals admired Villa for his courage and his picturesque cruelties, which served no political purpose.) The egalitarian Zapatists sought neither power nor wealth, but only land. Zapata's was the only voice which rang clearly in favor of social redress.

Within a few months, Mexico was without any central government, for Huerta was no longer in control of anything but Mexico City. The impromptu generals, whose manifestoes and laws were drawn up by pettifogging lawyers, governed as unscrupulous despots over the territory held by their bands. Either they recognized one another or they attacked one another, and in the end many of them were shot by Villa or Zapata partisans. Others tried to establish haciendas of their own. But sincere revolutionaries emerged among them, too.

In Washington, the spectacle of Mexico was disconcerting. Huerta was showing a good deal of favor to the British ambassador, although he owed everything to Ambassador Wilson. The American owners of mines, who saw their miners go off with the guerrillas, of trains, which refused to carry anyone or anything but guerrilla fighters, and of ranches, whose lands were occupied by the peons, exerted pressure on Washington on behalf of Huerta. But in 1913, Woodrow Wilson succeeded Taft in the White House, and President Wilson did not want to intervene openly because he felt some sympathy for the objectives, though not the methods of the Constitutionalists. Through a new ambassador, John Lind, he tried to convince Huerta to retire, but in 1914 Huerta held an election, in which he was not a candidate, with such grotesque results that he himself cancelled them and remained in office as provisional president. President Wilson, in order to favor the constitutionalists, lifted the embargo previously placed on the sale of arms to Mexicans.

Then, on April 9, 1914, the crew of an American ship was arrested in Tampico by federal troops. This gave President Wilson a pretext to move against Huerta. The *Ipiranga*, the ship that had carried Porfirio Díaz into exile, headed for Veracruz with a cargo of arms, only to find the port occupied by U.S. Marines. Two hundred Mexicans were killed opposing the American troops. President Wilson, who never understood the Mexican

Hernán Cortés

Indian portrayals of the Spanish invasion

Mexico City, ca. 1803, in a drawing by Alexander von Humboldt

Beníto Juárez

Francisco Madero

Emiliano Zapata

Plutarco Elías Calles

Lázaro Cárdenas

Mexico City

A peanut vendor

A farmer collecting guayule rubber

Industry in Monterrey

An Indian village

A Mexican family of Baja California

A boy reading in
Mexico City

Aerial photograph
of Palenque

An American tourist visiting Teotihuacán

The rain god Tlaloc, in the National Museum of Anthropology

A Lacandon Indian

psychology, was doubtless surprised when he learned that Carranza had condemned the occupation of the port, even though the order had been given to aid him, and Huerta, who managed with difficulty to seize the shipment of munitions, was able to pass as a defender of national independence.

Meanwhile, arms were crossing the border in quantity. Villa and Obregón won new battles with better equipment. Villa, seeing that his army was moving too slowly, due to his soldiers' wives going along as camp followers, organized a cavalry corps called the Dorados, and he seized the cattle on a ranch owned by Hearst, the American press tycoon, in order to sell the animals in Texas for money to buy more guns. The cities of Torreón, Coahuila, and Zacatecas fell like dominoes just as Obregón was entering Guadalajara and Querétaro. Mexico City was threatened from all sides. Carranza, wanting to make sure that Villa would not be the first to set foot in the National Palace, cut off the railroads' coal supply and thus deprived Villa of his principal means of transport. Consequently, it was Obregón who entered the capital on August 15, 1914, five days after its virtual collapse, following Huerta's departure into exile from Veracruz. He had been dictator for a year and a half. (He died soon after.)

At that point, the urgent need to win the war could no longer be used as a pretext to oppose revolutionary measures. The Revolution entered upon a new phase.

The Social Revolution

As we have seen, Madero did not have a very keen social conscience. He had said in his campaign platform of 1910 that the condition of the worker must be bettered by "creating trade schools, expediting laws governing pensions and workmen's compensation, and combatting alcoholism and gambling." As late as 1912, he declared:

Some newspapers have repeated so insistently . . . that sharing the land with the proletariat looms large in the promises of the Revolution and that the offer was made to divide up the latifundios still controlled by a few privileged men to the disadvantage of the needy classes . . . that I should like once and for all to rectify this

matter. . . . I have always advocated the creation of small landholdings, but this does not mean depriving any large landholder of
his property.

These words were spoken at the very moment when Zapatists
were burning haciendas at the gates of Mexico City and Luis
Cabrera was introducing a moderate agrarian law in congress. But
Madero called it extremely dangerous because, he said, he had
never believed that an agrarian problem existed in Mexico.

So it was Cabrera who raised the issue of land in all its bleak
reality before the Chamber of Deputies. A year earlier, he had felt
that the agrarian problem could be solved by partnerships imposed on the estates on behalf of the peons. But by December,
1912, he believed that the government must resort to expropriating the lands of the haciendas for public use, in order to reconstruct the *ejidos*. At the same time, Cabrera said, the predominance of big over small and medium-sized landholdings must be
combated by taxes that would induce the division of the latifundios. In Cabrera's judgment, the causes of the Revolution—
that is, the problems it must solve—were local bossism, peonage
(the servitude of the peons), industrial conditions (the servitude
of the factory worker), latifundism (the servitude of small landowners), "Scientism" (the servitude of small business), and foreign dependence. Only by solving these problems could the Revolution emphasize the mestizo character of the population (with
the help, besides, of such measures as divorce and legal recognition of natural children), and make Mexico a more homogeneous
country.

Cabrera's thesis, supported by a number of legal and historical
arguments, was echoed strongly in the various plans drawn up
during the Revolution, in accordance with Mexican custom. A
plan, in Mexican history, was always an attempt to simplify and
thus make plain to the masses the objectives for which its signa-
tories aimed. (Plans for conservative movements were always
more detailed and baroque than those for popular movements
precisely because the conservatives addressed a better educated
public.) The Revolution marked the end of plans, for it was in
the nature of a plan to defy existing law in order to replace the

current reality with the goals of those who rebel against it; and from then on, with a few exceptions, no attempts were made to depart from legality. During the Revolution, however, at least a dozen plans were put forth. Each time a new guerrilla leader emerged or some politician seized local power, he launched his own plan. Many of them were the work of schoolteachers, storekeepers, or provincial lawyers, preoccupied mainly with the agrarian problem; yet in spite of their obvious importance, the government and the capital tried to ignore them. In 1911, José Trinidad Ruíz led a rising in Tlaltizapan and issued a plan with the slogan: "Down with Monopoly: Of Land, of Mountains, and of Water." Molina Enríquez drew up the Texcoco Plan in 1911, which proposed the break-up of the haciendas, remission of workers' debts, and an eight-hour work day. In February, 1912, Braulio Hernández and others signed the Santa Rosa Plan, in which nationalization of the land was suggested for the first time. In March, 1912, Pascual Orozco led an insurrection against Madero and proposed the expropriation of uncultivated lands and a ten-hour day. (Later, even the reactionaries echoed the social question. The Tierra Colorado Plan of 1916, drawn up by partisans of Félix Díaz, espoused the return of their lands to the indigenous communities.)

But the man who stated Mexico's basic problem in unmistakable terms was Zapata in his Ayala Plan. Just as the Zapata movement, without winning battles, had played a decisive role in the Revolution's military victory, similarly, without a detailed program, it injected the agrarian question into the improvised revolutionary doctrine.

Zapata's Ayala Plan of November 25, 1911, drawn up by Otilio Montaño, a schoolteacher, demanded the immediate return of all lands usurped by the big landholders and expropriation of a third of the area of each hacienda, to be used for new settlements and *ejidos*. The estate of anyone opposing these measures would be nationalized. A later Zapatist document, the Milpa Alta Plan of August, 1914, defined the return of land more specifically and proposed that land be given free to those who fought in the Revolution or to their widows; that the recipient not be permitted to sell land granted by the state for fifty years; and that a Farmers'

National Bank be established. All these measures were both the fruit of experience and of the conversion of some intellectuals to Zapatism.

At the moment of Huerta's flight from the country, it had almost seemed that the Revolution was over. Indeed, it might have been if its sole object had been political change. Everything had been set in order by the presidential and congressional elections. But voting politicians into office and decorating generals could no longer satisfy the people. They were already in the streets. The peons were 'armed. The young intellectuals who had joined Obregón, Carranza, Villa, or Zapata knew that the task could not be left half done. Mexico had to shake off the dead weight of her anachronistic social structure and step into modern times, not only with railroads and factories, but by the government's leadership of the Mexican people.

Clearly, there was no direct expression of all these matters. Hidden personal motives stood in the way of settling the civil war and served to keep the Revolution going. Villa and Carranza, now *de facto* president in Mexico City, turned on each other, each accusing the other of being reactionary. Zapata, who distrusted Carranza as much as he had Madero, went on attacking the haciendas and distributing land. Obregón tried to mediate by negotiating with Villa, and they eventually agreed that Carranza would remain in power but would not be a candidate in the next elections. Carranza was not pleased by this accord; he called a convention in the hope that, awed by his prestige, it would support him. The convention met in Aguascalientes, a railroad center, instead of in Mexico City, in deference to Villa, who had a weakness for anything having to do with railroads, a major instrument for winning his victories.

Contrary to Carranza's expectations, the convention was dominated by Villa men. And for two weeks, these Villa intellectuals talked. But the military men, who composed most of the listeners, were concerned mainly with the immediate problem of how to wipe out Villa and Carranza at one blow. Villa himself went so far as to propose a suicide pact between himself and Carranza.

(But the chief of state, still in the capital, scorned the entire convention.) Finally the convention cut the Gordian knot by appointing as provisional president of Mexico a general from Potosí named Eulalio Gutiérrez (?–1940), an honorable and patient man. Gutiérrez had to rely for support on Pancho Villa, and thus the army of the north became the convention's strong right arm. These Villa forces soon marched on Mexico City. In December, 1914, Carranza moved his government to Veracruz, which the Americans had evacuated, and Villa entered the capital—only to find the Zapatists there ahead of him. The citizens were astounded to see that "those bandits," as the newspapers daily labeled the Zapatists, behaved with restraint and order. The Villa forces were not as orderly as the Zapatists from the south—not by any means.

That same December, Zapata and Villa conferred at Xochimilco, near Mexico City (a village, now a tourist attraction owing to the beauty of its floating gardens). Zapata told the northern guerrilla leader: "This Carranza is a cur," to which Villa replied: "With men like that [Carranza and his friends] we would have made no progress toward well-being or land distribution; tyranny would have ruled the country. It is my dream to see the territory of the rich fellows divided. God forgive me, isn't there someone who'll do that?"

The dialogue continued:

ZAPATA: The people have a great love for the land. They still can't believe it when one says to them, This land is yours. But as soon as they see that other people are getting a yield from those lands, they'll say: I shall ask for my own land and plant. That's the kind of love the people have for the land. As a rule, all the people feel it.

VILLA: They'll soon see what the bosses are like and who their friends are.

ZAPATA: They'll know if someone wants to take away their land, too. They'll know one thing all right, and that is that they've got to defend themselves. But you'll have to kill them to make them get off the land.

VILLA: Our people have never known justice, to say nothing of freedom. All the main tracts are held by the rich, while this poor naked little fellow has to work from sunup to sundown. I think he's going to have a better life in the future, and if he doesn't we might as well lay down our Mausers.*

Zapata developed into the authentic figure of the Revolution, though he was less spectacular than Villa, because his objectives were crystal clear. (In 1925, a group of Indians from Ecuador visited the Mexican ambassador in Quito to ask him to send Zapata down to organize them. They did not know that he had been assassinated.) To Zapata, as leader of the south, where many of the *ejidos* had been despoiled of their land, the main job was to return their property to them. To Villa, in the north, where great landholdings were the rule, the first step must be to break up the haciendas. To a great degree, the Zapata movement was Indian; Zapata himself was almost pure-blooded Indian and his forces were recruited from Indians on the plantations and in the villages. The Zapatist revolution, to a certain extent, had an Indian character, which Villa's revolution, in a region of mestizos, lacked. John Reed, the American journalist who marched with Villa for a time, wrote: "[Villa] is a peon who thinks like the peons more often than he reasons consciously toward the conclusion that the true cause of the Revolution lies in the land problem."

Villa did not stop at wishing, however. In Chihuahua, he handed out 75-acre tracts to anyone who asked and made them nontransferable for ten years. In 1915, he had an agrarian law drafted that included the statement that "the existence of great territorial properties [is] incompatible with the peace and prosperity of the republic." Carranza rejected it.

Indeed, with all this going on, Carranza had not adopted any measure that would satisfy the people's demands, though he spoke of social questions in a moderate tone not very different from Madero's. He was astute enough to keep abreast of events in such a way as to seem to be facing up to them. The Revolution owes its victories to laws promulgated by Carranza but also to laws that he opposed as long as he could. Carranza stood apart from the

* *Fuentes para la historia de la Revolución Mexicana,* edited by Manuel González Ramírez (Mexico City, 1954), pp. 87–88.

peasants' movement and later he persecuted the whole labor movement when he did not need its support. Each time he yielded to the social demands of the moment, he did so because Cabrera, one of his advisers, had persuaded him.

From the very beginning of the struggle, when the Guadalupe Plan was drawn up, Carranza had maintained that there was no need to talk of social questions just yet, because they would solve themselves "in the sweep of whatever revolutionary government may follow us." But as the struggle widened and the masses were drawn into it, occupation of the haciendas became inevitable. Carranza accepted this, but he tried to prevent the agrarian reform laws that would legalize the occupation. In the end, he could not avoid it, for, as he himself said in a speech delivered in 1913, "When the armed struggle is ended . . . the formal and majestic social struggle must begin, the class struggle; whether or not we ourselves want them and regardless of what forces may oppose them, the new social ideas will be imposed on our masses." He sensed that the people would make the final decision as to Mexico's future because they had the weapons with which to impose their will. "We need laws that will favor the worker and the peasant, but they themselves must promulgate [them], because they will be the victors in this struggle." Finally, on January 6, 1915, under pressure from the Villa and Zapata forces, Carranza proclaimed a law, drawn up by Cabrera, to restore the *ejidos,* and for decades, this law served as the foundation of the agrarian policy of the Revolution.

But though Carranza might yield when he had no other choice, and though he had announced that the social struggle would begin as the political struggle came to an end, when the moment came to act, he tried to prevent an exacerbation of the social conflict. In August, 1916, when his government was installed in Mexico City, a strike broke out against the foreign-owned electrical company. Carranza opposed the strike, declaring it illegal on the ground that "the workers have not wished to accept that they are but a small part of society, which does not exist for them alone; there are other classes whose interests they cannot lawfully violate since those rights are as worthy of respect as their own." By that time, the pressure was off Carranza's constitutionalist government. The constitutionalists had won out over the agrarians, thanks to the help of the labor movement, which supported Carranza at the very moment when he accused them of refusing to accept their status as a "small part" of society. But the moderate faction of the Revolution had achieved this victory only after a hard and dramatic struggle.

At the end of 1914, when Villa's forces had taken Mexico City, Gutiérrez had organized his government, with Vasconcelos as minister of education. But before he could do anything, the fighting broke out again. The members of the convention, realizing that they could not come to an agreement with Obregón and tiring of Villa's control, left Mexico City. Gutiérrez never was able to set up a real government, although he attempted to do so in several cities, and he eventually surrendered to Carranza. Some of his followers were executed; others went into exile. In the interim, Villa continued the struggle and appointed Roque González Garza as president. It was this move by Villa, as a matter of fact, that made Cabrera and Obregón pressure Carranza to yield on the social issue and proclaim the law restoring the *ejidos*.

At the same time, Obregón was negotiating with the leaders of the World Workers' House—who had never managed to influence the convention or put forth a program—to declare their support of Carranza. The workers, who had grown tired of Villa and were swayed by the city dweller's fear of Zapata's armed peasants, accepted the proposal. Luis Morones, an electrician, swung the meeting to Obregón. Six "red battalions" were formed to fight the Villa and Zapata guerrillas—an act which resulted in a permanent split between Mexico's peasants and industrial workers. In exchange for its support, the World Workers' House was given an old palace in the center of Mexico City for its headquarters, the Casa de los Azulejos (House of Tiles), which today contains a café patronized by tourists and intellectuals. This alliance, which momentarily reinforced the constitutionalists, cost the labor movement a very high price as time went on.

Carranza's new laws had upset the rightists, who otherwise might have tolerated, if not supported, his regime. Now they lined up with Villa, the foreign business community fancying that they could manipulate him to thwart the constitutionalists' reforms. Obregón, who remained loyal to Carranza, defeated Villa's troops in Puebla and retook Mexico City in January, 1916. Zapata went back to the country and Villa moved to Aguascalientes. Obregón demanded contributions from the rich, among them many priests. When the priests refused to pay, he enrolled 180 of them in his army as a punishment, a move which buttressed the steadfast opposition of the Church to the Revolution.

In April, Villa and Obregón met face to face. Obregón had encircled the city of Celaya with barbed wire, and when Villa flung his mounted Dorados against the city, the barbed wire halted them and Obregón's machineguns cut them down. For the next year, Villa's shrinking army was defeated again and again and he was forced constantly to retreat. His closest friend, Tomás Urbina, ran off with the war chest. Felipe Angeles, the only general still loyal to him, went to New York to seek help. Villa lost more engagements and finally took refuge in Chihuahua, where he was able to hold out for a time, although his influence on the march of events had ended.

With Villa out of the way, Carranza's chief enemy was Zapata. On his behalf, General Pablo González, who had never yet won a battle, tried to finish off Zapata by scorched-earth tactics. His soldiers burned everything left standing in Morelos and sacked the cities—all in vain. Zapata's resistance continued until 1919, not because he wanted power but because his peasants now held land and feared that the city people would take it away from them. During any respite from battles and skirmishes, the Zapatists cultivated their holdings with rifles slung across their shoulders. Then González hit upon a plan for victory. He sent Jesús Guajardo, an officer, to Zapata under the pretense of defecting to the peasant army, and ordered fifty-nine of his own men shot in order to inspire Zapata's confidence. But when Zapata arrived at his appointment with Guajardo, he found 600 rifles aimed at him; he was shot on the spot. That was on April 10, 1919. Guajardo was rewarded with a promotion and 50,000 pesos from the state treasury.

From the military standpoint, Zapata gave the victory to the Revolution, for neither Díaz nor Huerta had dared to use all their forces against Madero or later against Carranza for fear of the Zapatist bands, always at the door of Mexico City. From the political standpoint, Zapata also determined the course of events. To be sure, without him, Mexico would have seen a change in the political system; but thanks to him, the nation also underwent a social revolution—slow, vacillating, but viable.

During all this time, businessmen in the United States and Mexican rightists kept pressuring Washington to intervene. Cardinal Gibbons listed all the murders of priests, all the church-burnings, and even some nonexistent violations of nuns; but he never mentioned that those deeds came as the result of the Church's open support of Huerta. As in the days of the Reform, the rightists had entrusted their salvation to foreigners, but Ambassador Wilson was no Maximilian.

On the other hand, the outbreak of World War I benefited the revolutionaries. The White House, which had discreetly supported Carranza, did not care to have a military problem on its doorstep when a much greater one might emerge in Europe at any moment. To calm the American people, President Wilson issued protests and claims that Carranza refused to satisfy (because, in his view, foreigners in Mexico should be treated without any special privileges). Nevertheless, in October, 1915, Washington recognized the Carranza government, thus cutting off Villa's source of arms from the other side of the border. This so enraged the Villists that in January, 1916, they killed sixteen U.S. citizens traveling on a train which they had halted. Two months later, Villa raided Columbus, New Mexico (some historians have doubted the veracity of the reports of the raid published in the American press, believing that the news was invented as a pretext for action), and Wilson, on the eve of the presidential campaign, reacted by dispatching a punitive expedition under General Pershing to capture Villa. American soldiers entered Chihuahua but looked in vain for the wily Mexican. Carranza protested this violation of Mexican territory, and regular Mexican troops attacked one of Pershing's detachments, at which point President Wilson ordered his general to return. The subsequent entry of the United States into World War I put an end to these charades, and Villa retired to set up shop as a merchant. In 1923, long after peace had been restored in Mexico and the name of Pancho Villa was forgotten, he was shot by some of his enemies. His cinematic resurrection was still to come.

The time had come to stabilize and institutionalize the Revolution. Those of its veterans who had gone into government set to work to frame a constitution and a legal system that would define the course of the nation.

This was done under pressure. Some of the officials felt the pressure of the armed masses, even of the vanishing Convention, because the convention had made implicit promises and because the armed masses trusted those promises. To destroy the convention and to disarm the masses, the enemies of the convention found that they were obliged to abide by the convention's promises.

If ever the voice of the people had been heard, it had been in the convention. The concepts that the constitutionalists were to apply in the constitution and in their laws were first hammered out in interminable and apparently sterile debate there. The Zapatist representatives were particularly impassioned polemicists, and it was they who set out the platform for the convention, which may be summed up thus: to destroy latifundism; to return to the people the public lands and waters taken from them; to encourage the establishment of regional agricultural schools; to empower the federal government to expropriate real estate; to recognize the trade unions as legal entities; to offer guaranties to the workers; to protect children born out of wedlock (an important measure in the country where a high percentage of village people were not legally married) as well as the "women who were victims of masculine seduction"; to pass a divorce law; to give preference to the teaching of handicrafts; to reform the laws dealing with certain industrial corporations (the *sociedades anónimas*), a nationalistic measure; to grant the state a share in the output of the mines; to pass laws concerning workmen's compensation and retirement pensions; and to abolish the system of company stores and the use of scrip.

For several months the convention had worked to establish

guidelines for the future, awakening hopes that were to be thwarted later. Attempts were made to create socialist parties and even a League of Producer Classes, which would foster a cooperative movement and the municipalities' activities. Rafael Pérez Taylor, editor of *El Monitor*, the convention's paper, also came out for socialism; he considered the middle class "parasitic and womanish" and called for a strong revolutionary government to create reforms, asserting that the "revolution was not the daughter of liberalism" but had sprung from a "more profound credo," which only showed the decadence of liberalism and vitality of socialism. The Revolution, he went on, was ceasing to be political and was turning to an economic and social phase, backed by a proletarian army and the support of the trade unions, bent on destroying the great landholdings and creating small ones. The trade unions turned a deaf ear to his words.

The labor movement's strong anarchist tendencies and its weakness in numbers, plus the fact that the struggle had been carried on mainly in the rural regions, reduced its influence on the Revolution to a minimum. Its leaders could find no common ground with the peasants* and its ranks were isolated in the urban zones. Consequently, as we have seen, the labor movement was forced to ally with Carranza, who represented to some degree the distrust of the city for the country, and in doing so lost its apolitical character.

In a certain sense, the labor leaders looked upon the Revolution as a struggle between different capitalistic groups. And this feeling was only reinforced by declarations such as Carranza's to the workers in 1914, in which he counseled mutualism and said that trade unionism repelled him "as atheistic and an enemy of the fatherland." If, under Huerta, the Workers' House affirmed that "it has nothing to do and will have nothing to do with politics," it meant, at that particular moment, that labor would not come out against dictatorship, and when the Zapatists occupied Mexico City, the Workers' House stated, "We shall always condemn the

* When the Zapatists entered Mexico City, instead of sacking it, they had gone from house to house begging food, conduct which the World Workers' House organ *El Sindicalista* censured as "begging for alms from the bourgeoisie with a weapon on one's shoulder."

participation of the workers in armed movements. . . . We have always maintained . . . that only the collective effort of the workers, as elucidated by the official trade unions, will advance us slowly but surely toward the longed-for manumission."

This myopia weakened the Mexican labor movement for many years. When the unions tried to emerge from their isolation by accepting Obregón's suggestion that they ally themselves with Carranza and the constitutionalists, labor thereby turned its back on the people who were fighting for the remnants of the convention. Once the convention was defeated, the anarchist leaders tried to strengthen their own organization by establishing, at a famous congress in Tampico in 1917, the Mexican Regional Labor Federation, or CROM. This organization of traditional Bakuninist nomenclature supported the class struggle and direct action, but it revealed in its decisions that it was nationalistic above all else.* In this respect, the labor movement reflected a spirit that tended more and more to predominate in the constitutionalist movement.

The Nationalist Revolution

Little by little, the people laid down their arms, but the Revolution continued above them, in the government. Popular participation in the Revolution no longer resulted in spontaneous action; instead, action was directed by the government and by government groups. The Revolution, or the "revolutionary family" (a term then becoming current and still in use), began to function as a self-appointed guardian protecting the nation against foreigners, the Mexican against exploitation. For years, anyone who had taken part in the Revolution as a member of the constitutionalist band would find doors opened to him, privileges awarded him. Those on the side of the convention were accepted only after a time into the "revolutionary family," even though such men

* In fact, the congress at which CROM was founded marked the end of anarchist influence in the labor movement, but this was expressed in a rather odd fashion. Not a word was said about anarchism, but when the time came to decide on a name for the organization, two titles were proposed: Confederación Regional Obrera Mexicana (Mexican Regional Labor Federation) and Confederación Regional Obrera de México (Regional Labor Federation of Mexico). To the nationalists, the organization had to be "Mexican," to the anarchists, "of Mexico," and the nationalists won.

as Soto y Gama persisted in defending the agrarianist aspirations and hoped to see the power in the hands of the people rather than of their representatives in the "revolutionary family."

This tutelary character emerged openly and lastingly in the constitution of 1917 and in the legislation preceding and following it, particularly the state laws, which were the constitutionalists' first exercise of real power during the period of fierce struggle against the convention. In 1914, General Cándido Aguilar (1888–1964), the governor of Veracruz, had promulgated a labor code setting the work day at nine hours. And in Yucatán, General Salvador Alvarado (1880–1924), a man with vaguely socialistic leanings, codified a series of social laws in 1915—inspired by the laws of New Zealand, of all places—and favored the use of state funds to form workers' production companies. These moves, together with Carranza's agrarian law of 1915, influenced the framers of the constitution. As in the case of other historical manifestations of the Mexican personality, it might be said that there were several constitutions in the same document: the liberal; the ultramodern, inspired by ideas of statist control; and finally, an adaptation of colonial principles with regard to the ownership of land and mineral rights.

Carranza had won recognition as president of the entire country. He tried to control the numberless local centers of power that had emerged during the Revolution and to harmonize them with the federal power. But this was not always easy. Alvarado, in Yucatán, had organized the sisal workers there into a cooperative and, by taking advantage of the scarcity of fiber during World War I, had managed to raise sisal prices and thus make it possible to better the almost animal living conditions of the peons. Some governors had granted lands in accordance with the agrarian law; others bent their efforts to protecting the big landholders. The oil men of Tampico, where some IWW organizers had established unions, paid the governor to prosecute union members, although they themselves refused to pay taxes.

But Carranza had no talent for governing. He was energetic but not adroit. Obregón had returned to private life. The Revolution was in danger of fragmenting and disintegrating. At this point, Carranza decided (on the advice of his secretary of the treasury, Cabrera, the most lucid intellect in his government) to call an election of delegates to a constitutional congress. Cabrera hoped that by giving the delegates an opportunity to debate the various facets of the Revolution and to re-exert their influence, they might evolve a certain unity, even if only for the purpose of insuring their share of power. Thus they might keep alive the possibility of carrying out the unfinished work of the Revolution, which the revolutionaries had always postponed because they were too deeply involved in immediate struggles and maneuvers. Indeed, anything that the Revolution had accomplished until 1916 was the work of the people. Now, Cabrera thought, the moment had come when the administration must plan a governmental program and apply it.

In December, 1916, the constitutional congress met in a theater in the city of Querétaro. All the delegates were constitutionalists; there were no Villa men or Zapatists, although certain factions were beginning to be discernible. There were a few union members, a few independents, and a respectable number of intellectuals and lawyers. Another group, which might be called radical, was made up of followers of Molina Enríquez; their leader in the congress was General Francisco J. Múgica (1884–1954); and Obregón and Calles supported them *sub rosa*. This was the group that put the social and nationalist content into the Mexican constitution. When a ballot was taken, the radicals generally won, often with the support of the independents; but not until the final sessions of the congress did they succeed in winning approval of the two articles that time has shown to be fundamental: Article 27 and Article 123. On February 5, 1917, the constitution was approved and became the law of the land. It has been modified often since then, but never in any of its essentials.

The problem actually was not to draw up a new constitution, but to reshape the constitution of 1857 so that it would meet the country's new needs and, above all, stabilize the revolutionaries' desire to erase the overwhelming social inequality which, they believed, in one way or another, had been the cause of all Mexico's convulsions for more than a century. The delegates believed that a constitution must be much more than a mere declaration of principles; it must be an instrument for governing. But it could not be a sanctification of the concepts of the convention—that is, of direct participatory democracy. No one said this openly, but one of Carranza's trusted supporters, the engineer Félix F. Palavicini (1881–1952), stated in a series of articles written to justify the convocation of the congress: "We must flee from our everlasting leprosy . . . the consecration of historical lies . . . the trembling and cowardly abdication of good judgment before the dogmatic lies of the past." No one, he went on, believes in the infallibility of the people; conscientious citizens want a more or less extensive oligarchy so that all the diverse elements that the country contains may share in governmental life. The concept of guardianship shows up very plainly here. According to Palavicini, all Mexican revolutions had been the work of the middle class and the intellectuals; in short, they had been revolutions from above.

The delegates could not ignore the land hunger of the peasants, and this meant that they had to take up the whole issue of property and ownership. Now respect for private property was as inviolable to the revolutionaries as it had been under the Porfiriate. Molina Enríquez, therefore, laid the basis of the agrarian laws in such a way as to make this respect for property congruent with the necessity for granting land to the peasants. Paradoxically enough, he based it on concepts from colonial days. His thesis was that society creates the right to private ownership and it must be socially oriented for that reason. Property may be expropriated, then, whenever the interests of society so decree. The congress ruled that every expropriation must be paid for, but did not indicate whether payment must be made before or after taking over the property. As a matter of fact, the delegates preferred not to make prepayment a requirement, because in a poor country that would be tantamount to postponing a solution of the agrarian problem indefinitely.

At the moment when Article 27, which deals with the right of ownership, was put to the vote, Mexico had 7.5 million male citizens, of whom 3 million, or 65 per cent of the able-bodied population, were peons. These figures alone would show why debate on Article 27 could not be prolonged: no one could deny that after six years of fighting the longing for land was the motive force for most of the combatants.

The nationalist character of the Mexican Revolution was also clearly visible in Article 27, which in addition dealt with ownership of mineral rights, an issue to which Mexico could not be indifferent. Again, the colonial laws provided the formula. The subsoil was declared the inalienable property of the nation, which might concede its use to private persons.

Apart from the issue of property rights, the revolutionaries wished to break up the latifundios and to encourage ownership of small rural properties. The objective in restoring the *ejidos* was to provide the peasants with the means to maintain economic independence and learn to be landowners, but the *ejidos* were not considered the final solution of the agrarian problem. The delegates preferred to create a complex of small plots, farms, and ranches. But the heart of the matter lay in the concept that the land belonged to the nation, which might grant it as a gift that could be revoked, however, in the public interest. Finally, the constitution provided that no one person could own more than a given amount of land, but left it to the states to decide the amount, depending upon differences in climate, the condition of the soil, and the crops to be planted.

Article 27, which in the course of time would permit expropriation of the oil fields and which legalized immediately what had been already done toward distributing land, was passed in the final session of the congress—by candlelight, because there had been an electrical short circuit.

Article 123, dealing with labor matters, was passed a few days earlier, after a great deal of discussion. The debate did not revolve around the right to organize and strike but around the question whether or not the constitution ought to set the rules for applying these rights in detail. The labor delegates and a few radicals preferred to see all possible details covered in the constitution, even though the text might thereby lose a measure of legal elegance, and their wishes prevailed.

The delegates frankly acknowledged that they wanted the constitution to establish an equilibrium between capital and labor and to recognize strikes as a means of making and keeping this balance, with each side deferring its interests "to the moral interests of humanity in general and our nation in particular." In addition, the state should have the right to intervene as a regulatory agency, to protect labor in the matter of wages and hours. But under pressure from the radical group, the delegates acknowledged that a fair return for work cannot be computed on the basis of wages alone; it should be supplemented by the workers' sharing in company profits. That principle was embodied in the text of the constitution, but it was not applied until 1963. Its purpose was not to give the proletariat control over industry, but to prevent friction caused by too great an inequality. Another measure adopted in Querétaro, but not yet put into practice, was the establishment of a kind of homestead—not in land but in housing and savings—for workers' families.

Interestingly enough, in spite of the guardian spirit of the constitutional delegates revealed in the establishment of compulsory arbitration by the government and the measures to regulate trade-union activity, the congress still did not consider that it had achieved a just system of recompense even with regard to wages and a share of profits. The desire for a fair deal prompted the question of further benefits—social security, schools and housing for workers, medical care, retirement pensions, and terminal pay for unjustified discharge. All these were viewed not as concessions but as rights, economic rights, and it was understood that they must be in addition to wages. Also, Article 123 established a series of rules which may appear commonplace today but were quite advanced at the time: a ban on night work for women, the abolition of child labor, a minimum wage and maximum working hours, etc., but none of them was rigorously applied.

Other articles of the constitution guaranteed the usual basic freedoms and forbade re-election to public office, the reform that had been the starting point of the political phase of the Revolution. It also established the separation of church and state and civilian control of the government.

To some degree, the constitution was a paradox. Though it was born of revolution, it was reformist in tone; though nationalist, its primary concern was the special interests of labor and peasant; though tutelary, it recognized the interests of the lower classes as rights, not as concessions. It was the first constitution to recognize the rights of labor and the first to give the nation ownership of the soil and subsoil. Though it was the work of liberals, it abandoned the old liberal desire to wipe out colonial vestiges and even adopted certain principles of the Spanish colony. Though the work of the middle class, it set the social and national welfare above individual interests.

Many points of view converged in the drafting of the constitution—contradictory interests, opposing ideologies. What unified them all was not so much the debates and parliamentary maneuverings as a shared attitude, which kept emerging in speeches and analyses, on the very nature of the constitution. Mexicans had been debating for years—they are still debating—the question of how to characterize their Revolution. But all those who played a part in it already agreed on one point: that the political and social phases of the struggle, the questions of land and the rights of labor, and how the constitution handled both, were but partial aims, part of a general goal. The Revolution had begun without people being aware of that goal, but now it was beginning to be felt: the goal of creating conditions that would make possible the formation of a genuine Mexican nationality.

Mexico's history since 1917 has been the story of the steps taken toward that goal.

8 · Agrarian Reforms

THE PEOPLE HAD GONE HOME. Power was in the hands of the revolutionaries—men from the middle class, for the most part, doctors,
lawyers, teachers, some of whom had become military men. Some
were guerrilla fighters who had donned the uniform and grown
accustomed to urban life; some were businessmen who had left a
shop or factory to fight with the revolutionary forces; some were
laborers and finally, some were peasants turned politician or even
latifundistas, for everyone respected booty from the Revolution.
No one frowned at this general or that governor because he now
owned a big ranch or a range with herds of cattle. The important
thing was that his wealth did not automatically give him political
power or make him an oligarch.

This confused, diverse mass of men were united by three
things: participation in power, experience of the Revolution, and
the sincere desire to make the constitution something more than
a mere legal document.

Once the constitution had been approved and a large part of the army discharged, urgent problems arose: how to grant land to the peasants who had served as soldiers; how to organize the government with new elements; how to begin a normal political life with appropriate parties, programs, and elections.

Of all these problems, land was the one that preoccupied the people and dominated governmental life over a period of years. Some land had been distributed; much had been seized; haciendas had been burned. But latifundism still persisted, though the big landowners no longer retained any control over the government and many of them had left the country. Whatever the government might decide with regard to the land question would set the tone of its policies.

Ever since independence had been won, Mexico had suffered because of a defective system of land distribution and an equally defective distribution of population. Immigration was scanty but increased during the nineteenth century, although not as much as in Argentina, Uruguay, or Brazil, for example. In 1821, laws to encourage immigration and settlement of the desert regions had been passed, but they were of little avail.

Alamán had estimated that in his day the capital in mortmain amounted to upwards of 300 million pesos. The total population was about 6 million, and there were some 20,000 rural estates. On the eve of the Reform laws of 1854, the population numbered 8 million, and there were 21,177 estates. By 1878, under Díaz, the population had grown to 10 million, but the number of estates had shrunk to 19,500. Just before the Revolution, in 1910, there were 15 million people and 37,000 estates. Obviously, the condition had persisted and the problem had grown more acute.

The latifundio system had impoverished the country. During colonial times, latifundism was denounced, and Bishop Manuel Abad y Queipo had pointed out that because of it the country had come nowhere near producing enough clothing and shoes for even a third of the people. Spain took note of this situation, and before the Hidalgo insurrection in 1810, the tributes imposed on the Indians were lightened and they were promised some share in the land. But those pledges were never fulfilled because of the opposition of the great landholders. In 1812, the Cortes of Cádiz

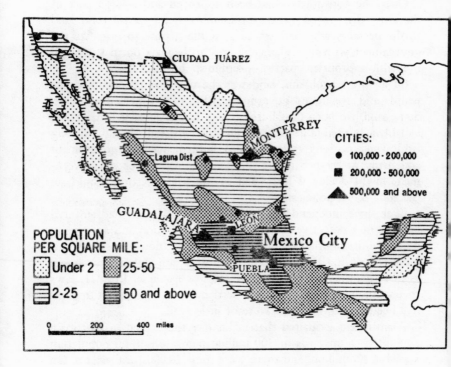

Distribution of the Mexican Population

had ordered a distribution of land to married Indians above the age of twenty-five; this promise was not kept either.

Hidalgo ordered delivery of the communal lands to the Indians, but he did not dare to free the peons of the debts that bound them to the haciendas. From then on, as far as the ruling class was concerned, the agrarian problem would have to be solved by opening new land to cultivation and settlement without disturbing the owners of the haciendas (with the possible exception, when the liberals were in power, of the clerical hierarchy). But the laws to foster settlement failed because European immigrants lacked the means to establish themselves in the countryside and because the Indians refused to move from their accustomed plots. Acreage under cultivation did not much increase until the Porfiriate, when more land was opened up, mainly in the south, thanks to work levies of Indians transported by force from the high plateau and the Pacific coast to Yucatán and other areas.

Some men outside the government had seen clearly the need for agrarian reform. Francisco Severo Maldonado (1775–1832), for example, proposed a law for the gradual nationalization of the land through purchase by the state, which would then turn over lots to the peasants. The novelist José Joaquín Fernández de Lizardi (1771–1827) had suggested fixing by law the maximum size for haciendas, with the government buying and distributing any land in excess of such limits. Even under the empire, proposals were made to offer land to the people. But none of these plans was adopted. All were predicated on government purchase or on prepayment to the owners, conditions quite impossible to fulfill in view of the chronic emptiness of the public coffers. The Reform laws might have solved the problem but for the dogmatism of the liberals, which had the contrary effect of aggravating it.

But until 1894, at any rate, there were some limitations on the enjoyment of property, even though they were seldom respected: the landowner was obliged to cultivate what he owned; he could not leave his land wild. Then in 1894, a law suggested by Díaz nullified this limitation, and thenceforth latifundism grew rapidly. At the same time, agriculture declined, as the land lost its fertility by erosion, owing to the failure to terrace the cultivated slopes. The wealth of the forests also was squandered.

At the outbreak of the Revolution, there were 56,825 communities within the boundaries of the haciendas and 82 per cent of them were entailed to the hacienda. Madero did nothing to remedy this situation. His parliament never even debated the few reform proposals put forth. When the Revolution turned into a civil war, the pressure of events expedited legislation. In 1913, General Lucio Blanco distributed land in Matamoros without bothering to promulgate a law. The Zapatists did the same. As we have seen, Villa issued an agrarian law in 1915, and the constitutionalists and the convention promulgated their own reform laws that same year. Everything coincided—the re-establishment of the *ejidos*, the limitation of property ownership, the distribution of excess land.

But when the delegates to the constitutional congress finished their work and went home, most of the rural population had not yet received land. Then it was up to the government to decide to implement the constitution and grant land.

The guiding principle for the task may be summarized in the words of one of the Revolution's theorists, Fernando González Roa (1880–1937), who said:

> The consequence of the latifundist regime is the division of society into a dominant minority, ready to commit any crime to maintain its domination, and a dominated majority, frequently on the point of rebellion. The aristocratic latifundism that predominates in Mexico is fatal. But the experience of the Reform demonstrated that land cannot be handed over to any but those capable of holding it. The communal property [the *ejido*] cannot, therefore, be considered other than a transitory solution for a backward people. Mexican land tenure, incompatible with the highest type of civilization, has been the cause of all the national ills, and the Revolution itself was due directly to the imperfect distribution of the land. It would be an act of folly to pretend to encourage widespread state ownership, in accordance with Marxist doctrine, just as any industrial development would have to be set aside if an attempt were to be made to nationalize industry, for any such step can be taken only when industry has reached its full development.

In Mexico, to govern meant to create small and medium rural landholdings, González Roa said.

Carranza accepted the constitution, but he had no intention of applying the articles covering social issues. What he wanted was to re-organize the machinery of government. His Porfirist origins came to the fore, in a way, and what he desired most was good administration. At that point, politics seemed pernicious to him. On the other hand, many revolutionaries, particularly those who had gone back to their old lives, considered that Mexico's prime need was to have a normal political life, with parties and elections, for only by such means would the government machinery develop rightly and administer the country in accord with the constitution. The national charter would have to be implemented gradually, and only gradually would the desire of those who had won the Revolution to promote the general welfare, and the needs of the various interest groups, be met.

In March, 1917, Carranza was proclaimed president of the republic—no longer provisional chief of state and without his former title of commander-in-chief of the constitutionalist army. One of his first measures was to restore to the nation ownership of the public lands that had been given away under Díaz. This was not difficult to do, for the majority of the hacienda owners who had gotten them had left the country. But when the land was again in the hands of the state, it was not distributed to the peasants. A National Agrarian Commission was set up to take charge of distribution and local authorities were deprived of the right to distribute lands; but this meant that state governors who were more radical than the federal government were prevented from making any grants. During the presidency of Carranza, only 450,000 acres were distributed to 48,000 families—an insignificant amount in a country as large as Mexico.

To escape the effects of the inflation resulting from the huge volume of paper money issued by the constitutionalists and the local governments during the Revolution, workers in Mexico City now called a general strike for higher wages. Carranza responded by closing the World Workers' House, arresting many of the leaders and threatening them with execution. One labor leader, Luis N. Morones, was sentenced to death, but Obregón interceded for him and managed to obtain a commutation of the sentence to a term in prison. José Barragán, in Tampico, was killed by army officers after he had organized the petroleum workers. I have already spoken of Zapata's murder. Some states appointed boards of arbitration to settle labor disputes in accordance with Article 123 of the Constitution, but the Supreme Court, filled with Carranza's men, nullified their powers.

Late in 1918, the world-wide influenza epidemic reached Mexico, where it claimed many victims. The wars of the seven preceding years and the epidemic together are estimated to have cost Mexico more than 1 million lives. But, oddly enough, the epidemic seemed to have swept away paper money as well as people, for gold and silver coins came back into circulation. Industries began to function again, too, but wages were lower than during the time of Díaz.

Many people began to ask themselves what good the Revolution had done. Had it all been in vain? Carranza's popularity was declining while Obregón, the other revolutionary *caudillo*, who had kept on the periphery of power since 1916, was winning support. The CROM, established in 1917 and controlled by the Action Group, led by Morones—a group organized some time earlier by a few socialist labor leaders and intellectuals—formed a Labor Party and planned to enter Obregón as its candidate in the forthcoming presidential election. The Catholics were beginning to organize politically, too.

Carranza, denied re-election by the very constitution he had promulgated, wanted to have a man he trusted follow him. He chose Ignacio Bonillas, the ambassador to Washington and a complete unknown in Mexico. Obregón realized that Carranza could use the governmental apparatus to throw the victory to Bonillas, and when, in 1920, Carranza sent troops to break a railroad strike in Sonora, he seized upon this as a pretext for an uprising. Adolfo de la Huerta, one of Obregón's friends and governor of the state, proclaimed the independence of Sonora on the grounds, he said, that the federal government was interfering in its affairs. In April, de la Huerta and Calles (who was then commanding forces in Sonora) launched the Agua Prieta Plan, which demanded Carranza's resignation and appointment of a provisional president to ensure an honest election. The police were sent to arrest Obregón, then in Mexico City, but he managed to slip through their hands and head for the Pacific coast.

The Calles forces moved southward, collecting men in each city they passed. Even the sinister Pablo González, who had acted as Zapata's trigger man, joined the Obregón group. Carranza, left alone, moved out of Mexico City toward Veracruz, escorted by a group of friends and soldiers and taking along part of the treasury's funds. He intended to set up his government in the Gulf port, but his train was attacked by troops of the governor of Veracruz. Carranza fled on horseback and paused to rest in the village of Tlaxcalantongo, where a local boss killed him in his sleep. Later the assassin gave out the story that Carranza had committed suicide.

Immediately after the Obregón forces entered the capital, they named De la Huerta to the presidency. De la Huerta's first act, which pacified Villa and the Zapatists, was to recognize the legality of the land distribution that had taken place. (Pablo González did not stay loyal to Obregón; he rebelled and was exiled. His lieutenant, Guajardo, Zapata's murderer, was executed.)

In November, 1920, after an uneventful election, Alvaro Obregón took office as president.

To an observer, the Mexican government appeared then no different from that of the Díaz period, with its politicians, demagogues, ambitious generals, big landowners (albeit new, uniformed owners who, as a rule, had seized their lands during the Revolution), small groups who disputed the executive power, and fraudulent elections. All this was too deeply embedded in Mexico by the thirty years of the Porfiriate to be conjured away in an instant. Nevertheless, the observer could note that young intellectuals filled some of the cabinet posts, there was great activity in the field of public education, and, above all, land was being distributed. Furthermore, the tone, even the physical appearance of those wielding power had changed; the new men were not the distinguished Europeanized white men of the Porfiriate, but men of the people, mestizos—"very Mexican," as they liked to say.

Meanwhile, a myth was growing up about Mexico: abroad, it was looked on as a country in radical revolution; indiscriminately defended by some, it was attacked by others as a Bolshevist nation—since at that time it had become fashionable in certain circles to identify new social reform with the nascent Communist movement. Actually, Obregón and his friends were trying to transform the country into a capitalist society, to pull it out of its agrarian feudalism, and to create the conditions necessary to modernize it. To do those things, they would have to give the working class in Mexico what it already had in some capitalist countries. This meant a twofold effort: to distribute land and to encourage education, thereby to create a rural middle class. While the United States watched Obregón with suspicion, he deported the first foreign Communists who had come into the country. (Much of the social agitation then going on in Mexico was fomented by the IWW and Communists from the United States.)

Obregón knew that he could not set up a democratic regime without destroying a number of obstacles, and without achieving some degree of governmental efficiency and economic stability. He would have to accomplish all this in the face of opposition from the Church and the boundless ambition of the "finger generals." He liked to say that "there is no general who can stand up to a cannonade of 100,000 pesos." New political parties were forming. (In addition to the Laborites, whom Obregón had rewarded with government posts, the Agrarian Party was formed. Its brain was Antonio Díaz Soto y Gama.) Parliamentary life was active and free. And although the president could execute and deport dissenters—with the tacit consent of the people if not legally—he used his power with moderation and respected freedom of the press; the newspapers, which were in the hands of reactionary groups, did not hesitate to criticize him sharply.

Obregón saw that the agrarian problem had a direct bearing on the nation's general welfare. In a speech in 1920, he said that farming landowners were using methods of cultivation that ruined the soil, even as they asked constantly for protective measures; that there would be no advantage in destroying large landholdings until small holdings could become established, for otherwise production would drop; and that the government would require from the latifundios whatever land should be necessary to satisfy the demands of the peasants, provided that the demands were presented "in such a way that whenever the great landholdings were broken up, their production would be replaced by that of the small landholdings and in the same proportions." Only a man with absolute assurance that he was in control and able to resist the pressures of the great landholders could present such a plan. At the same time, however, there were many dogmatic men in the government and on the National Agrarian Commission who tried to encourage collective ownership of property—collectivism was greatly in vogue then among aspiring imitators of the Russian Revolution. To offset this trend, Obregón proposed, in 1925, a law granting a parcel of common land as a patrimony to every member of the *ejidos*. The preamble to the bill affirmed that its purpose was to establish "common property in private use" and further declared that if experimentation in communal development of land was to continue, all efforts to reconstruct the country would be nullified by the mistrust aroused in the peasants and by the possible corruption of the directors of the communal holdings. The law would set out "to guarantee the peasant the enjoyment of the entire product of the investment of his labor or capital." Soto y Gama, Zapata's old friend, sponsored this plan and won approval for it.

The peasants' demand for land was growing, and so was the number of distributions, but the grants were being made in slow motion, partly because of bureaucratic obstacles (Mexicans have always been very clever at multiplying paper work, thus observing a long-established Spanish tradition), partly because the government was trying not to force the pace and to establish a certain balance between the land grants and new industries. And, although the number of peons had declined during the Revolution, when many of the haciendas were burned and their lands seized, nearly 1 million families were still dependent upon peons' wages. In the eyes of the law, the peon was a worker; therefore he should be unionized to enjoy the rights recognized in Article 123 of the constitution. Unfortunately, however, it was stipulated that this article should be applied by the state governments, with whom the big landowners were likely to have much more influence than the federal government. Consequently, the peon's miserable situation was not improved, and many people began to speak of the failure of agrarian reform when it had only just started. In the provinces, clashes frequently occurred between the hacienda owners' private police and bands of rebellious peons. The rebels attacked the priests, too, because they preached resignation and submission while they defended the hacienda owners. And the land barons refused to accept the bonds issued to them by the government as compensation for expropriated land, appealed to the Supreme Court, and consequently paralyzed the entire reform process. The bonds, which carried interest, could be used to pay taxes and were redeemable in twenty years, but the barons never took the Treasury very seriously. Expropriations were carried out nevertheless, and although many of the land-holders had left the country, some stayed (in the cities) and invested in Mexican industry, which by now they had come to consider safer than land.

In spite of everything, more land was distributed during Obregón's term than in Carranza's, some 3 million acres to 624 villages. Yet 320 million acres were still in the hands of the big landowners. The Revolution had not solved the problem, but it had created the conditions within which it might be solved step by step. Obregón's preoccupation, which he handed on to his successors, was to consolidate what had been accomplished in order to render the Revolution irreversible.

Obregón also had other problems to plague him. One of those was the trade-union movement. As we have said, CROM was formed in 1917 at a labor congress held in Tampico. CROM defined its international posture by "maintaining a diversity of tactics with a common objective" (still the traditional one of destroying the capitalist system), and indicated that "it would sometimes unite with the government and make the government's program its own [because] the government has always fought to defend not only the so-called sovereignty of the nation, but also the sources of public wealth, from which the economic liberation of the people must emerge and which constitutes the precise objective of the international assault."

In November, 1919, CROM, together with the American Federation of Labor, formed the Confederación Obrera Panamericana, or COPA (Pan American Federation of Labor) which held two congresses in Mexico City, one in 1921 and the other in 1924. But for all Mexico's membership in COPA and the prestige of the Mexican Revolution throughout the hemisphere, COPA never succeeded in establishing itself in Latin America or in wielding any real influence.

CROM supported Obregón in his candidacy and in his presidency, and he reciprocated by giving it every possible advantage. This was shown whenever CROM called a strike. In order legally to strike, the workers had first to exhaust all conciliatory measures, after which the Board of Conciliation and Arbitration would declare the strike legal. As the government representatives on the assigned boards (acting as presiding officers and as actual arbitrators) were appointed directly by the government, the boards always ruled in favor of CROM, whereas they branded as illegal strikes called by independent unions and other federations. This favoritism gave rise to bitter rivalries within the trade-union movement, so bitter that at times shots were exchanged. Nevertheless, by using the services of the boards, the workers succeeded in obtaining pay increases, though they came very slowly, and seeing to it that capitalization was not achieved entirely at their expense.

The labor movement tried at the same time to correct its sins of omission dating from the Revolution. The leaders of CROM were part of the projected Socialist Party formed in 1919 and quickly converted into the Labor Party to support Obregón's candidacy. They constituted the so-called Action Group which actually controlled CROM and the Labor Party, both of which in turn supported the government. By about 1928–30, the Labor Party began to fall apart and CROM lost strength because its contact with power and the possibility of winning victories without having to do battles had turned it into a bureaucracy. In 1924, one of its leaders said: "It is not a question of destroying capital; it is a question of a harmonious merger of labor and capital for the benefit of the workers." And in 1929, when a labor-management convention was held to study matters needing social legislation, Vicente Lombardo Toledano (b. 1894) on behalf of CROM defended compulsory arbitration, for, he said, "The workers have confidence in the government because it represents the interests of the Revolution."

Once CROM ceased to represent the working man by allying too closely with the government, labor unrest was exploited by a number of small political groups. Among the first of these were the socialist Grupo Marxista Rojo (Red Marxist Group); the antilabor Partido Socialista Mayoritario Rojo (Red Socialist Majority Party); the Partido Socialista del Sureste (Southeastern Socialist Party), organized by General Salvador Alvarado in Yucatán; the Ligas de Resistencia (Resistance Leagues), headed by Felipe Carrillo Puerto (1874–1924), an organization especially strong in Yucatan, in which the American Robert Haberman played a founder's role; the Partido Socialista Radical (Radical Socialist Party), in Tabasco, led by Tomás Garrido Canabal (1890–1943), a strong anticlerical. At about the same time, the Mexican Communist Party was established through the influence of M. N. Roy, an Indian nationalist living in Mexico City who had been converted to Marxism. The groups that Roy managed to bring together were oriented and indoctrinated by the Japanese Communist, Sen Katayama, while he was in Mexico in 1922, and later by Michael Borodin. Several party members in the United States, assigned to Mexico, controlled the Mexican party for several years until it was entrusted to a Swiss named Stirner. The Mexican Communist Party never succeeded in gaining much influence over the masses, although it enticed some intellectuals and artists—including the famous painters Diego Rivera (1886–1959) and David Alfaro Siqueiros (b. 1895).

All these groups kept Mexican political thought in ferment, but they never succeeded in winning the masses. On the other hand, the Confederación General de Trabajo (General Federation of Labor) was organized in 1921 by a group of anarchist-syndicalist leaders who were exasperated with the *de facto* monopoly CROM exercised in the union movement. The CGT practiced a peculiar anarchism, for some of its leaders ran for political office, and it became very aggressive, opposing the government on any number of occasions and winning some victories. It attempted to intervene on the side of the peasants, it organized the workers by industries, and it sponsored direct action without government arbitration. (In 1924, during a moment of crisis, the CGT decided that the workers should seize and operate businesses which had closed down.) As long as the CGT's dominance lasted, and as CROM lost strength, some hard battles were waged. For example, in Veracruz, the tenants organized and struck under the leadership of Herón Proal, a romantic and picturesque figure. But direct action demanded great sacrifices, since it was effected at the cost of the CGT remaining on the fringe of legality and renouncing the advantages of legal support. The CGT began to decline after

1932, although for several more years it was still a strong voice of protest.

After losing its powerful central organization, the working class —disillusioned with cooperating with the government (CROM) and disillusioned with opposition (CGT)—became disoriented. Several new organizations were formed but none was very important: the Confederación Sindical Unitaria (United Trade Union Federation), a Communist organization that existed only on paper; the Confederación Nacional Proletaria (National Proletarian Federation), and the Confederación General Obrera y Campesina (General Farmer-Labor Federation), led by Lombardo Toledano, who had broken with Morones and left CROM in 1932.

Obregón's government had a lasting cultural influence owing to the presence in it of a contradictory, picturesque, and extremely intelligent man: José Vasconcelos (1882–1959), whom Obregón appointed as minister of education soon after his election. Vasconcelos, who had first joined Madero and was later with Villa for a time, was very pro-Spanish and very anti-American, but in the end he became strongly Catholic and an enemy of the Revolution. Vasconcelos was minister during the days when Mexican mural painting was winning world-wide acclaim through the work of Clemente Orozco, Diego Rivera, Siqueiros, and later Rufino Tamayo, and others. Rivera, who believed that mural paintings were for the people, whereas easel painting was only for the rich, painted the murals in the Ministry of Education Building and the National Palace.

Vasconcelos contrived to make the education budget the most important single sector of the Mexican national budget, and it has remained so ever since. He also had a free hand to invite people from all over the world to come to Mexico and undertake every kind of experiment. He organized cultural missions, attracted important visitors like Gabriela Mistral, Ramón del Valle Inclán, and Pedro Henríquez Ureña, and built 1,000 rural schools that were planned to be the true cultural nuclei of their communities. Vasconcelos had the gift of inspiring rural schoolmasters with a sense of mission and with militancy, both of which were greatly needed, for the teachers often came up against hostility from the village priests and, not infrequently, from the old people, too. Many teachers were murdered by groups of fanatical Catholics; but many succeeded in awakening in the peasant youth the desire to learn and to transform the life of their communities.

At the same time, all the intellectual activity that the Revolution had thwarted—the intellectuals had been too busy acting as secretaries to the generals—now began to flower. Antonio Caso was teaching at the University of Mexico; his brother Alfonso soon started the excavations that led to the discovery of the astonishing ruins at Monte Albán, near Oaxaca; poets who had been formed in Europe were writing, publishing reviews, putting on plays, and establishing the Contemporaries group. Others, like the muralists, displayed an interest in social protest and signed endless numbers of manifestos and declarations. Students showed signs of social unrest, even the ones from privileged classes; eventually they organized a prolonged student strike that was marked by violent clashes with the police and that ended in success with recognition of the University of Mexico's autonomy. This meant that the university was allowed to appoint its own board of directors and the government intervened in academic life only to pay its expenses. The Universidad Nacional Autónoma de México (Autonomous National University of Mexico) and a number of provincial universities—while not for some time modern universities in the real sense of the word, falling short of true pedagogical effectiveness—were centers of intellectual agitation and forums for the spread of culture, at least to the middle class.

When this period is viewed closely, the astonishing thing about it is that so much was done with so little. The public treasury was ruined, and Mexico was in economic chaos. To try to establish some sort of order, and at the same time to satisfy the voracity of some of the influential politicians and generals, to preserve the peace, and on top of all this to pacify Washington was an almost impossible task. In Washington, the Republican Party was in power; Harding was in the White House and closely allied with the oil companies. And in Mexico, the oil companies were alarmed by Article 27 of the constitution, which gave the nation ownership of mineral rights. American hacienda owners were protesting the occupation of their estates by peasants. Obregón was reluctant to apply Article 27 because he knew that the situation was unfavorable to declaring that mineral deposits belonged to Mexico and that all companies must pay for them. As a temporary expedient, his government levied new taxes, one of which was on mining, whereupon the oil companies hastened to brand the tax confiscatory, even though it amounted to less than the taxes paid in the United States. Washington showed great lack of imagination here; the State Department failed to understand that many of the "socialistic" statements put out by certain elements of the Mexican Government reflected not what they thought but the need to pacify the radical groups. In Washington, there was much talk about the "Bolshevist government" of Mexico. Obregón served three years before the United States recognized his government. Even then, in order to be sure that Washington would not support a military coup against him, he declared that Article 27 was not retroactive and therefore would not apply to companies already established in Mexico. Washington responded by demanding that Obregón's declaration be recorded in a treaty; Obregón considered it insulting to doubt the word of the president of Mexico.

Luckily, the bankers were more intelligent than the diplomats. Adolfo de la Huerta, minister of finance, handled matters skillfully by assigning the income from the oil taxes to pay the interest on the national debt, thus opposing the banks and oil companies. The AFL used its influence on Mexico's behalf. Finally, in August, 1922, recognition was granted the Obregón government and a commission was set up to deal with the claims of U.S. citizens for damages caused by the Revolution. In 1934, when the commission's mandate expired, Mexico agreed to pay $5.5 million.

Obregón was a good executive, even-tempered and without demagoguery. He was also astute enough to choose a capable successor in Plutarco Elías Calles, his minister of the interior. Many deputies, unions not affiliated with CROM, and British companies all opposed Calles. Adolfo de la Huerta let himself be persuaded to run against Calles and resigned his post to do so and broke with Obregón. He did not even wait for the elections, however, and in December, 1923, two "finger generals," Guadalupe Sánchez, in Veracruz, and Enrique Estrada, in Jalisco, started an insurrection. They executed many officials (including Carrillo Puerto, the socialist leader in Yucatán, who became a legendary figure after his death), and returned land to the hacienda owners. The membership of CROM responded violently to this development, and Vasconcelos resigned his cabinet position in great indignation. It looked as if the Revolution was about to go under. But Obregón obtained arms in the United States (the American Government wanted no more disturbances in Mexico), and the peasants who had been granted land used the arms to fight the rebels. The conflict lasted three months. De la Huerta fled to the United States, not to return for ten years. The rebel leaders were executed, and Calles was elected president in 1924. Many of the "finger generals" left the scene and were replaced by fifty-four new generals loyal to the Obregón government. Thus the agrarian reform paid its first political dividends.

Obregón and Calles judged that with their regime established, the time had come to speed up the work of laying broad social foundations to support their government. Naturally this provoked a recrudescence of opposition and, in turn, the use of police methods against the opposition. The Calles government was at once very harsh (many prisoners were shot "while trying to escape," and many arrested men "committed suicide") and very progressive.

Calles was a former schoolteacher made a soldier by the Revolution. He was not a cultivated man, but he had sensitive political intuition and a keen nose to scent out popular feeling. He called himself a socialist, although in practice his politics were to encourage capitalism—within certain limits. Like all the political figures of that period, he became wealthy and bought land, but over and above his personal ambitions, he had, again like all politicians of his time, a certain feeling for the national interest and the people's welfare. To a great degree, political corruption abetted his program, for the ministers and politicians who grew rich established industries, especially of consumer goods, thus initiating a new stage of industrialization. Calles virtually ruled the country for twelve years through his hold over his successors, although he served as president for only the constitutional four-year term.

The economic situation improved, in spite of the fact that the army which had to be kept happy absorbed 300 million pesos, a quarter of the federal budget. Prosperity made possible the allocation of large sums for education, irrigation, public health, and roads, which were to end the isolation of vast regions. The distribution of land moved more rapidly: 8 million acres were granted to 1,500 communities during Calles' presidency. Since experience had shown that the peasants often found themselves at the mercy of the man in charge of the *ejido*, either a bureaucrat or a local *cacique*, Calles decided in 1927 that each person who received an individual or family plot would be forbidden to sell it—reasoning that if a peasant knew that no one could buy his land or expel him from the *ejido*, he would not submit to the bureaucrat. This was known as the law of Ejidal Patrimony. To reinforce further the peasants' independence and simultaneously to encourage the creation of small and medium holdings outside the *ejidos*, he established farm credit banks. In spite of them, however, the politicians managed through pressure and threats to channel a large share of the money in the banks into loans made out to themselves, with the result that the peasants again found credit tight.

Industrial workers enjoyed small wage increases and began to collect compensation for discharge or accident. The Action Group, ensconced in the bosom of CROM, encouraged the tendency for CROM to monopolize the labor movement and to incorporate as many unions as possible within it, and this trend was reinforced by official protection and augmented by the appointment of Morones as secretary of industry and commerce (with jurisdiction over labor matters). At that time, the unionized workers numbered less than 1 million. CROM claimed to control them all and 500,000 peasants besides, but not even as many as 20,000 paid their union dues.

Calles and Obregón, who always acted in accord, doubtless believed that they were taking the best course to achieve what might be called, in the jargon of the experts, the capitalization of the country. The people in government who were growing rich were converted to capitalism as they invested their wealth and changed their way of thinking, and the workers and peasants were benefiting along with the wealthy, albeit to a lesser degree. The regime was acquiring a solid foundation in the rising middle class. On the other hand, the old dissidents were still stirring, and Calles needed the strong props given him by CROM and the *nouveaux riches* among the military, who, even though they were wealthy, owed their rank to the Revolution and never had to undergo the leveling experience of barracks life. In other words, they retained some of their aggressiveness for all their wealth, together with a certain loyalty to the Revolution which had made them.

The Church—which had never ceased to be a church in the Spanish manner, that is, socially retrograde and riveted to dogma and ritual—the Church, let it not be forgotten, that had condemned Hidalgo and brought Maximilian to Mexico, collected around itself all the right-wing opposition to the revolutionary regime. The brutality of the government's repressive measures caused some sectors of the population, especially intellectuals and students, who might otherwise have kept faith with the Revolution, to lean toward opposition. The Church, however, could not count on prestigious figures or politically capable leaders. Consequently, Calles was able to hamstring it and to eliminate its power—and along with it went one of the continuing nightmares of Mexican politics. But this was achieved only after a long, hard, and sordid struggle.

The method of persuasion used by the Church from the very beginning in colonial times was to try to unify and harmonize the opposing creeds of paganism and Christianity. Probably this policy had arisen spontaneously, simply because it had been the easiest way to make Catholic ritual and doctrine acceptable to the Indians. What the Church did was to replace an idol with a saint, a goddess with a virgin, a pyramid with a church, a legend with a dogma. The great majority of the Mexican people were deeply religious, and they expressed their beliefs more naturally through superstition than through a real understanding of theological problems.

The ecclesiastical hierarchy opposed the Revolution from the start. The clergy pronounced an anathema on the agrarianists, supported Huerta, refused to condemn the assassination of Madero and Pino Suárez, and maintained a disapproving attitude throughout the struggle. While Carranza was in power, this attitude softened somewhat but was reaffirmed from the pulpits during the terms of Obregón and Calles, particularly on the issues of education and the agrarian laws. For centuries, the Church had enjoyed a *de facto* monopoly of education, especially in the primary grades, with the result that it turned a minatory eye on the Vasconcelos campaign to establish schools and train teachers in order to bring a lay culture to the countryside. Even the village priests, some of whom had worked for the Revolution, resented these secular, though not antireligious, educational efforts. On the other hand, the Church was no longer respected; in the villages everyone knew all about the priests' women and their natural children and all about how much funerals, baptisms, and weddings cost. Wealth and meddling in politics had corrupted the clergy.

When the Church set out to oppose the Revolution in toto, it felt sure that it could bring the people with it. But it found itself standing alone, without popular support; the people no longer respected it and, thanks to the ritualistic and superstitious brand of Catholicism that had been taught them, had no need of the clergy.

In 1921, as we have seen, the Church tried to organize its own trade unions, and the priests declared from the pulpits that membership in CROM constituted a mortal sin. Yet the Catholic unions never called strikes; the Church left it to management's conscience to decide whether or not to comply with the social precepts of *Rerum Novarum.* Thus, the workers—in spite of their religious fanaticism, which impelled them to cover endless distances on pilgrimages, to climb steep hills on their knees, and to flagellate themselves in public—refused to join the Catholic trade unions. They joined first CROM and later the CGT, which was outspokenly anticlerical.

The ecclesiastical hierarchy, exasperated by this desertion by the masses, and leaning more toward the boss-led groups and old

Porfirists, who still retained a measure of economic strength though they had lost their political power, did not hesitate to provoke conflicts with the government. In 1926, one of those confrontations became so bitter that a civil war might have ensued if the people had heeded the Church.

In that year, the press, for the most part privately owned and opposed to the Revolution, published at the behest of the archbishop a protest the clergy had drafted in 1917 against the constitution. The government considered that it could only be interpreted as a premeditated provocation, and Calles countered by ordering the immediate application of the articles of the constitution regulating freedom of worship and relations between Church and state. (The government had never bothered to put those articles into effect until then.) Calles also ordered the deportation of foreign members of religious orders—200 priests and nuns in all, most of them Spanish. He closed the religious primary schools on the pretext that the teachers had no teaching certificates, and reminded the priests that they must register at a special office of the government. The bishops believed that registry would enable the government to decide who could or could not perform clerical offices—a matter, they claimed, for ecclesiastical jurisdiction. They forbade the priests to register and threatened that if the government persisted in enforcing its order, they would keep the priests from administering the sacraments. That the bishops should have thought of this particular scheme demonstrates the degree to which strikes had become a normal feature of Mexican life of that period.

The government refused to yield. Calles decided that the civil authority could not surrender, because if it did, the Church would grow stronger, would become more demanding, and would try to recover its political influence. The Revolution, saddled with two powerful authorities, would sink without a trace, leaving the country to revert to a situation like that prevailing before 1910.

On July 31, 1926, the bishops ordered the priests all over the country to walk out of the churches (which were the property of the nation in the eyes of the law, to be held by the Church in usufruct). On August 1, for the first time since Cortés disembarked, no masses were said in Mexico. The government realized that the people were religious but not pro-clerical, and it ordered committees of parishioners to take charge of the church buildings and keep them open for the faithful. The people had never had any great need for the priests to help them with their devotions.

The priests' strike lasted for three years, but the Church gained none of its objectives. Violent incidents occurred, even battles between the police and groups of Catholics. There was talk of miracles invoked to punish the government. To Catholics all over the world, Calles was Antichrist. The Vatican supported the Mexican Church and condemned the government, but the people did not support its stand. In the main, the wealthy white Catholics came to the defense of the Church, and not infrequently, many of them received for safekeeping the jewels, chalices, and other valuables in the churches (and later many denied ever having received them, while they enjoyed the money obtained by selling them).

Some newspapermen and young Catholics from the cities moved to the villages in the north where the ranchers were very fanatical. Little wars occurred, to the cry of "Viva Cristo Rey" ("Long live Christ the King!"). The schoolteachers were offered up as sacrificial victims in this struggle, for whenever the guerrillas attacked a village, they hunted out the schoolteacher and tortured him by cutting off his ears or tongue or hanged him. The fanatics set fire to schools and public buildings. The bishops washed their hands of the activities of the *Cristeros*, as these guerrillas were called, but made no attempt to interfere with their activities, even though they knew the *Cristeros* would obey them if they ordered a halt. Indeed, there were priests among the guerrillas, who in 1927 did not hesitate for a moment before dynamiting a train and causing the death or injury of about 100 passengers. In reprisal, the government deported six bishops to Texas and started to organize a large-scale military expedition to liquidate the *Cristeros*, which ended by provoking new acts of brutality on both sides and many more casualties.

The generals, most of whom had been guerrilla fighters themselves, fond of recalling their days of glory during the Revolution, were in no hurry to end the *Cristero* rebellion because it gave them a chance to plunder the houses of the rich Catholics and to relive their days of youthful enthusiasm. Jalisco, Michoacán, and Colima, as well as parts of Mexico State, saw the bitterest of the *Cristero* fighting. In Jalisco, the local military commandant employed a tactic that was later adopted by the colonialist armies in Algeria and Indochina. He would isolate the rebels by creating rebel zones and ordering the peasants (60,000 in Jalisco) to move out of them.

The *Cristeros*, who were closer to the people than the priestly hierarchy, realized that if they were to rally support they must erase the impression that they were acting in opposition to the Revolution. One of their leaders, the journalist René Capistrán Garza, who later practiced his profession peacefully in the capital, was appointed commander-in-chief of the rebels. In January, 1927, he published, in the United States, a manifesto in which he promised to sustain the principle of no re-election to office, to respect agrarian reform, to nationalize mineral rights, to guarantee the right to strike, and even to maintain the separation of Church and state. The bishops—alarmed by the growing radicalism of their own combatants, the futility of their own efforts, which were steadily alienating the Catholic masses, and the support that Calles offered to priests who had not demonstrated solidarity with the Church and with whom he now proposed to found a national Mexican Church—gradually softened. Little by little the *Cristero* rebellion was stamped out, and it was generally believed that the resistance of the Church would come to an end with the inauguration of a new president. But the state of mind created by the Church was the cause of Obregón's assassination a short time afterward.

A political mistake on the part of Calles and Obregón provided a pretext for the crime. As no political figure with a strong personality was available to succeed Calles, he and Obregón came to an agreement that Obregón would offer himself as a candidate. This could be done only if they were able to persuade congress to amend the constitution so that the election of a former president who had been out of office for one term would not be considered re-election. At the same time, the term of office would be extended from four to six years (the period in force today). A reform of that kind alarmed many people who saw in it the danger that Calles and Obregón might thereby indefinitely hold on to the office of President. This disquiet was demonstrated by an abortive military coup. Two generals, Francisco Serrano and Arnulfo Gómez, were executed, the former for planning the coup and the second for proclaiming rebellion in Veracruz. The failure of the coup demonstrated that the militarism arising from the Revolution was losing strength. The people were opposed to reforming the constitution, but they felt no sympathy whatsoever for the insurgent officers.

Obregón could count on the support of the agrarian groups and the enemies of CROM. Morones, whom Obregón had rescued after Carranza had sentenced him to death, was now opposed to his savior's nomination, because he himself aspired to the presidency. In the summer of 1928, Obregón won the election.

Three weeks later, as he was leaving a restaurant called La Bombilla, on the road to Cuernavaca, Obregón was shot to death by a newspaper artist who approached him under the pretext of sketching a caricature. The killer, a young Catholic named José de León Toral, was shot down, too. The police arrested a priest, Fr. Pro, whom they charged with the instigation of the crime in collaboration with a nun, Mother Conchita. The priest was executed. Many people believed, however, that the leaders of CROM were responsible for the murder. Today, an ugly monument to Obregón stands on the spot where he was assassinated.

The political situation was very delicate. Calles could not constitutionally continue in office after the expiration of his term in December. In September, on the opening day of congress, when the president always reads his annual report to the legislators, Calles met privately with the state governors, the generals, and influential leaders—all those who were capable of making trouble, of rebelling or protesting. Calles read to this group a declaration stating that, for the good of Mexico, Obregón should be regarded as the last of the *caudillos* and that no one, not even Calles himself, should be permitted to govern as a virtual dictator. The moment had come when the democratic aspirations of the Revolution must be institutionalized. Many ambitious politicians and generals went away feeling defrauded, but no one ventured to dissent, and the country breathed a sigh of relief that snuffed out all the flickers of ambition.

The task of congress was to elect a new president, in accordance with the constitution, until new elections would be called in 1929. It was evident that the man chosen must belong to the Obregón group and be able to count on the support of the Calles men. Emilio Portes Gil (b. 1891), an attorney and former governor of Tamaulipas, was elected.

Calles left office with few conflicts unresolved. The Church, left standing alone, had been forced to submit to the law. The only other major problem, that of relations with the United States, had been solved—in part by the passage, in 1926, of a law providing, in accordance with Article 27, that the owners of oil-bearing deposits had to exchange their titles for fifty-year concessions, dating from the moment of purchase of the land. Many of the oil companies never had held valid titles; indeed, they had either seized the lands or received them illegally in the time of Díaz. The companies refused to apply for concessions, and the government started legal actions for the *de facto* nationalization of Mexico's mineral rights. This law was regarded in the United States as á breach of the promise Obregón had made in 1923 that Article 27 would not be applied retroactively. A widespread campaign against Calles was instituted in the American press, calling him a Bolshevik. Newspapers controlled by William Randolph Hearst, who owned huge haciendas in the north of Mexico, accused four liberal American senators, who had opposed any U.S. intervention in Mexico's affairs, of receiving more than $1 million from the Mexican Government. Catholics in the United States added fuel to the fire and demanded intervention. About then, two of the political figures most active in this anti-Mexico campaign became involved in the Teapot Dome scandal of the Harding administration, and eventually the campaign lost support through its very excesses.

In 1927, the State Department decided to take advantage of the furor to amend its policy toward Mexico. Dwight Morrow, charged with effecting this change, was the first ambassador from the United States who showed no signs of paternalism and never gave himself airs of superiority in Mexico. Morrow made it crystal clear at once that he did not intend ever to forget that Mexico was a sovereign state. (And fortunately for Morrow, soon after he arrived in Mexico, Charles Lindbergh visited there, and some of his popularity rubbed off on Morrow and his family, for the aviator had recently married the ambassador's daughter Anne.)

The Supreme Court of Mexico now ruled the law on oil concessions unconstitutional but also decided that the owners of land with oil-bearing deposits must relinquish it unless they were willing to develop its mineral wealth. Thus the U.S.-Mexican conflict was obliterated in a single transaction. Calles and Morrow became friends, and the atmosphere between the two countries changed for the better in the three years that Morrow was ambassador. This was important, because it helped to make the period following Obregón's assassination, which might have been a time of turmoil, one of relative tranquility and constructiveness. Calles held no official post, but he was rich (like all Mexican politicians leaving office), and a forceful personality, and he inspired and sustained government policy throughout this period. The people called him *Jefe Máximo*. No important decision was made without consulting him.

Calles knew from experience that the agrarian problem was the basic one. But like Obregón before him, and like Portes Gil, he was from the north and consequently was inclined toward a modern type of large-scale exploitation of the land. Although he understood the demands of the peasants, he felt that they were in some way foreign to him. To him, what really mattered was to step up agricultural productivity in order to improve the economic situation, for Mexico was burdened with foreign debts inherited from Díaz and increased by the Revolution, and there was no way to pay them. Nor could the treasury pay the amount claimed by foreigners as indemnity for damages incurred during the Revolution. This inability to meet her obligations debarred Mexico from access to international credit. The agrarian reform, which temporarily decreased the productivity of the land, required additional funds for equipment, livestock, and seed for the peasants. Money was also needed to continue building schools, roads, dams, and canals. The government enjoyed a few years of prosperity, during which it slowly extricated itself from this dilemma and even accelerated its policy of public works, particularly in school construction and irrigation. But when the crash on Wall Street came in 1929, foreign investment in Mexico and exports decreased, and many public works programs were paralyzed.

In 1930, Calles reviewed the agrarian situation in the country and concluded that the simplistic agrarian policy followed until then had failed because granting land to the laborers was only the first step, and it must be followed by providing the *means* to farm. He proposed that each time land was turned over to the peasants, or anyone acquired cultivation rights, a time limit should be set during which claims on the land could be made; at the expiration of this period, the new owner must have the assurance that his land would not be taken away from him. The suggestion aimed to encourage the farmer to cultivate and improve his holdings. As time went by, this was developed into a system whereby certificates testifying that specified lands had been inspected by the state, that titles were clear, and that they could not be expropriated as grants to *ejidos,* were issued by the Agriculture Department (the ministry responsible for the agrarian reform created later) to owners of small and medium tracts.

Some sectors of Mexican society received these statements of Calles' with welcome relief; others with revolutionary zeal. The Communists, whose influence as a party was small but whose following among the intellectuals (frequently persecuted by Calles) was large, accused him of betraying the Revolution, which they characterized as bourgeois.

Calles realized, however, that if democracy was to be institutionalized and reforms were to be controlled and reoriented, the exercise of power could no longer be based on the strength and prestige of the one man who held it or on scattered groups of his supporters. It must depend upon the organized support of the people. He knew that the system now functioned on a basis of favor. The *caciques* in good odor with the National Palace could count on the designation of public works in their domain; schools and clinics would be provided. These favors were indispensable to the maintenance of order, for many of the old guerrilla fighters had kept their arms, and they still felt a strong nostalgia for the days when they had dashed across the plains on horseback and bivouacked in the mountains under the stars. But a boss, whether civilian or soldier, realized that if he lost the confidence of the National Palace all financial aid stopped; and the people knew that whenever a public works project was shut down, it meant that the local *cacique* had lost power and that an aspirant to succeed him would quickly step forward. All this provoked conflicts and frequently bloody clashes, but in the period of transition following the chaos of revolution, it proved an effective means of gradually establishing order and later a degree of governmental efficiency.

Nevertheless, Calles judged that the time had come to close this chapter in Mexican history—particularly in view of the international problems posed by the depression, and Mexico's domestic problems following the assassination of Obregón and the painful wounds inflicted by the religious conflict. Indeed, Calles' historical greatness lies in the fact that under circumstances that might have led any other politician of his day to think of reinforcing the mechanisms of power or even of acting dictatorially, he understood—in the Mexican context, with the memory of the Revolution still vivid—that a period of crisis must not be handled harshly by the men in power; on the contrary, they must grant increased participation in power. On the whole, Calles trusted the people in spite of his skepticism—or realism.

He expressed this trust in a manner that might seem paradoxical to anyone not acquainted with Mexico or prone to measure the country by rules applied to the United States or Europe. Calles wanted the people to face up to the crisis of the depression by participating in the government. He did not intend to erase the government's tutelary character; he meant the people to receive directly the benefits of its guardianship, which would be adapted to their wishes. Calles believed that success in this undertaking depended upon changing the political party system. Mexico had always lacked the tradition of popular political parties; politics, even for the liberals, had been manipulated by urban minorities and rural *caciques*. The people had been awakened suddenly to fight the Revolution, and they believed that the Revolution was their own accomplishment, but the many revolutionary parties that emerged from the struggle no longer suited the times. It would be more appropriate to polarize all the political forces and offer guaranties to the nonrevolutionary groups. Accordingly, Calles established a party that would unite the "revolutionary family," the phrase then fashionable, and tried to mitigate the official neglect of people who were not members of the "family." He attempted also to grant a share to the outsiders in the practical benefits deriving from the government, but without letting them get a foot in the door. His new policy abolished the requirement that a man had to be a revolutionary in order to get contracts, concessions, or official protection. Of course, this provoked new accusations and wove around Calles the legend that he had turned counterrevolutionary. What he had really done was to normalize the Revolution, to transform it from a privilege to a shared blessing. That in itself is why Calles is a decisive figure in Mexico's history; he stands out unquestionably as the most wholehearted revolutionary of the years following the armed conflict.

During Obregón's presidency, several political parties had been represented in congress. The most important were the Agrarians, who supported the measures adopted by the government to distribute land; the Liberal Constitutionalists, the opposition party; and the National Cooperatists, who gained popularity rapidly, then split, and ended by lining up with Adolfo de la Huerta and supporting his coup. Under Calles, the Labor Party was the main support of the government, but as CROM lost support among the masses, it also waned. The several socialist parties—of Yucatán, Tabasco, Tamaulipas (the last-named founded by Portes Gil)—never succeeded in acquiring any national influence. Consequently, the Revolution found itself with a government but without any organization that would bind it to the people. In the main, the parties were used as tools of opposition or as means of preparing candidacies. Now Calles intended to give the Revolution an instrument of its own.

After his term in office, Calles toured Europe, where he became very interested in German socialism and in the peculiar organization of the British Labour Party. On his return home, he founded a new party called the Partido Nacional Revolucionario (PNR), the National Revolutionary Party, in 1929.

The PNR remained under Calles' control, although it elected its own officers. In the same way that labor legislation tended to establish harmony between capital and labor and to grant the government a tutelary role over both elements, the PNR established political harmony and fulfilled the tutelary function over the diverse and contradictory forces that had surged up from the Revolution, and controlled local bossism, too, integrating the *caciques* into the national system. The PNR was not a party that used strictly democratic methods, for that was impossible as long as the men who had won the Revolution by force of arms were still alive. But it did create new conditions, and in time the methods employed by the government became more refined. Naturally, all the existing parties attacked the very idea of the PNR; the press and the public named it and its offshoots the "official party." Only the agrarians and various socialist organizations were able to fuse with the PNR without losing their local individuality in the process.

President Portes Gil gave a new impetus to the land distribution program. It was evident that many of the revolutionaries who had grown rich were thinking of investing their money in land, not in industry, so it was imperative to grant land quickly to prevent newly grown latifundios from wielding too much influence. Great properties were not inherently evil, it was now realized; actually, they were more productive than the small holdings and the *ejidos*. But the danger was that the small and medium holdings could not serve as a counterweight to them. Also, the great landholdings prevented the development of the small ones. Small properties had to be protected, and the bureaucrats in charge of settling the peasants' petitions for land would have to make haste.

With regard to labor legislation, however, things were more difficult. Portes Gil opposed revolutionary trade unionism, even as he affirmed his desire to protect the workers, for he was wary lest it encourage the aspirations, then beginning to be expressed, to transform a capitalist society into a socialistic one. He also decided to end the overweening influence of CROM, and to do so he saw to it that strikes called by CROM would fail, while those by the other federations would succeed. By 1932, the imposing edifice of CROM had crumbled, and its influence had dwindled to controlling the textile industry in Puebla and Veracruz, where the workers had a longer trade-union tradition.

The Church, for its part, agreed to negotiate on the situation arising from the 1926 conflict (Morrow evidently had some influence on that decision). Portes Gil promised that if the priests would register, and thus eliminate the legal origin of the conflict, the Church would be allowed to retain its spiritual independence and to teach doctrine within the churches, if not in the schools. The Church agreed, and masses were said again on Saint Peter's Day, June 29, 1929.

Portes Gil, who was considered a leftist and who called himself a socialist, was thus able to restore amity between the government and the Church and to finish off CROM. Thanks to his successor's reputation as a moderate, the government was able to pass a law aimed at preventing the Church from regaining political influence. The states began to set legal limits on the number of priests who could perform their offices within each state. In Tabasco, General Tomás Garrido Canabal's "Red Shirts" blacklisted the priests in 1931, and by 1932, only 197 priests were able to say mass legally. The Church could allege persecution, but it chose to bide its time, for the violent struggle had greatly weakened it. Only a few mutinies, protests, and expropriations occurred.

Portes Gil worked with Calles in forming the PNR and ordered all government employees to contribute a small percentage of their pay to its support on the theory that by admitting them to the bureaucracy, they were considered partisans of the Revolution—automatic members of the PNR. At the same time, he attempted to undermine the influence in the new party of such outstanding old leaders as Soto y Gama and Morones and to isolate them.

The PNR chose its first candidate in the summer of 1929. Everyone thought the choice would fall on Aaron Sáenz, a financier, but Calles preferred a more neutral figure, Pascual Ortiz Rubio, an engineer who had never been involved with big business. General Gonzalo Escobar did not accede to this idea and started an insurrection in Sonora, but Calles, who was serving as secretary of war, put it down in short order. Calles also executed several Communists, among them José Guadalupe Rodríguez, who tried to take advantage of the situation by organizing peasant and soldier soviets in a mechanical application of Moscow slogans that cost a number of soldiers their lives (some before a firing squad), and prison terms for some leaders in the penal colony of the Marías Islands. The agrarian leagues, led by Ursulo Galván, a convert to Communism for a time, supported Calles and broke with the Communists, and a Labor and Peasant Bloc set up by the Communist International was simultaneously dissolved. Its president had been Diego Rivera.

But crushing the military rebellion did not suffice to re-establish normalcy. A group of intellectuals and young people put forth a candidate of their own, José Vasconcelos, who had done so much to revive the culture of the country as Obregón's secretary of education. Vasconcelos declared himself an anti-re-electionist, saying that Ortiz Rubio would be nothing more than a puppet of Calles. He accused the government of corruption, of selling out to the United States (citing as proof of the latter the friendship between Calles and Ambassador Morrow), and of maintaining a tyranny worse than Díaz'. These accusations were so exaggerated that, even though Vasconcelos was very popular, he lost the election. At any rate, the official figures showed that Vasconcelos received only 20,000 votes. Vasconcelos immediately charged that the elections had been fraudulent and marched off to the United States, where he waited for his supporters to rise up in arms. He was following the example of Madero, but there was no Pancho Villa or Pascual Orozco to come to his aid. Later, Vasconcelos became a convert to Catholicism and a theorist of the right wing and returned to Mexico City, where he lived for another quarter of a century, working on his memoirs, attacking the government, and managing a library.

Meanwhile, Calles, Morrow, and others were living in Cuernavaca, which had become a playground for the revolutionary élite. The people called the street on which their houses stood the "Street of the Forty Thieves." Ortiz Rubio presided over the government under the thumb of *Jefe Máximo*. Calles was worried over the economic failure of the agrarian reform: agricultural productivity did not increase; the peasants were earning an average of only 44 centavos per day. It was at this point that he declared that the agrarian reform must come to an end. (Many people believed that Morrow had convinced him that U.S. capitalism should be taken as a model for Mexico.) Portes Gil had distributed 2.5 million acres of land, but Ortiz Rubio's grants totaled only 500,000, and many of the states had set a time limit of a few years after which land distribution would cease.

In September, 1932, Ortiz Rubio tried, like other new executives, to prove his independence by replacing some high officials who were friends of Calles. As soon as Calles learned of this, he announced to the press that Ortiz Rubio had resigned, and the president hastened to write a letter of resignation—or at least, that is how people say it happened.

Congress appointed a banker and businessman, also a "finger general," named Abelardo Rodríguez (1889–1967), to succeed Ortiz Rubio. The group of Callistas-turned-conservative had triumphed. Yet these conservatives, let it be clearly understood, conserved what the Revolution had achieved. They had no wish to turn back the clock; their only desire was to hold back new changes and to consolidate the nation's economy and make Mexico an orthodox capitalist country.

A new generation was beginning to play an active part in politics. These younger men had been children at the time of the Revolution, and they did not feel the same sentimental loyalty to it as the men who had fought beside Villa, Zapata, or Obregón, or the participants in the debate over the constitution. To them, the Revolution was not an achievement crowning their ideological or personal aspirations; they had not grown wealthy from it nor had they ever tasted power. On the whole, they considered the Revolution only a first step; they were discontented and impatient with the slow pace of agrarian reform; and they did not like the idea that the state must remain neutral in labor disputes. This generation had been dazzled by the Russian Revolution, and they blindly believed its propaganda—a reaction to the Fascism then appearing in Europe and, fleetingly, in Mexico. The home-grown Fascists, quickly quelled by the government, were the anti-Semitic Camisas Doradas (Gold Shirts); they had no real ideology.

This new generation—which included many schoolteachers who were dissatisfied with low salaries, intellectuals who dreamed of making readers of the masses, agronomists trained in the Agricultural School of Chapingo, where Diego Rivera's murals decorated the walls—later found a protector and teacher in the successor of Abelardo Rodríguez. These young men hoped to carry agrarian reform to a successful conclusion within a few years. From 1917 to 1933, some 4,000 villages containing 750,000 families had received land grants totaling 19 million acres. But, said the engineers, 2 million families were still landless and 300 million acres not yet distributed. Even so, the situation had radically changed from the Díaz period. Ownership of land no longer meant control of political power; Mexico was no longer an oligarchic society.

In 1933, on the eve of the presidential elections, the government brought some of these young people into a participatory role in governing. One of them, Narciso Bassols, became secretary of education, and some of the others were put in charge of drawing up an agrarian code, a task to which they responded promptly and vigorously. Still others were appointed to high office in the farm credit banks, which were reorganized and extended.

The new generation was thinking more of what was still to be done than of what had been done. Yet what had been done was no small thing. Aside from distributing 19 million acres of land, Obregón, Calles, and their successors built 7,000 schools attended by one-third of the school-age children in the rural areas. Illiteracy had shrunk from 69 to 59 per cent. Article 3 of the constitution had been amended, calling for socialistic education before there was actually any education at all. (Later the article was amended again to modify the dogmatic phrasing.) Calles never looked kindly upon the change, but he tolerated it so as not to alienate the new generation. The Catholics, however, were well aware that the term "socialistic" meant anticlerical, modern education. They fought the reform energetically, to the point of tolerating the murder of schoolteachers, of whom eighteen were killed by fanatics in isolated villages.

On balance, all this represented no small achievement. The fundamental freedoms were respected and consolidated. The people, accustomed for several generations to violence and arbitrary police power, began to realize that neither was necessarily normal. The pressure of the authorities on the press was diminishing as the newspapers resisted it stubbornly; indeed, neither Obregón nor Calles ever had the support of the press—or needed it. Justice was still corrupt and expensive, but young lawyers protested and offered plans for reform. The Supreme Court, still a servant of the executive branch, gained some prestige owing to the quality of the men appointed to the bench. Intellectual life was bubbling, stimulating, and beginning to take on a tinge of cosmopolitanism, yet it also moved closer to the people.

Best of all, the country was no longer experiencing the shocks of militarism. Obregón's coup against Carranza was the last military insurrection to succeed. Trade-union and peasant organizations collaborated with the government to put down rebellion, and the armed forces finally realized that the period in Mexico's history when it was possible to rebel at no risk, when their only antagonists were an apathetic police force and a lethargic garrison, was a chapter that had closed.

In 1933, the "finger generals" still headed the army but a new generation of officers was coming up, trained in the general-staff school and not thinking of power as their ultimate professional ambition. This was a far cry from 1920, when Obregón had had to deal with 80,000 soldiers belonging to several semi-autonomous armies. Then, he conquered the resistance of their leaders and incorporated them all in the federal army, which granted them an officer's pay. Many of the "finger generals" died in the de la Huerta insurrection in 1923; others went into exile; and Obregón replaced them with young officers who had studied in Europe or were graduates of the Colegio Militar at Chapultepec, which had re-opened in 1920. Then, with one stroke, he reduced the size of the army and the military budget.

Joaquín Amaro, one of the "finger generals," an Indian and a very strict officer, completed this task when Calles appointed him secretary of war in 1924. After six years, the army had been reduced to 50,000 men and the military budget was half its former size. Amaro eliminated many of the political generals and raised professional standards, educational requirements, and discipline. Little by little, the old generals found themselves surrounded by young officers better prepared than themselves, loyal to the government, and originating from the people, particularly the poorer sections of the middle class. When the political generals attempted coups in opposition to these reforms in 1927 and 1929, the army itself subdued them with the help of the agrarian leagues and the trade unions. In 1923, half the officers had joined the rebels; in 1929, only a quarter of them, and in 1937, when the last insurrection occurred, the rebel general had no supporters in the army. The old *caudillo* tradition had died. The only *caudillo*, from 1934 on, was the president, simply because he was the president and regardless of his personality.

Nevertheless, a general was elected president in 1934: Lázaro Cárdenas (b. 1895), a veteran of the Revolution who had fought for Carranza against Zapata, later governor of Michoacán, a cabinet member of small accomplishment, and head of the PNR, in 1930, while still under forty. He was considered to be sympathetic to the new generation that formed the left wing of the PNR. To mark the importance of having an elected president again after two executives chosen by congress, Calles suggested the need for a plan of government that would signalize Mexico's political modernization. The plan—called the Six-Year Plan because the presidential term had been extended to six years—aroused the enthusiasm of the youth, for it promised to speed up agrarian reform and extend educational development.

Two candidates without a chance of winning ran against Cárdenas. One was Antonio Villarreal, who opposed "continuity," which meant that he was against the continued direction of the government by Calles; the other was the Communist Hernán Laborde (1894–1956). Their weakness notwithstanding, Cárdenas ran as if they were seriously threatening him, and the young men in the PNR had a chance to present their ideas to the people. Cárdenas was elected in July, 1934, and took office in November, appointing a cabinet recommended by Calles. Nevertheless, it was Cárdenas who had been elected, even though many people said the vote had been manipulated. And Mexico had arrived at a stage in its political evolution when the fact that a man knew he was elected could transform him.

9 · Nationalizations

CÁRDENAS FOUND HIS COUNTRY quite different from the Mexico he had known in his youth, which, after half a century of political and social paralysis, had not changed except in its outward appearance. From the time of the Revolution until the administration of Cárdenas, a sweeping transformation had taken place. Under Madero the people had dressed differently than under Juárez, but they lived and thought in the same way. In Calles' day the people dressed more or less the way they had in the time of Madero, but they lived and thought very differently.

Cárdenas found a country with innumerable unsolved problems, all of which were important but none menacing. The means to solve the problems gradually came to hand, and the experience accumulated over fifteen years made possible an approach to solutions. Some of the remedies failed; some succeeded. The PNR was a tool for governing and for mobilizing the masses, and Cárdenas had no cause to fear any further interference from the military establishment. He could rely on the faith in the Revolution that was still alive in the peasants, the middle class, and the workers. Even the sense of impotence that had paralyzed reactionary elements in the country since the settlement of the conflict between Church and state could be turned to his advantage. In a world of economic and political crisis, plagued by fascism and widespread unemployment, especially in Europe, he could count on the stimulus of Roosevelt's New Deal and on a kind of economic stability caused by the fact that Mexico was still an agricultural country. Cárdenas had other support in the prestige, experience, and political imagination of Calles, to whom he owed his office and the idea and content of the Six-Year Plan. Added to that, Cárdenas rose to power at a moment when one generation was losing control and another gaining it, and when ideas and programs were beginning to be debated within the PNR, that is, when political life was ready to profit from a larger dose of democracy.

During the six years of the Cárdenas government, events of transcendental importance occurred in the world, and their influence on Mexico was great. Civil war broke out in Spain; Roosevelt was re-elected, and a new generation of young New Dealers played a part in the government; World War II burst over the globe. Within Mexico itself, events of equally great importance were occurring: the influence of Calles and the generation who had fought the Revolution came to an end; the railroads and the oil industry were nationalized; and agrarian reform quickened its pace.

At the time of his election, Cárdenas was neither popular nor widely known, and he had never shown any evidence of great political acumen or initiative. But the enormous power that accompanies the office of President of the Republic, and the election victory itself, transformed Cárdenas into a reflective man capable not only of controlling events but of turning circumstances to account (and also of refusing to be dominated by foreign interests).

As soon as Cárdenas took office, he ordered a more rapid distribution of land. Conciliation boards began to rule on the side of the workers in labor disputes, and strikes multiplied. Calles reacted by summoning many of his friends in the Senate to his home in Cuernavaca, warning them that the epidemic of strikes was dangerous to the country (a "marathon of radicalism," he called it) and making references to Ortiz Rubio's resignation. This was in June, 1935, six months after Cárdenas took office.

Cárdenas was quick to reply. He allied himself with Portes Gil, whom he had appointed leader of the PNR, and changed his cabinet, selecting men who were not considered Callistas: both General Saturnino Cedillo, the right-wing *cacique* of San Luis Potosí and a convert from agrarianism to Catholicism, to succeed Garrido Canabal; and General Francisco J. Múgica, one of the authors of Articles 27 and 123 of the constitution and a member of the extreme left wing of the PNR. Cárdenas stated that the period of anticlericalism was past. Then, when Garrido Canabal's Red Shirts greeted a demonstration of Catholic students in Tabasco with gunfire, the federal government stepped in, as the constitution authorized it to do, and Garrido had to leave the country. The Red Shirts were dissolved, and one by one, in a similar manner, the governors who were considered Callistas disappeared.

Calles did not rise to the challenge. He moved to Mexico City, where he issued statements announcing his retirement from politics. Meanwhile, Cárdenas won over the congress, as the deputies and senators saw that Calles' power was waning. But Cárdenas needed support in the streets, too, and to obtain it he started some behind-the-scenes moves to establish a single labor federation and a national peasant organization. The workers organized some demonstrations against Calles and Morones, who had remained loyal to him. Then in April, 1936, Cárdenas used the need for public order as an excuse to invite Calles and Morones to leave the country and provided them with an escort to the airport. Calles stated when he reached Texas that he had been exiled because he was an enemy of Communism, but from that moment he never again became involved in politics. He died in exile, nine years later.

Cárdenas had made himself complete master of his office, and now he had to use his power. His first step was to cast off his allies General Cedillo and Portes Gil, both of whom returned to their respective strongholds in San Luis Potosí and Tamaulipas, where they resumed their activities as local *caciques*. Congress supported him, and the Church, freed of the nightmare of Calles, supported him. Cárdenas now initiated a somewhat novel style of governing—which consisted of saying very little, disregarding abstract questions in favor of solving concrete problems, traveling all over the country, especially to the villages, and keeping the presidential authority (virtually an absolute authority) intact yet respecting freedom of the press, speech, and assembly. The Gold Shirts were left alone; the Communists were not persecuted; and the newspapers attacked Cárdenas ceaselessly with complete impunity.

In order to be able to pursue this policy, Cárdenas had to seek new allies, and he found them in the most radical sector of the new generation. Congress was tamed—it had ceased to be the forum for great debate it had been under Obregón and Calles, and indeed had become a body of yes-men—and now Cárdenas set out to win the support of the peasants and workers. To succeed in that aim, he had to vitiate, to a certain degree, both the agrarian reform and the labor movement.

Cárdenas used Lombardo Toledano to form a union federation loyal to the administration. Lombardo Toledano, a lawyer who had started as a Catholic, later collaborated with Morones and finally broke with him and CROM in 1932, had kept up an impassioned dialogue with the Communists throughout the 1920's. In the course of one encounter, in 1929, he said to the Communist Siqueiros:

> As long as the Communist group fails to demonstrate to the proletariat of Mexico that it is capable of transforming the present bourgeois regime and seizing power, the workers of Mexico can point with reason to the Communists as a group of delinquents, for to contribute to the failure of the labor organization, with premeditation, is a form of crime. As long as the Communist group fails to demonstrate that conditions in Mexico are such as to permit the working masses to carry out a radical and abrupt change in the actual order of things, the Communists deserve nothing from the

Mexican workers except the name of perverse agitators, men of little honor, and false leaders.*

In founding his own federation in 1933, rallying the dissidents in CROM and the CGT to his side as members of the new Unión General de Obreros y Campesinos (General Farmer-Labor Union), Lombardo Toledano argued that the Mexican workers were not ready to take over power and that any talk about social revolution was utopian. Instead, he urged them to fight for the enforcement and broadening of social laws favorable to the workers. He saw his new federation as a means to carry out his ideas, to unite existing unions, and to support Cárdenas. Naturally, he expressed his views in radical terms, since the younger generation was receptive to Stalinist rhetoric, yet it did not draw on Communist ideology and its concepts were not Marxist in origin. Its Marxism went only as far as its rhetoric. Ideologically, the younger generation was closer to the Fabian Society, but in the Mexican manner, with a weakness for phrases and formulas and a strong desire to participate in power without relinquishing the right to criticize the men in power.

In the beginning of the struggle between Cárdenas and Calles, Lombardo Toledano had formed a National Committee of Proletarian Defense to support the president. In February, 1936, this committee summoned a congress for trade-union unification, out of which came the Confederación de Trabajadores de México (Mexican Federation of Labor), with Lombardo as president and Rafael Piña Soria, who had an anarchosyndicalist background, as its most active and popular figure. In its declaration of principles, the CTM demanded worker participation in the administration of the economy, but given local conditions in Mexico, the document said, the immediate objective of the proletariat was economic and political freedom for the country, although its ultimate aim was the abolition of capitalism. The CTM also declared that it would invoke a general revolutionary strike against any attempt at dictatorship, the reason for this being that there was a false rumor that friends of Calles were planning a coup. The motto adopted

* Cited in Víctor Alba, *Las ideas sociales contemporáneas en México* (Mexico City, 1960), p. 381.

by the CTM was "For a Classless Society," and a few years later, Lombardo Toledano affirmed that the federation had been guided by the general principles of socialism. He defined its relations with the government as follows: "We are in agreement with Cárdenas today; I feel sure . . . that we shall agree with him to the end. Agree, not submit. . . . I hope so, and we shall agree later with other men. But there will come a time when the proletariat of Mexico will not need to agree with anyone." In truth, however, the CTM did submit to the government, and its subjection is not yet over. What is more, the federations not affiliated with the CTM and some less important ones, which were founded later (the Confederación Nacional Proletaria and the Confederación Obrera y Campesina de México), and the old CROM and CGT, reduced to skeletons, all submitted, too. Cárdenas regarded his instruments of support as exactly what they were—instruments.

For several years, the CTM served the immediate interests of the workers because the government supported it. *De jure* working conditions improved, but *de facto* betterment was not considerable. Industry was still small-scale and the working class was numerically weak. Yet the government's sympathy for the CTM made it easy for labor to overcome the resistance of many companies, especially foreign ones, to unions among their own workers. For a while, the public favored the CTM for keeping union leadership in honest hands; they could see the contrast between the union leaders' honesty and the corruption that pervaded CROM; but they did not see the fundamental dishonesty in a union movement that was directed by the government. The CTM later became a bureaucracy and became corrupt, too, but in the early years when it was full of young enthusiasts, it carried out the important work of educating its members, training militant leaders, and attracting the sympathy of intellectuals, students, and others to the workers' problems.

Marxism became increasingly fashionable. These were the days when the Spanish and French popular fronts were winning elections, and when in Spain, the only passionate battle against fascism was being waged, soon to turn into a civil war. Most Mexicans looked at these happenings elsewhere with completely indifferent eyes. Fascism never worried them; indeed, they felt a certain passive sympathy with it because they believed it was anti-Yankee, and they considered it "very masculine." To the intellectuals and the new political and labor leaders, however, these questions were of burning concern to be widely debated—with a great abuse of the Marxist vocabulary. The whole furor sometimes gave the impression that Communists had great influence in Mexico. The truth is that there were Communists and many fellow-travelers in important positions, but they never determined the government's policy.

The Mexican Communists were never able to produce a theorist of any importance. And they never succeeded in penetrating the masses. When they split off from the CGT in 1921, they isolated themselves from the labor movement, and their "united" federation, created a few years later, was only a paper organization, like their Anti-Imperialist League. After a transitory success with a Labor and Peasant Bloc, the Communists were isolated from the rural workers, too. If they won some sympathy among the intellectuals and the youth in the PNR, they never succeeded in imposing their discipline on these elements. The party itself was divided into factions, and it was weakened by the expulsion of the Trotskyites. Actually, its only effective field for action was among bureaucrats and schoolteachers, with whom it did acquire a certain measure of influence.

When Cárdenas became president, the Communists said that his government was "in duty bound to carry forward the Calles Six-Year Plan, the program for turning the country Fascist and reinforcing Yankee domination of Mexico, while hiding behind the screen of the leftist Cardenistas, who represent a deceitful and scandalous socialism." In 1935, at the Seventh Congress of the Communist International, which adopted the new tactic of the Popular Front, the leader of Mexican Communism (later expelled) Hernán Laborde declared that the democratic-bourgeois Mexican Revolution had been betrayed and that it was up to the Communists to set it in motion again. He recognized he had been mistaken in placing Calles and Cárdenas on the same level, yet he insisted—at the very moment that Cárdenas was shaking off Calles—that "the maneuvers [of Cárdenas] toward the left are in great part concessions that bourgeois national reformism is obliged to make in order to ensure the support of the working class and the petty bourgeoisie because it lacks strength of its own, owing to the smallness and weakness of industry in Mexico." In Moscow, Laborde said, it has become necessary to advocate a popular front with the anti-imperialist bourgeoisie and petty bourgeoisie. In Mexico, the Mexican delegation to the Moscow Congress pointed out, "being the semi-feudal country that it is, the popular front must take on an anti-imperialist character [as a means] of completing the national revolution; only then will the proletarian revolution for the establishment of socialism come."

The new popular front tactics, then, determined the Communist Party's position, but not the policy of Cárdenas. In 1937 Laborde stated in a speech:

> It would be false to say that we are under a socialist regime or that the Cárdenas government is equivalent to the dictatorship of the proletariat. It is not, but we cannot refuse to recognize that thanks to the peculiar conditions in our country at this moment of its history, and within the revolutionary policy of President Cárdenas, fundamentally democratic, antifeudal, anti-imperialist in character, we have those traces, those very weak but indisputably socialistic forms, if you like, which represent the true foreshadowings of a higher stage of the Revolution, and which may permit us from now on to create conditions that will, at any given moment, make for a more rapid transformation of the Mexican Revolution in the socialist sense.

But the Communists still clung to many of their clichés. For example, while they were in Moscow, two of the Communist leaders, Alberto Lumbreras and Vicente Guerra, prepared several theses on the Indian question in which they harked back to theories fashionable in the United States during the period when the American Communists were proselytizing for the founding of a Negro state. (The Communist Party in the United States, incidentally, had been assigned the task of watching over and systematically orienting the party in Mexico.) Lumbreras and Guerra maintained that the problem constituted an acute form of the national question. The surviving Indian tribes, in their view, were national groups among whom the Communists must agitate for the achievement of free indigenous republics, even though that would involve the risk that petty-bourgeois nationalism of the Yaqui, Tarahumara, Zapotec, or Tarasco people would dominate such republics. In the meantime, the Communists must fight both the oppression of the Indians by the whites and the Indians' petty-bourgeois nationalism. Obviously, this schematic application of Stalinist concepts to the problem of nationalities signaled a complete departure from reality; for at the moment when Lumbreras and Guerra were writing their papers, Cárdenas was distributing land to the Indians and trying to protect them through a new Department of Indian Affairs.

Cárdenas was fully aware that the Marxist talk of many of his supporters and the presence of Communists in some of the minor positions in his government, not to mention the major posts held by fellow-travelers, led many people to accuse him of being a Communist or playing the Communist game. To correct that mistake, he offered sanctuary in Mexico to the exiled Bolshevik leader Leon Trotsky, when he was told by Diego Rivera (for several years a Trotskyite convert) that Trotsky had been forced to leave his refuge in Norway owing to Stalin's maneuvers to have him expelled. The Communists protested. Lombardo Toledano, who in the heat of the popular front was rapidly drawing closer to Moscow, added his name to the protests. Nevertheless, Cárdenas offered Trotsky a house, police protection, and full liberty to write and publish. When the old Bolshevik was assassinated in 1940, Cárdenas published a note saying: "The government of Mexico is not Communist. . . . Nor is any postulate that may aim to protect the working class under doctrines which admit of industrial progress and law at all strange to our environment, nor has it been since before Communism appeared in Russia."

To speak of the land question during the Porfiriate was to speak of the hacienda; to speak of it in Cardenist Mexico or the Mexico of today is to speak of the *ejido*. As we have seen, the *ejidos* were portions of land set aside under Spanish colonial law for the Indians. They were considered communal property and were worked individually or by family for a communal end. At the time of the Reform, the *ejidos* were broken up and distributed among their members, but as the Indians had no notion of the meaning of ownership, they sold their holdings or let them be seized. The *ejidos* that remained intact were later taken by the hacienda owners under various legal pretexts or without any pretext at all. The return of the land to the *ejidos* was Zapata's principal objective.

When Cárdenas came to office, he was confronted by two schools of thought on the agrarian question. The agrarianists themselves wanted socialization of the land as a final and accepted fact: the break-up and distribution of all large landholdings with guaranties that the haciendas could not be reconstituted, and consequently the application of Article 27 in full force to establish that the *ejido* would be not a transitory institution but the definitive form of land tenancy in Mexico. The young men adopted this radical point of view. Another stand was taken by the men who fought in the Revolution and who contended that at that time not even the agrarianists wanted the *ejido* as a permanent institution. The modern agrarianists were, largely, trained agriculturists. Calles and the former secretary of agriculture, Luis León, expressed the feeling of the veterans who viewed agrarian reform as something less than a continuous series of triumphs—for many peasants still had no land and many were unable to subsist on the allotments they had been granted—and who viewed the *ejido* as a school for landowners, a transitional institution. To them, the latifundio was not a bad thing per se, apart from the political influence it could wield. Indeed, the Mexico that emerged from the Revolution might need large tracts of land for technical reasons, and possession of it would not necessarily mean the exercise of political power.

The agrarianists and veterans argued bitterly while the Six-Year Plan was being drafted in 1933, and the debate went on until the Agrarian Code was made law in 1934, before Cárdenas became President. The code offered an eclectic solution, in the end, and it satisfied no one.

Calles had a clear vision of the agrarian question. To him, the *ejido* was a first step toward small ownership, and communal labor on the *ejidos* was to be only an interim measure until individual parcels were increased and the haciendas were converted into farms. The father of agrarian reform, Molina Enríquez, said that the *ejido* was a stop-gap to make it appear that the government wanted to solve the land question without actually doing anything about it; in short, it was an escape from the difficulty of taking effective measures.

In 1927, Calles had believed that the *ejido* would function better if it were given the guaranties stipulated in the law of Ejidal Patrimony. The theory was that the peasant would feel the joy of ownership, knowing that he could not lose his allotment. In 1934, a system of farm credit through the Ejidal Bank was created for the people on the *ejidos*, but this step did nothing to modify the *ejido's* ambiguous structure.

The *ejido* posed an insoluble problem. The parcels of land seldom were large enough to support a peasant family in any degree of comfort. As time went by and the children of *ejido* peasants increased in number while the tract remained the same, the inadequacy of the land to support them and their families became more marked. Demographic growth alone would lead to the disruption of the *ejido*, which also felt the pressure of the burgeoning bureaucracy built up around it during the Cárdenas regime. Some figures of 1937 will show to what degree the *ejido* proved inadequate at the very moment when the Cárdenas government gave the agrarianists the green light to go ahead with their solutions. In 45 per cent of the *ejidos* the individual parcels of land were from 2½ to 10 acres; in 13 per cent, less than 2½ acres; in 20 per cent, from 10 to 25 acres; and in the remaining 22 per cent more than 25 acres.

To correct this situation, the agrarianists proposed that the *ejidos* be worked collectively, especially those that had sugar mills or processed their own harvests. Luis Cabrera, the author of the agrarian law of 1915 that had revived the *ejido*, rebelled against this idea and thought that Cárdenas was vitiating everything that the Revolution had sought to accomplish; the Revolution understood "through sheer instinct," he said, that the *ejido* was the only means of transition from large to small property ownership; Cárdenas was converting the *ejidos* into a chain of large collective latifundios administered by the Ejidal Bank, to whom the people on the *ejidos* were nothing but peons with a new landowning boss, the bank itself. The *ejido* had not emancipated the peasant; it had merely changed him back into a peon. The essential step was to change the peasant into a farmer.

Within the agrarianist groups themselves doubts soon arose as to whether they were following the right road. A short time after Article 27 of the constitution was amended to admit the collectivist *ejido* into the legal system of land tenancy, a Cardenista named Florencio Palomo Valencia, governor of Yucatán and later a senator, aired the agrarians' doubts. His experience as governor had shown him that the men on the *ejido* wanted absolute ownership of the land, but as they were not permitted to sell or bequeath their "patrimonies," they could not leave to settle elsewhere or become factory workers; in short, they were tied to the land, like serfs. A man on an *ejido* was also expected to pay off the value of his land (in practice, this was never done), and he was all the more tightly bound to the *ejido* by this obligation. According to Palomo Valencia, it was necessary to cancel all this kind of debt and to give each *ejidatario* a title of full ownership. Once the peasant felt that he was a real landowner, he would be less submissive to the bureaucracy, which, in turn, would lose its arrogance.

The bureaucratization of the agrarian reform had, in fact, increased fantastically within a few years. Each *ejido* had a commissioner—a guardian appointed not by the peasants but by the authorities. These commissioners were not fired with missionary zeal; on the contrary, they tried to jog along with the fewest possible headaches and were regarded as virtual *caciques*. Above them were the technicians and agricultural engineers, most of whom were strong agrarianists who greeted any opinion on the agrarian question with the sacred phrase: "It is a very delicate subject for those who are not technicians." The Ejidal Bank told the peasants what, how, and when they should cultivate and fixed the selling price of the harvests. Hence nothing was done that would give the peasant the mental attitudes of landowners; on the contrary, everything tended to perpetuate their status as wards. The Department of Agrarian Affairs, established by Cárdenas to accelerate reform and control the *ejidos*, still further accentuated the bureaucratic trend. The Confederación Nacional Campesina (National Peasant Federation), founded by the Cardenistas to unite the old-style agrarian leagues into a single political organ, never put up a real fight against the bureaucrats.

To sum up, the agrarianists' objective had been to make the *ejido* a means of emancipating the peasants, but as they became bureaucrats, their objective shifted to a justification of the existence of the *ejido* bureaucracy. Mexico was no exception to the rule that bureaucratization follows revolution.

On the other hand, Mexico was an exception to the rule that bureaucrats can silence opposition and crush dissidence. For reasons that will be set forth later, Mexico achieved a revolution with an exceptional capacity for reforming its own reforms, for adapting itself to new needs without losing sight of its fundamental aims. Obregón reformed Carranza's agrarian reform; Calles reformed Obregón's; Cárdenas reformed Calles'. Cárdenas' successors went on to reform the Cardenista reforms, although their task was more difficult because the bureaucratization of the *ejidos* tended to paralyze all reform and to convert the *ejidos* into a sacrosanct and untouchable myth.

In 1940, when Cárdenas completed his term of office, the agrarian situation could be seen in the following figures: some 40 million acres were under cultivation of which 47 per cent were *ejido* lands; 140 million acres were in pasture, of which 24 per cent were *ejido* holdings. During that year, cattle, fowl, and honey were marketed to the value of 1.14 billion pesos, of which 225 million, or 19 per cent, came from the *ejidos*. A quarter of the population of the republic, that is, some 5 million people, were living on *ejidos*. The rural workers in the whole country numbered 3.83 million, of whom 1.6 million were on *ejidos*. In other words, 42 per cent of the farm workers of Mexico accounted for only 19 per cent of the cattle, fowl, and honey and still less of the corn and other crops. Peonage still survived, but of course it lacked the quality of servitude that marked it in the nineteenth century and even in Madero's time. Of the 3.83 million Mexican peasants,

1.9 million were day laborers. Half the active agricultural population, then, were peasants without land.*

The uneven distribution of the land had not been corrected entirely, even though Cárdenas distributed more land than any president before him: 45 million acres among 750,000 families in some 12,000 settlements. Of the 18,000 *ejidos,* some 500 were organized as collectives at Cárdenas' orders. His most important experiment, however, was carried out on 600,000 acres in the Laguna region, a cotton-growing area where the plantation workers went out on strike in 1936. The following year, cooperatives were set up for the sisal workers of Yucatán, like those established in the past by General Alvarado, except that his cooperative effort had been unable to prevent the resurrection of a sisal oligarchy. Both experiments failed, for different reasons and under different circumstances. The price of raw materials fell on the world market, and there was too much bureaucracy. Today, many of the people on the *ejidos* of Laguna have been moved away to settle virgin tropical areas, a new experiment of which the results cannot be predicted at this time.

In any case, Cárdenas' agrarian policy brought an immediate groundswell of popularity, which enabled him to confront successfully the riskiest test of his government: nationalization. In the long run, however, the agrarian policy had unfortunate economic consequences.

In 1909, the Mexican Government, under the advice of Limantour, bought two-thirds of the stock in the railroad companies backed by British capital. Since part of the price was still unpaid at the outbreak of the Revolution, British and U.S. investors constantly demanded redress. They were still applying pressure when Cárdenas became president, and, in the hope of escaping new problems and of improving the obsolescent rail network, he de-

---

* The figures on this subject and expositions of opposing points of view on agrarian problems and the *ejido* can be found in *Problemas agrícolas e industriales de México* (Mexico City), V, No. 4 (October-December, 1953). The figures given above are from Gabriel Ferrer de Mendiolea, "La cuestión mexicana desde el ángulo de la sociología rural," in *Hechos y problemas del México rural* (Mexico City, 1952).

cided in June, 1937, to nationalize the railroads and consolidate their debt with the national debt. (This did not include the minor lines, temporarily left to their own devices, though later they too were incorporated into the national network.) Administration of the railroads was turned over to government officials. By May, 1938, these officials and the unions had developed so many differences that the president decided to place the railroads under union administration and appointed a committee of seven railroad-union leaders for this task. This move created an unforeseen problem for the labor movement. A doctrinal position on the question had to be thought out at the same time that union leaders carried on an internecine war for position and brought some sort of order to a network that was not only antiquated but also disorganized by the Revolution and by the later negligence of the companies.

Rodrigo García Treviño, one of Lombardo Toledano's colleagues, who broke with him when he began his flirtation with Communism, was assigned the task of formulating a basic theory that would support the government's position. In a capitalistic society like Mexico's, he said, no industry, even if administered by unions, can escape the laws of bourgeois economy, much less when the companies are compensated for nationalization. The railroads were bankrupt, and the union officials were obligated to make an effort to increase revenue, yet they could not use it to satisfy workers' demands. However, nationalization of the railroad and oil companies demonstrated the value of the labor movement as a centralizing force, for wherever union administration was put into effect, the trend toward centralization emerged spontaneously and the economic value of the operation increased. Union administration under a capitalistic system was a step toward progressive reform of the system; in effect, it was state capitalism. But, García Treviño warned, there was no cause to cherish any illusions: if a nationalized industry went bankrupt, the workers were the losers, whereas if it flourished, the state gained. This did not mean that the union should reject its administrative role; it meant only that union management could not be regarded as a panacea; instead, it should be seen as a means by which the

laboring class could learn to administer and participate in par-
liaments, municipalities, cooperatives, and the like.*

The Communists opposed "labor administration" because "it
endangers the independence and freedom of action of the trade
unions. . . . Administration of the large-scale enterprises that have
been nationalized must be left in the state's charge, with the
cooperation of the trade unions and with a system of worker
control." These words were contained in a resolution passed by
the Party's Central Committee.

The whole unforeseen situation so disconcerted everyone that
the opinion of Leon Trotsky, then residing in Mexico, was sought.
He responded in favor of trade-union administration because he
considered it a step up the ladder of power.†

Clearly, the passing of a nationalized enterprise from the hands
of the state to those of the trade unions was a progressive move,
but it was equally clear that if the companies were to be handed
back to the state, the result would be regressive and prejudicial
to the labor movement. This was precisely what happened. The
trade unions never succeeded in reorganizing the nationalized
companies, nor did they satisfy the demands of the workers.
Cárdenas decided to incorporate the railroads as an autonomous
unit under state control and to permit the unions to participate
in running them—which came down in the end to a merely con-
sultative role in their administration. The unions were greatly
relieved to be freed of a burden for which they did not consider
themselves prepared and which they had not anticipated. The
railroads had not been nationalized for the purpose of turning
them over to the workers, of course, but because the country's
political needs impelled such a step. Handing over the industry
to the unions had been an expedient dictated not by principle
but by the failure of administration: The unions failed too, after
which the railroads were organized on a purely commercial basis.
Little by little, they worked their way out of bankruptcy. After

* For further information concerning the debate on nationalization, see
Víctor Alba, *Las ideas sociales contemporáneas en México* (Mexico City,
1960), pp. 393 ff.

† The text of Trotsky's reply, obtained by the author from the person
who consulted him may be found in Víctor Alba, *La mouvement ouvrier
en Amérique Latin* (Paris, 1953).

twenty years, they were still a state-owned enterprise, but as the lines were modernized slowly, they began to produce a profit. It is interesting to note that while, in the decree of nationalization, the state had claimed to have nationalized the railroads because the railroad officials had neither the ability nor the power to direct their activities so as to "promote the social welfare, first and foremost," as a public service should be expected to do, the trade unions never raised the question whether it was fair of the state to allocate a quarter of the profits from nationalized companies to build up the retirement fund without considering the cost to consumers, the distribution of the profits, or the effect on railroad administration. Doubtless this was one of the reasons for the public's indifference toward nationalization of the railroads and for the briefness of labor's period of administration.

But by the time the petroleum companies were nationalized, the lesson had been learned. The history of this step has often been distorted—sometimes by those who opposed it, who considered it an act of irresponsible dogmatism; sometimes by partisans of nationalization, who regard it as the product of considered policy. In fact, it was a clever improvisation dictated by circumstances. Cárdenas decided to nationalize the oil industry because the companies themselves had made that step inevitable. Everyone in Mexico welcomed it with enthusiasm, public opinion unanimously supported it, even though the country was deeply divided over the government's social policy. The move was not regarded as a socializing, nor even as a nationalist measure, but rather as the response of wounded dignity—which it was.

In 1921, Mexico was producing one-quarter of the petroleum consumed in the world—193 million barrels annually. Then, as we have seen, conflicts arose around the application of Article 27. Calles and Ambassador Morrow reached agreement in 1926 that the foreign companies exploiting Mexican oil (mostly British and American, which had first come into the country during the Díaz period) would tacitly recognize Mexico's ownership of her own mineral rights, in exchange for which they would be permitted to continue exploiting the land on which "positive acts" had been taken, but they could not aspire to new concessions. Most of the deposits then being exploited were in the region of

Tampico. The companies opposed, often with force, the attempts of the industry's 13,000 workers to organize, but nevertheless twenty-one unions were established, one for each company, each with a different contract. (Fifteen companies were affiliated with the great international oil consortiums, three were oil-tanker companies, and there were several small independent companies.)

By 1935, production had shrunk to only one-fifth of what it had been fifteen years earlier. That same year, the twenty-one trade unions joined to form the Sindicato Nacional de Trabajadores Petroleros (National Union of Petroleum Workers), which affiliated with the recently founded CTM the following year. At the same time, the government established a company of its own, Petroleos Mexicanos (Pemex), to look for new deposits. In November, 1936, the Sindicato presented a demand for a contract with all the companies, stipulating that such a contract must conform to the existing labor code based on Article 123 of the constitution. Some of their demands were: an increase in pay, an eight-hour day, double pay for overtime; schools for the workers and their children; sanitary and adequate housing; paid vacations; inclusion of the office workers in the union; and a closed shop. The companies decided to negotiate as a united front; they were ready to grant some of the demands, but they considered that the pay increase asked for was excessive, and they roundly rejected the inclusion of office employees on the ground that it would be tantamount to letting the union know all the details of management's accounting.

In November, the union called a strike. Cárdenas intervened and proclaimed a six-month period for negotiation. But everyone was growing angry and restless, and by May, 1937, the alternatives were clear: a contract or a strike. On May 28, the strike began.

Mexican law distinguishes between a strike and an "economic dispute," the latter occurring when the imbalance between capital and labor in an industry is so great that one of the two parties is left defenseless. The unions therefore defined their strike as an economic dispute. On June 9, the conciliation board ruled for the unions, setting aside the companies' protests. Actually, the companies did not want arbitration, even if it was obligatory in economic disputes, for like the old anarchosyndicalists, they preferred direct negotiation. Now the question was put before the Federal Board of Conciliation and Arbitration, and the strike was halted pending the board's decision.

The board appointed a commission to study the entire situation in the oil industry in order to be able to arbitrate with full knowledge of the facts. The commission concluded—somewhat exaggeratedly, some people thought—that the companies were making a profit of 16 per cent in Mexico but only 2 per cent in the United States, and that a part of the profits earned in Mexico must be applied to the betterment of the workers' condition. The commission proposed that half of the 16 per cent profit, amounting to some 26 million pesos per year, be set aside to increase wages and pay the costs of complying with the labor laws. On August 18, after a study of the million or so words in the report, the board ruled as the commission recommended and ordered the companies to sign a collective contract that would raise wages by 27 per cent and permit the white-collar employees to join the unions; set a 40-hour, 5-day work week; approved a pension system, vacations, insurance, and housing; and finally, ordered the companies to provide their employees with work clothes. The dispute had been settled according to the law, and the board's decision, which had the force of law, had to be complied with. But the companies appealed the board's decision to the Supreme Court, knowing that as long as the court had the case before it, nothing could be done. The companies claimed that they were not able to pay the cost of applying the ruling because it would amount to 100 million pesos, not the estimated 26 million. The dispute was thus shifted from a conflict between union and management to one between the companies and the government.

The unions, which until then had not had much support from the people, now stated the question in nationalistic terms, and the response was immediate. An all-out campaign of agitation followed. The companies withdrew a portion of their bank deposits. Both sides tried their best to influence the Supreme Court and government. But on March 1, 1938, a year and a half after the dispute began, the court ruled that the companies must comply with the board's decision. The Federal Board of Conciliation fixed March 7 as the date when the companies would have to comply. The companies tried to bargain by offering pay raises amounting to 24 million pesos, but they refused to allow their white-collar employees to join the union. The unions and the government were on the point of yielding; Lombardo Toledano, leader of the CTM, and the Communists demanded intervention in the companies if they failed to comply, but they did not ask for nationalization.

Cárdenas declared that the companies' offers were acceptable and promised their representatives that no new workers' demands would be heard as long as a contract remained in force. The company representatives then asked to have this promise in writing. Cárdenas considered this an insult to the president of the republic and a personal affront. As soon as word of this meeting with company officials reached the streets, everyone became indignant. On March 15, the new date set by the Board of Conciliation for compliance, the companies told the board they refused to comply with the ruling. According to the law, they then became liable to a fine amounting to the total wages paid for three months, about 100 million pesos. But the companies believed that if worse came to worst, the government would intervene and pay the wages out of the treasury and would ultimately yield to diplomatic pressure. They were mistaken.

Cárdenas had sent a representative to Washington to inform the U.S. Government of what was happening and to warn that the Mexican Government might take over the oil companies, but only temporarily—a move intended to avert misunderstandings and prevent a new anti-Mexican campaign in the United States. But before the envoy arrived in Washington, Cárdenas was told of the companies' defiance, and he made up his mind that he could not tolerate their outright refusal to comply with the court order. The companies had made a major error in demanding total victory and closing off any possibility of retreat by the government. This—and their insolence—forced Cárdenas to seek a recourse never used before: nationalization. The president called a meeting of his cabinet at 10:00 P.M. on March 15, and also informed the country in a radio address that he proposed to nationalize the oil companies "in the national interest." He acknowledged that this was unheard of, but affirmed that it was the only possible way of resolving a situation affecting the national honor.

The very next day the companies offered to comply with the law, but Cárdenas did not deign to answer them. On March 18, the decree of nationalization was proclaimed. It was a great moment for collective Mexican emotion, for a generalized enthusiasm. Any president with a feeling of national pride would have done as Cárdenas did, but his particular forcefulness won him a place in history and a popularity that was to stand him in good stead many years later. All of Mexico agreed that the expropriation had affirmed their national character, and every year since, on March 18, an official celebration is held in which the Mexican management renders its accounts of the oil industry, demonstrating that the profits from its control have contributed a considerable share of the country's capitalization and modernization. In 1938, however, no such happy ending was foreseen, and it could not have been known that the economic consequences of this decision would work to the great advantage of the Mexican economy. But it did prove the resourcefulness of the Mexicans in improvising solutions to problems hitherto unknown to them, while emphasizing the harmful effect the oil companies had had on the national economy.

At the time of the expropriation, Cárdenas explained to his people that their country's national sovereignty was at stake. He showed that the companies' investment had been small and that the industry had in fact been established largely because several Mexican administrations had granted them special exemptions and privileges. But the companies had never reciprocated by reinvesting their profits in Mexico; they had done nothing to further the nation's progress; on the contrary, they established a humiliating discrimination toward their Mexican employees and had resorted to violence and even crime to prevent the organization of their workers. The companies reacted to these revelations by opening an anti-Mexico campaign in the United States and Great Britain. They implied that the Mexican government had permitted the establishment of foreign industry there because of the "inability of the Mexicans themselves to progress," only to appropriate the companies later. They also appealed the expropriation order to the Supreme Court, but on December 2, the court ruled that it was constitutional. The only move left them was to provoke the intervention of foreign governments, which they attempted heartily, while making every effort to ruin Mexico by blacklisting buyers of Mexican petroleum, by refusing tankers to transport Mexican oil, by seeking court orders that would permit confiscation of it abroad, and above all by bringing pressure to bear on the White House in the hopes of persuading President Franklin D. Roosevelt to force Cárdenas, through diplomatic means, to reverse himself.

Meanwhile, Cárdenas took advantage of the country's emotional state to reaffirm his power. In 1938, he transformed the PNR and renamed it the Partido de la Revolución Mexicana (Party of the Mexican Revolution), rebuilding it as a fourfold entity in which the peasants, the workers, the military, and the middle class (the bureaucracy to whom Cárdenas granted the right to organize but not to strike) would all participate.

By including the military, he probably meant to guarantee against army adventures of one kind or another. His strategy was successful except in the case of General Saturnino Cedillo, the rightist *cacique* of San Luis Potosí whom Cárdenas had invited into his second cabinet. Cedillo rebelled in May, 1938, whereupon the government ordered him out of his bailiwick. The insurrection was put down quickly, almost without a struggle, since Cedillo found no support from the Church, whose cause he claimed to defend, or from the army. He surrendered and was killed. This rebellion—the last coup attempted by an army man— preceded the change of the PNR to the PRM, which reflected a general change in the country's political situation. To integrate the PRM, Cárdenas was able to count on the CTM, organized under his aegis, and the Confederación Nacional Campesina, also founded at his behest.

Still, Mexico was in an extremely difficult position. She had no tankers in which to transport her oil, and the companies refused to sell spare parts for the machinery in the oil fields. This obstructiveness meant that Mexico, in the midst of the world depression, could export only silver and petroleum; and, with oil production temporarily curtailed, the national income was reduced drastically. (The companies even tried to cut down on the sale abroad of Mexican silver, in spite of the fact that it came from mines owned by Americans. Of course, the mining men were making every effort to offset the maneuvers of the oil men because they feared that if the Mexican Government were sufficiently aroused, it might nationalize the mines, too.) On the day of the expropriation, however, Cárdenas announced that the oil companies would be compensated and that Mexico would meet the obligations of her foreign debt. Public collections were set up to raise money. People contributed their gold rings; the Church—even the Church—gave some of the jewels in its treasure vaults; the closed caste of the far-right Porfirists contributed precious metals; and the peasants brought turkeys and corn to sell in Mexico City and donated the money to pay for their drop of oil. Of course all this was very touching, but it was not enough. So Cárdenas wrote a personal letter to President Roosevelt; the State Department let up some of its pressure; the Mexican congress studied new ways to pay the debt. The oil industry, now organized as an autonomous governmental enterprise (in which the unions played no important part), succeeded in renting some tankers and offered petroleum to whoever would buy it, which meant Italy and Germany. This trade established the paradoxical situation in which Spanish Republicans fought with arms from Mexico (among other countries), while Franco used petroleum products supplied by Germany and Italy which also came from Mexico.

The international situation was now so black that the United States and Great Britain were eager to avoid any new complications. London might have adopted energetic measures in the Mexican situation, but Washington was not ready to support them, so that in the end Great Britain had to modify its stand. A series of diplomatic maneuvers followed. First London assumed an attitude of superiority, desiring to teach Mexico a lesson in international law that it would not soon forget by setting a value of $250 million on El Aguila Company, belonging to Shell. This was followed by a demand for the payment of $82 million owed to British subjects according to the terms of the 1935 agreement on compensation for damages caused during the Revolution. Mexico answered immediately with a check accompanied by a note pointing out that Great Britain had repudiated her own war debts and stating that because El Aguila had been founded as a Mexican company, no claim on its behalf could be presented by a foreign government. Mexico broke off diplomatic relations with Great Britain, not to reinstate them until World War II. Interestingly enough, however, there was no resentment of England among Mexicans, in spite of her arbitrary behavior.

The United States was more flexible. Roosevelt's "good neighbor" policy had gotten off to a successful start, and the Mexican situation threatened to mar it. Demands of American companies for the return of their Mexican property and for compensation for them and for the petroleum not yet extracted were heard with less sympathy in Washington than the English companies had received in London, although the American press campaigned violently against expropriation. The United States was in an awkward position, for the government had accepted the principle of nonintervention agreed upon at the Pan-American conferences and had acknowledged that foreign companies operating in any Latin American nation could be treated no worse and no better than national enterprises. And as Mexico had expropriated the property of many Mexicans, the fate of foreign petroleum interests was no worse than that of the Mexican companies. Cordell Hull, then secretary of state, approached the question indirectly by opening negotiations with Mexico to enable American citizens whose lands had been expropriated to collect indemnities, which he estimated at $10 million. Mexico agreed to negotiate and made an advance payment of $1 million. Roosevelt, for his part, stated that the oil companies were entitled to compensation only for the properties expropriated, minus depreciation, in no case for petroleum not yet extracted. Cárdenas promised that Mexico would honor its commitments, adding that the attitude of the United States had won the esteem of the Mexican people. In March, 1939, the companies sent a mission to Mexico to negotiate directly with Cárdenas. The mission demanded the immediate payment of $260 million. When Mexico refused, counterproposals were made, such as leasing the oil-bearing lands for fifty years or founding mixed Mexican and American companies. Those suggestions were rejected, too.

A short time later, World War II broke out. The diplomats from the Axis countries went into action in Mexico, and a fascist movement called Sinarquismo sprang up. Washington foresaw the moment when for military reasons it would need Mexican raw materials; agreement on the issues dividing the two countries became urgent. Cárdenas was followed by a conciliatory president, Manuel Avila Camacho (1897–1955). Meanwhile, the sale of Mexican petroleum to the Axis countries continued.

In 1940, Sinclair, one of the U.S. companies, decided to accept the Mexican position and obtained a promise to receive $8.5 million for its expropriated property, but not for the petroleum not yet extracted; and in November, 1941, the two countries reached a general accord which provided that Mexico would pay $40 million for all the damages due to the Revolution, at the rate of $2.5 million a year. (By 1956, the debt was paid off.) At the same time, the United States offered long-term credits at low interest rates from the Import-Export Bank for the acquisition of American capital goods. A bi-national commission, established by the accord, fixed the indemnities to the oil companies at close to $24 million, less than 10 per cent of the amount they demanded, which was based on obviously inflated figures. (In 1947, that obligation was paid off within the time limit set by the accord.)

After the war, Petroleos Mexicanos bought up the small companies that were not yet expropriated. (Expropriation had affected only companies that refused to comply with the court's labor ruling.) By 1956, there was not a single foreign oil company in Mexico.

A new agreement was reached in 1947 to settle the British claims. Mexico promised to pay the sum of $8.5 million a year until a total indemnity of $81 million, plus interest, had been cleared away. This promise has been kept, too. All in all, the expropriation of petroleum has cost the country $172 million, which included interest and the cost of purchasing the small companies. Pemex and its profits are paying off this sum.

All this success was not easily achieved, owing to a lack of administrative experience, for one thing, and to the demands of the petroleum unions (under Communist control for ten years) for another. The unions, claiming that the expropriation procedures owed their success to the unions' struggle against the companies, had increased their wages fourfold within a short time. But when the war ended and the Cold War began, they called a political strike. President Miguel Alemán (b. 1902) declared the strike illegal on the grounds that the maneuvers of a handful of union leaders could not take precedence over the interests of millions of consumers, and the public turned against the unionists, who were arrested and imprisoned when they refused to call off the strike. The union then elected non-Communist leaders, who have since maintained good relations with Pemex. But the oversubmissiveness of the new leaders and their corruption gave the Communists a pretext to take over control of the union again after ten years. Again the Communists were eliminated when they attempted to use the union for their own political ends.

In that same decade, Pemex, freed from international pressure (exerted by the companies and then from the war), was reorganized on an efficient, business basis, and it modernized and improved its installations. A few figures will show the results obtained: in 1922, 182 million barrels of oil had been extracted, of which 2 million were set aside for national consumption, while by 1932, production had declined to 32 million barrels (of which 12 million for domestic use); in 1946, at the start of the reorganization, 49 million barrels were extracted, of which 10 million were exported. Thus, national consumption had risen sharply as industry, stimulated by the war, used more and more oil. In 1951, petroleum production was up to 78 million barrels, of which 22 million were sold abroad. Since then the figures have doubled, as new refineries were built in Atzcapozalco, Reynosa, Salamanca, Poza Rica, and Minatitlán and many of the by-products, formerly refined abroad, are being produced at home. New oil fields have been opened also, and pipelines for oil and gas have been laid. (The principal oil regions, all near the Gulf Coast, run north and south from Reynosa, Tampico, Poza Rica, to Minatitlán.) Pemex workers are among the best paid in the country; they enjoy good housing, schools, cooperatives, and other benefits. Pemex has demonstrated that a nationalized industry can function success-fully and efficiently without raising the price of the product, for oil sells in Mexico at a lower price than in the United States. Con-versely, a nationalized industry can offer its workers better treat-ment than private enterprise and can bring not only economic but budgetary benefits to the country, for Pemex turns a portion of its profits over to the national treasury.

The Cárdenas administration became the period of nationaliza-tion owing to force of circumstances, not because it was fore-seen. The measures taken were not revolutionary, for it was a matter not of giving society control of the means of production, in accordance with the socialist formula, but of giving it the means for extricating the country from a dilemma, for solving unexpected problems. After Cárdenas, demands were made—sometimes by unions, sometimes by leftist groups—for more na-tionalizations of insurance, electrical power, telephone, aviation companies, and so on. But what was done amounts to a "Mexi-canization" by Mexican purchase on the open market of shares in companies held by foreign interests and by agreement between the interested parties.

10 · Reforms of Reforms

THE PERSONALITY of Cárdenas and his policies have been judged in many ways and never disinterestedly. He has his fervent partisans —who give the impression at times that they are using his prestige rather than serving him. And he has his consistent detractors, who nevertheless seem proud that Mexico should have had a president of his caliber. No one, in either camp, can doubt that his six years in office marked the end of one era in Mexican history and the beginning of another.

Cárdenas pacified the country and bound up the wounds inflicted by the struggle between Church and state, but he never permitted the state to play second fiddle to the Church. His policies were a continuation and consolidation of the work of Calles, who never wished to persecute the Church, only to prevent it from paralyzing the state. Cárdenas did away with militarism by taking advantage of a situation in which positions of command were assumed by a new generation of officers who were not products of the Revolution. This, too, consolidated the policy of Obregón and Calles, which was always to keep the military integrated in the system and punish any military who tried to attack or ignore it. Cardenas never resorted to police brutality or illegal means to enforce compliance, and this moderation added luster to the Revolution's progress toward institutionalization, begun by his predecessors. In nationalizing the railroads and oil, he transformed the spirit of the 1917 Constitution, which crowned the Revolution, into a daily reality, accepted by everyone. He quickened the pace of agrarian reform and changed its character, thus proving that social change stemming from the Revolution could be achieved without violence. He laid the bases of a social security system and set up the Federal Electrical Power Commission—both of which were essential to a more rapid industrialization of the country.

Like every Mexican president since 1917, he actively intervened in the selection of a candidate to succeed him, for he wished to assure Mexico's internal peace at a moment when the world was plunging into war. Considered as a revolutionary (and later, by supporting Castro and permitting himself to be used by hard-core anti-Americans, emphasizing this aspect of his reputation), he was in reality neither a leftist nor a revolutionary. He was a conservative in the true sense, trying to keep what the Revolution had gained and consolidating what his predecessors had begun.

To date, the presidents who have followed Cárdenas have been conservatives in the same sense, also true to revolutionary principles. Consciously or not, they directed their administrations toward reforms, conforming the Revolution to the new realities of the country, new currents in the world, and new needs emerging from general technological advance. Meanwhile, the means of popular expression have been expanded as the political process slowly and cautiously has become more democratic. Cárdenas undoubtedly hoped to move the country into a new period of history, his own period, but in fact he was a president of transition. The post-Cárdenas period has a quality of its own, which might be characterized as a reform of reforms, without violent upheavals. The Mexican Revolution, like all revolutions, had solved no problems; it had destroyed the obstacles that had prevented solutions in the earlier system. The post-Revolution governments found and applied some solutions. But, as the country changed, the problems changed too, so that the first solutions no longer served their purpose. Unlike the liberals of nineteenth-century Mexico, or the Stalinists in Russia, the Mexican revolutionaries did not become dogmatic, but discovered—more through political instinct and a sense of power than by reflection and forethought—ways to infuse into the system a means whereby they were ready to adapt to the new form the problems took as earlier solutions were effected. The continued need to reform the reforms demonstrates that each reform fulfilled its function.

In 1939, as the world entered World War II, a crucial question in Mexico was who would succeed Cárdenas. Some of the people wanted a man who would continue Cárdenas' policies and emphasize even more its social aspects—a political figure favoring the rapid expansion of agrarian reform, supporting the trade unions, perhaps nationalizing other important industries. Some of the people wanted a man who above all would make every effort to keep Mexico out of the war while collaborating vigorously with the anti-Fascist forces. Others, finally, wanted their future president to establish a period of rest, so that the country would have the opportunity to assimilate the changes and reforms of the past twenty years.

If Cárdenas had had his choice, he would have picked a Cardenist president who would apply a Cardenist policy and over whom he would have had some influence. His followers not only wanted the same type of man, but also hoped that Cárdenas would be able to help them retain their own political positions and influence. And evidently they persuaded him to support the revolutionary General Francisco J. Múgica, one of the authors of the basic articles of the 1917 Constitution. But a strong majority in the Mexican Revolutionary Party, wanting most of all a period of stability in which to digest reform, buttressed their views with the argument that Mexico was feeling the economic repercussions of the world situation and would be unable to absorb new changes without jeopardizing the economy. Cárdenas eventually swung around to this theory, to the great disappointment of his followers who had begun to campaign for Múgica.

The candidate finally chosen by Cárdenas and the upper echelons of the PRM was secretary of defense in the Cárdenas cabinet, General Manuel Avila Camacho (1897–1955). Avila Camacho was from a traditionalist Catholic family in Puebla. If he became president, power would pass out of the hands of the groups from the north—the region of the great cattle-raising haciendas of the past—to the people from the meseta, a strongly Catholic and industrially advanced region. This geographical shift was not a crucial factor, but it was not unimportant in a country as extensive and diverse as Mexico, where friendship and local relationships are of considerable importance in political life.

The trade unions and peasant organizations were not attracted to Avila Camacho, but they supported him. Their help and that of the PRM were his only political assets except for what he could get from the governmental machinery. The younger members of the PRM, wanting a new look in political methods and style; the conservatives; possibly many of the workers and peasants; people of the provinces; and many intellectuals hoped that the predominance of the "official party" would be ended and believed that the time was ripe for this change. If they could nominate a winning opposition candidate outside the ranks of the "revolutionary family" but not antirevolutionary, they believed, the world situation would make it impossible for the government to ignore the election results and prevent his taking office. So this diverse group, united only by a desire to win the election of an unofficially selected candidate, threw its support to an interesting, though not precisely charismatic figure, General Miguel Andrew Almazán, who had been popular as commander of operations against General Escobar in 1929 and who later had become a millionaire through public-works contracts. Thanks to his money, he was able to finance a very dynamic and energetic campaign, in the course of which he accused Cárdenas of tolerating Communists and was himself accused of being a fascist. When the votes were counted, Avila Camacho had 2,265,199; Almazán only 128,574.

Many people, knowing that Almazán was very popular, were convinced that there had been fraud. The defeated candidate said so in a tone that hinted at a desire for a fight. People rushed into the streets, and the National Palace was virtually besieged. Cárdenas went out alone to confront the multitude—who, deeply impressed with him, dispersed. Almazán left the country. Roosevelt announced that he would send Vice President Henry Wallace to attend the inauguration ceremonies of Avila Camacho. Calm was restored, but the election had disillusioned a whole generation about political life. Perhaps this was a good thing for Mexico, for that generation went into business at the end of World War II and created the basis for a new stage of Mexican industrialization.

General Avila Camacho, whom the people called "the unknown soldier," turned out to be a more capable president than anyone had expected. The influence of Cárdenas on his administration was clear but never decisive. Neither was that of Avila Camacho's brother, the secretary of communications, whom many people regarded as capable of using his office for personal benefit and as not averse to using brutal methods in doing so.

Mexico's situation was far from simple. The United States was preparing for war, and Mexico, knowing that the United States would step in to fill a vacuum, had to take a stand. After the United States entered the war, there was talk of German and Japanese submarines off the coast of Baja California. The Mexican Government sent troops there and appointed Cárdenas chief of operations in the area, thus preventing the United States from patrolling the Mexican coast. At international meetings, Mexico voted in favor of war measures as long as they could not be interpreted as intervention.

Avila Camacho had declared in the course of his campaign that he believed in and favored small property ownership. His administration carried out that platform, under a modified Department of Agriculture policy which established fewer *ejidos* and issued more titles to small property owners. Peace with the Church was reinforced. Avila Camacho's successors have, with some variations, followed his policies.

Many grievances were assuaged by the president's strategy, but many still lingered. Almazán's most active supporters, undeceived about their candidate (who soon returned to Mexico and his business), still considered Avila Camacho as a creature of Cárdenas. In reaction, many of them turned toward Germany, and among the people there was strong sympathy for the Third Reich, which they regarded as a power capable of bringing forth men who would crush the United States. Besides, it was *"muy macho."* The Stalin-Hitler Pact contributed to this opinion by encouraging an acceptance of Germany, at the urging of the Communists. On the other hand, many fellow-travelers, disconcerted and undeceived, deserted the party.

In April, 1941, Avila Camacho issued a clear statement that he opposed the fascist "new order." At the same time, the government continued the Cardenist policy of refusing to establish diplomatic relations with the government of Generalissimo Francisco Franco, on the ground that it had won the Spanish Civil War through Italy's and Germany's intervention. The Cárdenas administration had supported the Spanish Republic at the League of Nations, and, when the civil war ended in 1939, Cárdenas welcomed exiled Republicans in spite of strong popular opposition and the protest of the many Spaniards already living in Mexico, most of whom were pro-Franco.

These Spanish exiles began their acclimatization to Mexico during Avila's term. Their adjustment was not easy, for the unions made it difficult for them to find work, even as they welcomed them with anti-fascist demonstrations. The standard of living of Mexican workers was low compared with that of Europeans (even Spaniards, long accustomed to poverty), and the refugees had to turn to business. Many prospered quickly because they were industrious and because the peculiarly favorable circumstances of the world war eased the way for them. A large number of them were intellectuals and university professors who were welcome in the Autonomous National University. Some founded publishing firms; some worked on newspapers and in radio. On the whole, they made an important contribution to Mexico's cultural life, which continued and intensified in the following decades, as they abandoned the hope that they would be able to return in triumph to Spain when peace came. (The Franco government openly favored the Axis, though it remained officially a nonbelligerent.) The Spanish refugees, except the Communists among them, lived on the fringe of Mexican politics, as most of them—being principled Socialists or anarchists—were demoralized by the need to start businesses of their own and exploit workers. Their political ineffectualness in Spanish affairs reflected this demoralization, and it isolated them from the Republican refugees in France (where the greatest number of Spanish political exiles lived), who existed in misery, some of them persecuted and others dedicated to the resistance against the Nazis, which was the equivalent for them of fighting Franco.

Avila Camacho's government seized Italian and German ships, restricted trade with the Axis, and finally broke off economic relations with Germany in August, 1941. During the following month an espionage law was passed to control the activities of a new group favoring the Axis. Their organization, the Unión Nacional Sinarquista, emerged during the Cárdenas administration following doctrines similar to those of the Spanish Falange. A little while earlier, the Communists had carried on an energetic anti-American campaign, hoping to turn popular feeling against the United States to their own advantage and offset the Mexican Government's anti-Axis measures. Three weeks after one of their attacks (directed by Lombardo Toledano, head of the CTM, but not yet openly pro-Soviet), Germany attacked Russia. Lombardo, like the Communists, became overnight a warm friend of the United States as he discovered the virtues of Roosevelt's Good Neighbor Policy. Later, he made a tour of Latin America and came back to defend the dictators of the day, whom he labeled "paternalists" and "well-intentioned" because circumstances had placed them on the side of the Allies. At this point, the Communists were trying to prevent strikes (and even antidictatorship activity throughout Latin America) lest they damage the war effort and thus the allied aid to the Soviet Union.

The war helped to bring to a happy ending the negotiations between Mexico and the United States over claims resulting from the Revolution and the nationalization of oil. After Pearl Harbor, Mexico broke off relations with Japan and seized German, Italian, and Japanese property throughout the country. Avila Camacho said that Mexico must be an arsenal for democracy, but his ringing words fell on indifferent ears.

Mexico shipped great quantities of oil to the United States even as German submarines were halting ships and the German government was threatening Mexico with "grave consequences" if this trade continued. On May 14, 1942, a German submarine sank the Mexican tanker *Potrero de Llano* off the coast of Florida and destroyed another tanker a week later. All told, twelve Mexican seamen lost their lives. A wave of indignation swept the country, but many people still did not favor entry in the war. Avila Camacho convened congress in extraordinary session and summoned the state governors and the generals to the capital. The people demonstrated, demanding a declaration of war. Convinced of the country's readiness for such a step, the congress declared war on the Axis on May 30 and suspended constitutional guaranties for the duration.

The man charged with sustaining the country's morale, and keeping second-rank politicians from using the suspension of civil rights as a means to make themselves petty dictators, was the secretary of the interior, Miguel Alemán. His task was not easy. Alemán had to impose a truce in the struggle between the various labor federations to avoid a decrease in production rates. He had to stop the activities of the fifth columns, active among the many Germans and Italians—economically strong, well organized, and well liked. To strengthen national unity, Avila Camacho called together all the living ex-presidents to help celebrate Independence Day—September 16—and the Mexican people were able to see Calles side by side with Adolfo de la Huerta, who had led a rebellion against him; Cárdenas beside Calles, whom Cárdenas had exiled; Ortiz Rubio, who had been virtually destroyed by Calles; Abelardo Rodríguez and Portes Gil, who had abandoned their protector, Calles. A Supreme Defense Council was founded in which the unions, management, the army, and other groups were represented. The council was to draw up plans for mobilization, resources, and defense. Little by little, the people accepted the war.

With the war came an acceleration of Mexico's economic development.

When the United States entered the conflict, the Latin American nations were deprived of their usual source of manufactured goods, and imports from the U.S. dropped drastically. But the shortage of goods, although it threatened momentarily to impair the comfort of those prosperous enough to buy imported products, favored Mexico's progress in the long run. Here was Mexico's opportunity to create domestic industries that would supply the domestic market and have enough left over to export elsewhere—the Caribbean and Central America, for example. Both the government and Mexican businessmen recognized their chance. Their desire for an easy, quick profit engendered many hastily improvised enterprises offering products of mediocre quality that would not have had a hope of competing successfully with American goods in normal times. Nevertheless, they supplied the Mexicans with what they considered essential to urban life, and, at the conclusion of the war, the country had its own industry, still somewhat small but employing an increasingly skilled and specialized labor force. Some markets, which had grown accustomed to certain Mexican goods, were well established. Thus, the absence of imports from the United States, especially light industrial products, created conditions that started a new wave of industrialization, and the Mexican economy was guided in a new direction.

The development of new industry permitted Mexico to collaborate to some extent in the United States war effort. The general outlines of this partnership were worked out in Monterrey during an interview between Roosevelt and Avila Camacho in April, 1943, on board a train. This was the first time an American president had ever been on Mexican soil, and it was only the second interview between presidents of the two countries. Roosevelt said tactfully: "We know that the epoch of exploitation of the resources and people of one country for the benefit of one group in another has definitely passed." A Mexican-American Committee for Economic Cooperation was set up to expedite production of raw materials essential to the war effort and to speed shipment of necessary machinery and parts to Mexico. The

United States supplied experts to collaborate with Mexicans in increasing agricultural productivity so that they could raise enough food to supply themselves. A mixed commission, empowered to reorganize the railroads, abandoned its task in 1944, because the lack of discipline among workers in nationalized industries made its effort futile. President Avila Camacho then issued a series of decrees granting the railroad administration extraordinary powers, but not much order resulted, and it was not until the succeeding administration that a serious campaign to modernize the railroad network was even possible.

Mexico could offer the United States minerals and fibers—and, more important, labor, since so many American workers had been mobilized. *Braceros* (also known as "wetbacks" because they entered the United States by crossing the Rio Grande) had worked in the southwestern United States illegally ever since the termination of slavery; now they flocked across the border in enormous numbers and could be seen in Chicago, Kansas City, and throughout California. Special agreements legalized their status and regulated the work contracts of some 200,000 of them, but they were still relegated to a position of inferiority. The U.S. trade unions tried to champion the Mexican workers' rights, largely to protect their own members, but without much success. Not until a later administration were the *braceros* given legal protection of a kind.

These Mexico-U.S. agreements had a curious sequel. One of the decisions between the two countries provided that Mexicans in the United States could be drafted into the American Army and Americans residing in Mexico could do their military service in the Mexican Army without impairing the citizenship of either group. Americans doing business in Mexico for American firms were indignant at having to live in the same barracks with "poor Indians," for whom they felt a disdain they made no effort to disguise. (Their chagrin was especially deep if they were from the southwestern states—as many of them unfortunately were— where social and cultural discrimination against Mexicans was and is entrenched and widespread.) A quarter of a million Mexicans were mobilized in the United States Army, of whom 14,000 engaged in actual combat; one thousand won the Purple Heart and one the Congressional Medal of Honor. Meanwhile, Mexico, which had raised an army of volunteers, established universal military service for a year and reinforced the garrisons on the Pacific coast under the command of General Cárdenas. Indirectly, these moves made the army more professional, though it reduced the number of fighting men to some 52,000. And Mexico sent an air squadron to participate in Pacific operations, manned by volunteers and armed with matériel bought in the United States on credit for the purpose of modernizing the Mexican armed forces. But Avila Camacho was astute enough to suppress the military arm of the PRM and to prevent the deputies and senators in uniform from establishing a special bloc in congress, and actually turned the world war to his country's advantage by taking a new step toward suppressing the militarists' ambitions.

World War II affected Mexico in another way by opening its doors to the world. Except in the case of the Spanish Civil War, Mexico had never before participated in international politics, but now she began to play an active role in Pan American conferences. Chapultepec Castle, once Maximilian's royal palace and later the president's home, was opened to the Inter-American Conference in 1945, at which the foundations were laid of the present-day inter-American system. During the conference, Mexico collaborated closely with the United States yet maintained an independent position permitting her to defend consistently the principle of nonintervention, the cornerstone of Mexican international policy already set before the war in the Estrada Doctrine, named for the Mexican secretary of state who formulated it, which stated that the establishment of a government was each nation's internal affair, and diplomatic relations between Mexico and other countries would continue regardless of the regime, as long as such relations did not violate Mexico's national interest.

On the whole, Mexico benefited by the war. The economically active population increased by more than 11 per cent; the gross national product doubled; the minimum wage rose by 14 per cent. On the other hand, the cost of living tripled and inflation and corruption increased. The middle classes, like the proletariat, grew in number, while the economic situation of the farm workers remained static and inferior. Little land was distributed (only about 7 million acres during Avila Camacho's presidency), and the social security system, set up in 1943, could not develop owing to the scarcity of capital. But as capital increased with the establishment of new industries and the spread of corruption (since war profiteers, unable to invest abroad during the war, were forced to put their gains back into the Mexican economy), industry was strengthened. The *nouveaux riches* flaunted their wealth so offensively that the government had to call them to account.

The administration, casting aside the rhetoric of free enterprise, founded the Nacional Financiera, a governmental investment banking enterprise that would control investment and through it a program for economic progress (not yet called development). It turned inflation to good account by liquidating the national debt and sending a part of its dollar reserves abroad, not so much to relieve inflationary pressures as to decrease the foreign debt. By the end of the war, the country's financial situation could be considered relatively healthy, and the economic situation was very good with prospects of growing better. Headlines in the Mexican press reflected prosperity and emphasized economic rather than political news. The government's economic measures were given good coverage; later, when money was plentiful enough for public works, news stories covering the inception of such projects were emphasized. The Mexicans' day-to-day interest in political wrangles began to wane as their enthusiasm over economic matters grew. Students enrolled in economics and technical professions in growing numbers.

All this did not mean that political problems had vanished. The influence of Sinarquism spread among certain groups of peasants, particularly in the rich region of the Bajío. The Axis fostered this movement, and the Catholic hierarchy, not yet resigned to the outcome of the long struggle against Calles, secretly supported it. The Sinarquists established agricultural colonies in Baja California possibly to serve as submarine bases for the Axis, but they were a failure. Their sympathizers were watched but not persecuted.

The Communists, for their part, indicated their readiness to support the government once Russia was forced to enter the war. Lombardo Toledano sang the praises of Roosevelt and proclaimed the friendship of the Mexican people for the United States. As head of the CTM, he won approval of a peace pact with management organizations. The war was also reflected in the resumption, in 1942, of diplomatic relations with the U.S.S.R., which the Mexican Government had suspended in 1927 when the Soviet Embassy intervened in Mexico's affairs. Alexandra Kollontay was Russian ambassadress at that time. The presence of a large Soviet diplomatic contingent exasperated the Mexican rightists, but the government tried to prevent an extreme polarization of attitudes. Indeed, one of Avila Camacho's major preoccupations was to maintain national unity during the war and to try to appease everyone—the workers by the social security system, and the poor urban masses by a system of subsidies to purchase crops at a decent price and to sell food at low prices. On the whole, his policies were successful, since nothing spectacular happened. He pacified the Church with a new revision of Article 3 of the constitution that eliminated the expression "socialist education." Insofar as possible, school construction was increased, and it grew during succeeding administrations. At the end of the war, the government renounced the extraordinary powers granted it by congress, and a new electoral law was drawn up in 1945 in the hope of attracting a greater number of voters to the polls and making the elections cleaner. Proof of the success of this conciliatory program was that in 1946, for the first time, elections went off without incident (although shortly before the polling a bloody encounter took place between Sinarquists and soldiers in Léon), and also for the first time since the Revolution, a president was elected who had not participated in the Revolution and who had never worn a uniform.

The election to the presidency of a civilian signified one step in Mexico's evolution. Another was taken in 1946 when the PRM decided to dissolve and created in its place the Partido Revolucionario Institucional (PRI), composed of labor, peasant, and middle-class branches.

Two men from the new PRI ran against each other in the election campaign of 1946. One was the party candidate, Miguel Alemán; the other, the outgoing government's secretary of state, Ezequiel Padilla, ran as an independent candidate. Padilla had the sympathy of the right-wing and the antipathy of the left-wing, which considered him too pro-American. Alemán won 1,786,901 votes to Padilla's 443,537, the largest losing vote since the Revolution, and many Mexicans interpreted this as another step toward democratization.

Alemán, a young man surrounded by a group of loyal and energetic friends, represented the spirit of the new generation that had not lived through the Revolution. His father had been a local revolutionary leader who was killed in combat. A group from Veracruz rose with Alemán to power, which that region had not tasted for many years. This lent a somewhat different tone to politics. People still talked of the principles of the Revolution, but they spoke mainly in terms of government activity, especially in economics. Mexico had on hand a moderate dollar reserve, unlike most of the Latin American countries that had accumulated dollars during the war. But while the others were squandering their dollars on the importation of luxury goods and refusing to worry about liquidating their foreign debt, Mexico was paying off most of her debts and starting new industries. This enabled the Alemán government to concentrate on public works and to encourage the opening of more factories. U.S. capital, once more available, was invested in considerable amounts.

Alemán appointed two energetic administrators as heads of the two great government enterprises, Pemex and the railroads, with a mandate to reorganize both. He also drew up a grandiose irrigation plan, with a central project similar to TVA called the Papaloapan Dam Project. It entailed displacing some of the indigenous groups in order to serve a region larger than any Central American country.

To accelerate industrialization without friction, the cooperation of labor was needed. Lombardo Toledano favored a pact with industry, but Alemán refused to entrust control of the unions to the Communists. Leadership of the CTM was finally won by a group headed by Fidel Velázquez and called the Five Little Pigs (because its members were all chubby), who expelled Lombardo Toledano and later split the CTM off from the Communist CTAL to affiliate with the International Confederation of

Free Trade Unions. While this was going on, Alemán took advantage of a political strike of the oil workers to jail the Communists who led it, whom the union replaced with nonideological officials. Alemán knew that social peace depended not on labor leaders but on labor's participation in the benefits of development. Accordingly, he speeded up the work of the Mexico Institute of Social Security, which then began to build clinics and assistance centers and to extend its services each year to cover a greater number of urban workers.

Industrialization was not planned, but neither was it left to the will of God. The government's effort to control industrialization through the budget, by the offer of tax exemptions to new industries, and with public investment made through the Nacional Financiera and the Housing Bank, was successful. Two devaluations of the peso gave the products of new industries a chance to compete on the foreign market and increased the sale of Mexican raw materials abroad, both of which, in turn, made available to Mexico large amounts of currency for the purchase of imported capital goods. This was important since, after four years of "austerity," the *nouveaux riches* hungered for imported cars and other luxury items, and, for its part, the government was eager not to alienate them by forbidding such articles, and yet to limit the dollar hemorrhage.

People say that corruption became common during Alemán's term in office and that no important business could function unless official elements had a share in it. It seems certain that many of the president's friends became wealthy, but as the proceeds of corruption were invested in the country, capital was created and Mexican capitalism grew strong enough to offset the damaging effect of the influx of foreign investment. Mexico's stage of development at that time was not dissimilar to that of the United States seventy or eighty years earlier, during the "Gilded Age," when corruption moved hand in glove with developing capitalism. In truth, corruption can act as a policy of capitalization, provided that it does not last and is confined to small segments of society that invest their profits in the country, and provided that it does not lower the standard of living of the weakest economic groups. Such conditions were present in Alemán's time. The

Compañía Exportadora e Importadora Mexicana, Sociedad Anónima, or CEIMSA (Mexican Export-Import Company), later converted into Compañía Nacional de Suminstros Populares, or CONASUPO (National People's Supply Company), an autonomous government enterprise, bought basic goods and sold them at low prices, thus providing the public, especially workers from the country who entered new industries, with articles suited to their means.

Of course, this had some social effect on Mexico, as the figures released by Alemán's secretary of the treasury indicate: in 1939, profits accounted for 26 per cent of the national income and wages for 30.5 per cent. In 1952 (at the end of Alemán's term), the share of profits had climbed to 41.4 per cent, while wages had shrunk to 23.8 per cent. But the public was unaware of this because the gross national product had risen so sharply that the people's standard of living in absolute terms was visibly better, especially in the cities. The development of industry permitted diversification, and, thanks to the increasingly active Nacional Financiera, investment was directed into both heavy and light industry and into mechanized farming. In the country, small property ownership was encouraged, but the creation of new *ejidos* was now avoided. Plantations were laid out—virtual latifundios, but without political power—for the introduction of new agricultural products, such as olive oil, and for the expansion of already existing crops, such as cotton—all this in spite of an epidemic of hoof-and-mouth disease that had decimated the country's cattle.

Conditions favorable to foreign capital, subject always to the law specifying that 51 per cent of the capital of any enterprise must be in Mexican hands, were thus created without the risk of foreign intervention in national policy. These measures later helped Mexico gradually to free herself from dependence on imported agricultural products. In fact, the country's economy was being transformed and was assuming the form it retains today: a balanced mixture of private initiative and indirect state planning, of private and public investment. Nevertheless, as we have said, the portion of the national income paid out in wages decreased by comparison with the share that represented capital. Unmistakably, Mexico was following the road to capitalism.

Of course, this trend perturbed the left, which had been hoping that eventually the Revolution would turn toward socialism. Alemán had to cope with pressure from this group, which organized into the Partido Popular, led by Lombardo Toledano. In order to prevent this group from disrupting the economic development of the country, the government discreetly favored labor leaders who indicated their readiness to collaborate in development without neglecting the interests of the workers. Men of this type finally displaced the pro-Communist elements in the CTM and other labor federations.

The right wing, composed of traditional capitalists and the remnants of the Porfirists, were concerned, too, by the thought of a directed economy, and many of its members joined Acción Nacional, a rightist party founded some years before. To counteract their influence, expressed most strongly through the Federation of Chambers of Commerce, the government, again discreetly, favored the Chamber of Manufacturing Industries, a modern and very nationalistic body. The banks, grateful for a policy of easy credit (at a high interest rate, in accordance with Latin American practice) supported the government.

By the end of his term, Alemán's policies had enabled his friends to achieve economic power. They used their power to campaign for the restraint of anti-Americanism and for the maintenance of pressure so that the pace of development would not slow down.* But they blundered by launching a campaign at the end of Alemán's term to amend the constitution so as to permit his re-election. The campaign was a failure, for one of the few things a Mexican president cannot do, for all his enormous power, is to get re-elected. Alemán's secretary of the interior, Adolfo Ruiz Cortines (b. 1890)—a compromise candidate between the Alemán group and the still influential Cardenistas—was elected

---

* In 1952, Mexico's gross national product had risen to 183 on a scale with 1939 as an index of 100. Domestic consumption of farm products jumped from 100 to 170; corn production almost doubled; sugar tripled; cotton quintupled; and real per-capita income increased to 161. One hundred thousand people were absorbed by industry, an important event in a country with a rapidly growing population.

president with 2,713,419 votes, in spite of the very active opposition of General Miguel Henríquez Guzmán, who received 570,745, a respectable number for a loser; of Lombardo Toledano, who ran as candidate of the Partido Popular; and of the Acción Nacional, which put up a candidate, too.

Alemán—a flexible man with a sense of humor, strong character, and a distinct personality—gave his government certain touches that lasted (with modifications) past his term. His impact was the result not so much of his virtues as of the fact that his government reflected the country's true needs. Perhaps his greatest merit was his ability to recognize those needs and to satisfy them without destroying or vitiating the essential objectives of the Revolution, grown old after forty years. Those qualities were clearly visible in Mexico's international policy.

In March, 1947, Alemán had received President Harry S. Truman of the United States (who made the gesture of laying flowers at the monument to the *Niños Heroes,* the military cadets who gave their lives to oppose the entry into Mexico City of U.S. troops a century earlier). On a more mundane level, the United States offered credit, supported the peso, and respected the political and economic life of the country, even though Washington regarded it as contrary to the principles of free enterprise. Alemán, in return, supported the international policy of the United States. This state of accord was to strengthen as each new Mexican president visited Washington and received in Mexico each president of the United States. John F. Kennedy, in 1962, was greeted with the most spectacular welcome ever seen in the capital, and during it the first steps were taken to resolve the question of the Chamizal—a piece of land that a change in the course of the Rio Grande had left on the American side of the border—which was settled in 1964 by restoring the land to Mexico. American property owners affected by the return of the Chamizal were compensated.

Yet Mexico has maintained her policy of independence in international affairs. In 1954, Mexico refused to approve the action taken by the United States against the Arbenz government in Guatemala. Similarly, she has maintained relations with Castro's regime in Havana, even though the Organization of American

States passed a resolution recommending that all Latin American countries break off relations with Cuba. (Later, however, Mexico supported the United States in the crisis over Soviet missiles in Cuba in October, 1962.) And Mexico has never recognized the government of Generalissimo Franco; indeed, in 1946, Spanish deputies in exile were welcomed to a meeting in which they formed a government in exile, which Mexico has recognized ever since (which policy has not impeded active trade with Spain). Later, President López Mateos tried to diversify Mexico's international politics, with visits to South America, Asia, and Europe, with the invitation to General de Gaulle to come to Mexico, and by active Mexican participation in the United Nations.

In 1959, when President López Mateos visited Washington, journalists asked him what was Mexico's principal problem, and he answered ironically: "The United States." But in truth, the United States is less and less a problem to Mexico, since Mexico needs outside aid less and less and since her own capital development permits the absorption of foreign capital without peril to her own and enables her to resist diplomatic pressures. Mexico has not established diplomatic relations with mainland China, but she trades with all the Communist countries (albeit on a rather small scale), and maintains relations with them. All in all, Mexico offers unequivocal proof that economic development—in a society capable of change in response to that development and to internal needs, and yielding a profit, large or small, to all social groups—can make economic and political independence possible without any spectacular demonstrations of nationalism.

Nevertheless, Mexican nationalism became accentuated during this period as it became more refined. The Mexican people have gained confidence in themselves, and they express it in their attitude toward foreign countries. They have no warm liking for the United States: indeed, the average Mexican always looks with some satisfaction on any event that bothers the United States. The lamentable history of Mexico's relations with her neighbor to the north is ever present in the schools and in Mexican memory. Yet the old bitterness has waned, and the Mexican people have learned to differentiate among American policies, and to view the Cold War in its world context and no longer as an expression of an American desire for dominance, which was the popular Mexican consensus on the issue after World War II.

Another trait of Alemán's politics that has lasted till today can be seen in the relations between the administration and the opposition. The Mexican government now realizes that a real opposition party must exist, for the good of the country, and discreetly tries to encourage it. For years, the government has given financial help to the newspaper *El Popular*, a pro-Communist opposition organ, and it is said, though no one can prove it, that the rightist paper has received similar aid. Be that as it may, the government has never used the enormous power concentrated in the president's hands to silence the opposition, even though in some cases the opposition may injure the president. Insults to the chief executive are always ill received in Mexico, where it is permissible to joke about him in private but never to attack him in public. Even so, when the pro-Castro and pro-Soviet magazine *Política* in 1962 accused President López Mateos of "serving Yankee imperialism," one of the worst imaginable insults in Mexico, its normal quota of paper, imported by a semigovernmental company, was not affected, and no attempt was made to quash it. This restraint marks a forward step in Mexican terms.

On the other hand, as the economy grows stronger, the government has tried to foster the democratization of political life. This deliberate policy, handed down from one president to another, has served to unify and characterize this period of civilian presidents.

Ruiz Cortines was more conservative than his predecessor. (In selecting him, the PRI had instinctively applied the pendulum theory—after a dynamic president, a cautious one who would prepare the ground for another dynamist; after a period of pressure to accelerate the rate of development, a period in which to consolidate the progress achieved.) But his administration marked a cautious, not very large, step toward democratization of the regime. The step taken during his term was woman's suffrage.

As we have seen, certain institutions, marginal in other countries but fundamental in Mexico, had been created: social security, CEIMSA, and Nacional Financiera. In countries where there is much poverty, systems of assistance are more important than political systems; in a sense, they constitute the very foundation of the government.

Ruiz Cortines' government took office on a platform that promised to clean up the administration and to dedicate itself to the strengthening of what already existed rather than innovation. As usual, the first problem to be faced was the agrarian problem. Production on the *ejidos* was still low. Their boundaries were fixed, but not the number of people who lived on them. And, as people continued to have children, they wanted more land or jobs in the cities. Owners of small and medium holdings felt threatened by pressure from the *ejidatarios*. Ruiz Cortines tried to create no new *ejidos* and to amortize the existing ones. At the same time, he encouraged small property ownership and increased the number of certificates of inaffectability issued by the Department of Agriculture, which guaranteed that small and medium holdings would not be expropriated for incorporation in an *ejido*. No large-scale irrigation works, like those carried out by Alemán, were undertaken, but small irrigation projects were built to serve a locality and raise its productivity. Because the work force exceeded available factory employment, the government went so far as to order the use of hand labor on public works whenever possible. Construction of schools and clinics continued, and the Ciudad Universitaria, started in Mexico City during the preceding administration, was completed.

Thus the rhythm of economic activity was normalized, but to Mexicans, it seemed a time of recession. The government controlled imports, limiting them to "indispensable" items. The value of the peso was maintained, and the rate of economic growth, slower than during the preceding few years, still exceeded the rate of population growth. During this same quiescent period, Pemex began to exploit natural gas and laid pipelines not only to the probable markets for gas, but even to regions where there were no purchasers but where gas would be used as a source of electricity and would thereby enable the rural population to better its living conditions. But no private company would have risked its capital on such a venture.

As the government won the cooperation of labor leaders,

Adolfo López Mateos, then secretary of labor, managed to avert many strikes, but at the price of arousing the workers' dissatisfaction with their leaders. Thus, labor discontent gave the Communists a chance to offer themselves as adversaries of the "immoral leaders" and win over some unions. Violent strikes followed—of railroad and oil workers and schoolteachers—all led by Communists. The new president who succeeded Ruiz Cortines, in 1958—and it was López Mateos himself—had to act with energy. He jailed some Communist leaders, who received sentences running to as many as eight years on a charge of "social dissolution."

López Mateos was another nominee for the presidency chosen as a compromise between the Cárdenas and the Alemán groups. As always happens in Mexico, the year before the election was a time of recession. No one wanted to open a new business without knowing who the next president would be and what economic policy he would follow. In the months of the preliminary political moves, everyone always pretends to know who will be the future candidate. All possible aspirants to the office are discussed, and as their friends hand out publicity on their behalf, launch their names, and set up organizations, many candidates prematurely rush into the fray, are disqualified, and come out with "burned fingers." All this electoral folklore has little to do with the selection of a candidate however. The deciding influence is wielded by the outgoing president, and the choice of candidate depends largely upon his political acumen.

After the pause granted the country by Ruiz Cortines, the time had come for a dynamic administration, and as the country was well capitalized by then, the president would have to give particular attention to living conditions. López Mateos was the man to do just that. His only opponent was the candidate chosen by Acción Nacional, but he won 6,767,754 votes to his opponent's 705,303. The total vote was greater than before because women exercised their suffrage for the first time in a national election.

The six-year term of López Mateos from 1958 to 1964 saw an expansion of governmental activities geared to the people. Social security coverage increased and entered the rural regions; CEIMSA changed its name and structure from an emergency to a permanent institution to regulate the prices of basic goods; a literacy campaign was launched on the national level, with Jaime Torres Bodet, the poet and former director of UNESCO, as secretary of public education; and the program for school construction was implemented. The tourist trade was fostered, as many new hotels were built by private initiative; the labor leaders, heeding the lesson taught them by the Communists, became more aggressive in order to prevent the Communists from seizing any new chances to displace them; and the industrial workers' standard of living somewhat improved. The enactment of workers' sharing in management's profits, foreshadowed in the constitution of 1917, contributed to this betterment. Public works once more became a source of jobs; cities were growing rapidly. (Mexico City's population reached 6 million, and several provincial cities doubled in size within twenty years.) The government gave special attention to its own bureaucracy by promoting housing plans and organizing a special social security system for them. All in all, Mexico made a good start toward setting up modern administrative machinery and a career bureaucracy—now much better prepared than when Cárdenas established a permanent administrative career base in the government.

During López Mateos' term, industrial expansion had spurted forward, and much of this development was channeled into the provinces. New American, German, French, and Japanese capital moved in. By government purchase of shares in electrical companies, these were "Mexicanized" and integrated into the national electrical grid and in turn helped to provide new industries with needed energy. The telephones were "Mexicanized," too, not by the government but by private capital. The fiscal system was revised to make it more progressive and less susceptible to tax evasion, and in 1963, for the first time since 1910, government bonds, valued at $40 million, were offered on the U.S. market.

The rural regions had advanced little, however. Small property owners were still protected, and the fewest possible number of ejidos were established. Huge, half-abandoned tracts in the north, some of which were owned by foreigners, were expropriated. A campaign was started to move peasants from regions on the high plateau, persistently parched by drought, to the tropical zone of Chiapas. But the rural problem was still difficult, owing to the *ejido* bureaucracy's opposition to any reform of the system under their jurisdiction. Each time the question was raised, the cry of "counterrevolution" arose, and since the prestige of Cárdenas was still high, the bureaucrats had enough influence to block any advance on the agrarian problem.

But Cárdenas made a series of damaging mistakes during this period, which caused him to fall from the pedestal where he had stood for so long. One of his gravest errors was to speak repeatedly in favor of Castroism and even to offer to go to Cuba to fight for the Castro regime at the time of the abortive Bay of Pigs invasion in 1961—just as Mexico was taking a difficult international stand with respect to Cuba, not breaking off relations with Castro and continuing air service to Havana, but not supporting him either. Cárdenas had collaborated in the "pacifist" Stockholm Movement in former years and accepted the Stalin Peace Prize, and now he let himself be used by a group of intellectuals calling themselves Castroists, who formed a National Liberation Movement. Cárdenas' son was one of its leaders. Pro-Castro feeling, strong in 1959 and 1960, dropped rapidly in the autumn of 1962 after the missile crisis and in response to a campaign by the Church under the slogan of "Christianity Yes, Communism No." People began to realize that the controversy over Castro might bring back many old Mexican problems—like the problem of Church intervention in politics—and this fear greatly lessened their respect and liking for Cardenas.

On the other hand, the government, which the pro-Castro elements considered leftist, had to deal energetically with the Communist leaders of certain trade unions, break a railroad strike organized by them, and sentence many of the Communists to prison—among them the famous painter David Alfaro Siqueiros, who had seen the inside of a prison once before, in 1940, after taking part in an attempt to assassinate Trotsky. In 1963, the Communists launched an international campaign on behalf of Siqueiros, and were joined by many non-Communists, believing that fame as an artist endowed one with special political privileges.

(Siqueiros himself petitioned the president for a pardon, which was granted.)

The fact that the campaign brought Communists and non-Communists together in opposition indirectly benefited the government by strengthening its reputation for diplomatic independence, for no one could now accuse the administration of yielding to Communists. This independence was made more patent by Mexico's refusal to sanction the landing of U.S. Marines in the Dominican Republic in April, 1965. Only Venezuela and Chile went along with Mexico in the meeting called by the OAS. This attitude, taken by a quiescent government that represented a backward swing of the pendulum after the administration of López Mateos, was another demonstration of Mexico's stubborn and persistent loyalty to the principle of nonintervention.

The new administration that took this stand was headed by President Gustavo Díaz Ordaz, former secretary of the interior under López Mateos and the candidate of the PRI. The Díaz Ordaz congress contained, for the first time, many members of the rightist opposition in Acción Nacional and many deputies of the left-wing Partido Popular. The new make-up is the result of a law passed on the initiative of President López Mateos that marks a new step toward a more democratic political system. According to this law, any party obtaining 2.5 per cent of the vote cast has a right to appoint five deputies in addition to those chosen by direct balloting, plus five more for each additional 2.5 per cent of the total. It is hoped that this will give representation to important political minorities that never succeeded in attracting enough voters in any one electoral district to elect their own candidates. Basically, it is a combination of proportional representation and direct district representation.

In Díaz Ordaz' campaign, he stated that the agrarian problem was the one most important to the country, not because agrarian reform had failed, but because the time had come to adapt it to new realities. The *ejidos* were scarcely mentioned. Later, his administration parceled out some of them to give each man on an *ejido* his own allotment in an attempt to restore the *ejidal* system to what it was in the beginning: a school for future owners of small tracts.

Thus, under successive presidents, periods of dynamism and rapid industrialization have alternated with periods of caution and consolidation, as reform of the reforms deriving from the Revolution has continued. In this sense, it may properly be said that the principles of the Mexican Revolution guide the nation still. But Mexico is very different from what it was during the Revolution and after. It is now an industrialized Mexico, no longer in need of outside aid, and it is becoming a capitalist country with mixed private and public ownership and political institutions slowly evolving toward democracy.

11 · What Is a Mexican?

TODAY MEXICO is the only Latin American country that is generally stable. There are others that enjoy a measure of political stability, but none has achieved an economic and social stability comparable to Mexico's. Latin American oligarchs, once accustomed to exporting their capital to Swiss banks, tacitly acknowledge Mexico's position by exporting their funds to Mexico to avoid the fee charged by Swiss banks. Mexico, in turn, invests whatever portion of Latin American capital she cannot absorb in Central America, Venezuela, and Puerto Rico. In the near future, Mexico, the country that has insistently required that foreign capital must submit to its laws, may be forced to demand security on its investments in Central and South American governments. President Díaz Ordaz's visit to Central America in 1966, though nothing more than a good-will tour, doubtless was intended to create an appropriate climate for Mexican investment and foreign trade.

In Mexico, there is no one, even among the people of the far right, who can doubt what has become an axiom of the nation's political life: that the country owes its stability to the Revolution, which directed Mexico onto the path toward a capitalistic democracy. To be sure, the capitalist aspect became manifest more rapidly than the democratic, but democracy does exist and is gradually being perfected as structural changes in society render less necessary the tutelary and protective functions of the state. Yet the moment is still far off when the government can cease to act as a guardian, and equally remote is the day when all groups in Mexican society will participate actively in the decision-making process. Still, the time draws nearer.

Mexico's national income has increased fivefold in the past quarter of this century—from 20.7 million pesos to 102.5 million pesos in 1965. Except for mining and related industries, all economic activities have grown. The number of acres under irrigation has risen from 390,261 to 8,896,911; steel production from 103,000 to 1,115,000 tons annually; electrical capacity from 543,000 to 2,470,000 kilowatt-hours; the network of roads from 2,500 to 37,000 miles. In the same period, the birth rate jumped from 44 to 46.9 per 1,000, while the death rate dropped from 23.8 to 13.3 per 1,000. The population has doubled within a quarter of a century and in Mexico City has almost quintupled. Each year 1 million more people live in Mexico, of whom 350,000 are in need of jobs.

After Alemán's term in office, which gave a great boost to industrialization, the guardianship policy, exercised through such institutions as social security and minimum wages, and CONASUPO, checked the tendency of profits to absorb an increasingly large portion of the national income.

Year	Wages*	Profits*
1939	30.5	26
1949	22	49
1959	24	41
1965	25	41

* As percentage of national income.

During the same twenty-five years, consumption of the necessities of life grew by 31 per cent and of luxury items by 68 per
cent. At the same time, production of consumer goods increased
by 57 per cent and of capital goods by 156 per cent. That Mexico
is becoming a modern country is further indicated in the break-
down (in percentages) of the gross national product:

agriculture	22.9
mining and oil	29.5
industry	30.2
services	17.4

All this is also reflected in the changes in the composition of
society. Howard F. Cline* estimates the various social groups as
percentages of the entire population as follows:

Class	1895	1940	1950	1960
Upper	1.5	2.9	2	6.5
Middle	7.8	12.6	25	33.5
In transition	—	6.5	20	20
Lower	90.7	78	53	40

Mexico's capitalism, however, is adapted to Mexico's needs (the
first of which, in the view of Mexicans, is the tutelary function of
the state) and at the same time is an outgrowth of the colonialist
tradition of a directed economy. The legal basis for this protective type of capitalism is expressed in two laws drawn up during
Alemán's presidency by one of the most intelligent men in Mexico, Ramón Beteta (1901–66), Alemán's secretary of the treasury.
The first law was passed to further the development of essential
new industries (but it also limits the scope of business and its
intervention in the government, as Cline points out); the second,
dealing with the power of the executive branch over economic
affairs, establishes the ways and means by which the state may
intervene in the economy. Intervention functions particularly,
but not exclusively, through investments made by the Nacional

* Howard F. Cline, *The United States and Mexico* (Cambridge, Mass.,
1963), p. 410.

Financiera to balance industrial development against agricultural progress—an aim not achieved thus far. On occasion, the Nacional Financiera may also serve as a political instrument. Its investments have risen within a quarter of a century to some 15 billion pesos, distributed as follows: 52 per cent in the development of public utilities—electricity, communications, transport; 18 per cent in basic industries—petroleum, cement, steel; 20.3 per cent in manufacturing; and the remaining 9.7 per cent in other activities. Agriculture is stimulated through the Agricultural Credit Bank and the Ejidal Credit Bank and construction by the Housing and Public Works Bank. Meanwhile, international public investment in aid, credits, and the like, very important several years ago, has shrunk greatly because it is no longer absolutely necessary and is now channeled mainly through the Nacional Financiera.

The precise role played by foreign capital in the Mexican economy is difficult to evaluate. Data on this subject are almost always questionable, owing to the conflicting desires to sanctify foreign capital or decry it as imperialistic. If we take the figures of the economist José Luis Ceceña, who leans toward the latter view, we shall see the blacker picture and so be guarded against surprise.

Ceceña says that there are some 2,000 medium-sized and large companies now in Mexico (meaning those that sell goods worth at least 5 million pesos [$400,000] per year), whose total sales amount to 56 billion pesos ($4.48 billion). Of these 2,000 firms, 400 represent the base of the economy; 160 are controlled by foreign capital; 73 have strong foreign participation; 128 belong to independent Mexican businessmen; 39 are government-controlled. The 128 independent private firms have 20 per cent of the total sales of the 400 firms.

The mining industry is in a state of decline, although it is still important. A large amount of foreign capital, especially that of American companies, is invested in mines; among the American firms are American Mining and Smelting, Anaconda, and American Metal. The foreign share of the total capital invested in the lead mines comes to 90 per cent; in copper mines, 98 per cent; in zinc mines, 97 per cent; and gold mines, 47 per cent. Foreign interests also have a share in coal, iron, and sulphur mines, but the investment is smaller.*

Today, the volume of national investment is able to tolerate foreign capital without endangering the economy. By law, the Mexican Government may direct foreign investment in such a way that it cannot jeopardize the country's development. Relations with the United States have been stabilized to a degree that makes unlikely the occurrence of friction great enough to cause political interference by Washington in the foreseeable future. Nevertheless, Mexicans in the government, and in the leftist opposition groups, of course, are somewhat perturbed by the continued high rate of foreign investment. Their concern prompted President López Mateos to try to "Mexicanize" mining by the purchase of shares and by exemptions to enable the Mexicans themselves to exploit new mines. The campaign to promote such a move was not entirely successful, because mining in present-day Mexico cannot offer rapid and immediate returns. Similarly, energy and money were invested prodigally to irrigate and cultivate the land in the northern Altar desert, but the campaign through which Ruiz Cortines hoped to encourage the fishing and shipping industries—which had it been more successful, might have prevented American, Cuban, and Japanese fishermen from exploiting the wealth of the seas around Mexico and cut off profits going to foreign merchant marines from Mexican freight—evoked an apathetic response because most Mexicans have never shown any great fondness for a life at sea, and the country's coasts are the least dynamic and modernized regions today. Few people appear to be attracted to the development of the coastal region, except for the tourist industry. Acapulco and other spots have become famous as suburbs of Hollywood, and Mexico takes in almost as much money from the tourist trade as from oil.

During the past few years, investment in Mexico has been made easy for Japanese, West German, French, British, Scandinavian and Italian interests. Nonetheless, the volume of capital coming in from those countries is not half so great as from the United States. At present, the United States accounts for 70 per cent of all foreign investment in Mexico; Italy for 13 per cent; France,

* José Luis Ceceña, "La burguesía nacional," *Siempre* (Mexico City), January 5, 1966.

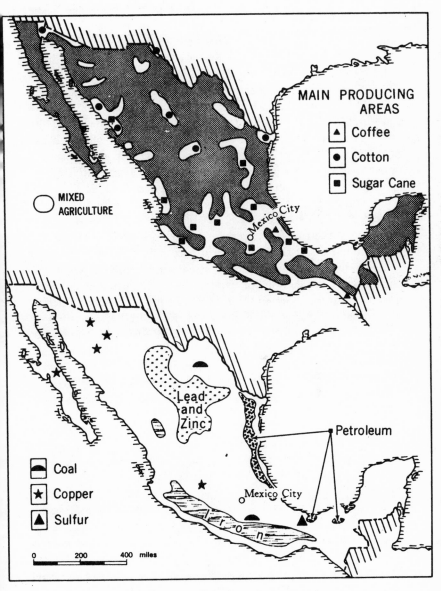

MAIN PRODUCING
AREAS

▲ Coffee
● Cotton
■ Sugar Cane

MIXED
AGRICULTURE

Mexico City

Lead
and
Zinc

Petroleum

Coal
Copper
Sulfur

Mexico City

Iron

0   200   400 miles

Agriculture and Industry in Mexico

8 per cent; Switzerland, 4 per cent. But one thing has been achieved—the rate of reinvestment has risen. In the past few years, reinvestment of foreign capital has been at the rate of some $500 million to $700 million, half of which goes into existing industry. During the past fifteen years, Mexico has received loans from the Export-Import Bank totalling $347 million, and $121 million of other public international loans. The World Bank lent Mexico $30.5 million with which to modernize the railroads and $130 million for electrification. If all this money can be absorbed by the economy without endangering the country, it is because national investment has increased simultaneously. Domestic national investment, which totaled 4.675 billion pesos in 1954, rose to 8.733 billion pesos in 1960. In the same period, private investment increased from 5.4 billion to 12.435 billion pesos. Meanwhile, the country has been amortizing its foreign debt; in 1950, it amounted to 1.6 billion pesos; ten years later it was only 490 million.

Meanwhile, the government is attempting to diversify its imports and its production for export, the object being to stabilize the economy still more and to maintain its policy of independence by gradually reducing the influence of the United States as buyer and seller. The importance of the United States as a seller to Mexico is decreasing, partly because Mexico is already producing many articles that were once imported, partly because new legislation requires importers to assemble their machinery in Mexico and to manufacture parts domestically whenever possible. This is particularly relevant to the automobile industry, which now assembles all its vehicles in Mexico and will be forced increasingly to manufacture parts under a plan for "semi-Mexicanization" of the industry. On the other hand, imports from and exports to other countries are being encouraged: Japan absorbs a portion of the Mexican cotton crop (though it buys through an American firm that controls the cotton market in Mexico). West Germany, France, Great Britain, and, to a lesser degree, countries of East Europe, Scandinavia, and Asia also buy from Mexico. In former years, Mexico sold appreciable amounts of cotton textiles to Africa and the Near East, but this export is threatened as those areas become industrialized. For trade purposes, Mexico has joined the Latin American Free Trade Association, and has a payments agreement with the Central American Common Market.

A decrease in the importation of food has been achieved, even though the rural standard of living is still very low. Corn is no longer imported*; neither is sugar, rice, nor meat. On the contrary, some of these products are exported; cattle, for example, are shipped north to the United States by truck. But all this is not enough to make the farmers a rural middle-class. In this respect, there is still a long way to go.

But, in spite of a certain restlessness in rural zones, Mexicans in general are convinced that their goals will be reached. They may criticize the country's political system, but they all admit that it gives them confidence that the way still to be traveled will not be as rough and steep for them as it has been for other countries that developed in the past century. The vehicle is official action, not by the federal government alone, but also by the governments of the thirty states.†

The national budget reflects this official action and also governs its direction. Taking as an example the budget of 1963, a year when the economy was normal, we find that expenditures rose to nearly 14 billion pesos.‡ Of this total, the following sums were allocated to these sectors:

SECTOR	(in millions of pesos)
Department of the Interior	86
National Defense	958*
Communications	881
Education	3,012
Health and Welfare	607
Agriculture	360
Irrigation	852
Public Works	927

* Much of this in pensions.

* Some 12.5 million acres of Mexico's entire cultivated land surface are planted with corn, the Mexican's daily "bread." The corn crop comes to between 4.5 million and 5 million tons per year.

† The municipal governments, however, are somewhat lifeless and powerless. The people living in villages and cities participate in only a minimal way in political life; not infrequently, local officials are appointed by the governors even though the law stipulates that they must be elected.

‡ In 1945, expenditures in the national budget were 1 billion pesos; in 1950, 2.7 billion; in 1955, 5.7 billion; in 1960, almost 10.3 billion; in 1966, seventeen times greater than it had been twenty years earlier.

In addition, 1,240 million pesos were set aside for investment and 1,009 million for interest on the public debt. Clearly, the amounts that might be considered income-yielding—education, irrigation, public works, communications, and health—took the lion's share of the budget. How were the needed funds raised?

	(in millions of pesos)
income taxes	5,000
exploitation of natural resources	230
taxes on industry	900
taxes on trade	1,500
import taxes	1,500
export taxes	700
exploitation of national properties*	826
Total	10,526

* Such as the national industries, which also paid normal business taxes.

Indirect taxes, still high and ubiquitous, made up the remainder.

What is the nature of the political system that has brought such stability and progress to Mexico?

A schematic Mexico could be divided horizontally into geographical regions, all profoundly different, and similarly it could be sectioned vertically into different economic, political, and social levels. Mexico City and the other major cities live in the twentieth century, fully politicized. But as one moves from the urban centers and the comfortable residential districts, as one comes to the shanty towns, to the hamlets in the southern mountains or in the ranchland of the north, another Mexico is discovered—submerged, closed in on itself, silent.

Politically, we encounter three superimposed countries: first, this submerged Mexico of the Indian and mestizo masses, indifferent to politics, with awareness of the world shrunk to the dimensions of a village. If one day Mexico's industrial life were paralyzed, and the factories, railroads, cars, and airplanes, the telephone and radio all ground to a halt, this voiceless Mexico would go on living almost unaware of the catastrophe.

Another Mexico, the intermediate one, is in process of evolution, being transformed gradually but still in contact with the submerged Mexico from which it evolved. It can be found in the provinces and the poor quarters of the cities. It is a minority, composed of small nuclei, but it is on the rise. Its political interests are local. This is the Mexico of the *caciques*, whose world extends only as far as where authority resides, authority that can give power or take it away: in the state capital. Little by little, this Mexico is shaking off the rule of the *caciques* and entering upon what we might call the rule of local opinion. It is a realm where the large problems of the country and the world are neither heard nor answered, for problems there do not go beyond the municipal or state level. Struggles occur—over simple ideas or immediate interests—and they are already political struggles.

This Mexico of local opinion is very slowly dragging the submerged Mexico into contact with broader public life. A village that is dissatisfied with its mayor (known as the municipal president) depends for action upon a certain number of its residents who protest, send telegrams, publish in the newspapers, or send spokesmen to the state capital. These are the active people who listen to the radio and rouse the masses from their indifference, often unaware that they are doing so. By their actions they are being graduated from a kind of political preparatory school to lend their voices to the Mexico of public opinion.

This third Mexico of public opinion is found in the cities —among businessmen, bureaucrats, professionals, intellectuals, and students, people enjoying some degree of economic comfort, union leaders and militant union members, and at times among schoolteachers, priests, and the owners of small or medium tracts of land in the provincial towns or villages. These are the people who buy magazines, newspapers, and even books. Their numerical size may be indicated, more or less, by the daily press run, in this country of 37 million people, which does not exceed 1.5 million. This is the size of the Mexico that is aware of problems, that debates solutions, directs the country, and marks the road to the future.

This Mexico may be said to occupy the seat of power, for popular sovereignty seems impossible in a country where at least 25 million people—two-thirds of the whole population—take no part in political life. Before anyone can become interested in politics, he must be able to live on a certain economic level and must maintain a minimum of communication with other people, other communities. This is true in both local and national affairs, and I mean by the latter that world in which public opinion is alive to the national character of problems, more or less aware of what is going on in the world, and familiar with the interplay of interests and ideas.

But if Mexico does not have popular sovereignty in the strict meaning of the term, neither does it have dictatorship. Mexico is a democratic country, though the majority of the Mexicans will say among themselves that it is not. The country is democratic in its prevailing mode of life, in its great social mobility, even in its political system, which is based on the sovereignty of public opinion, if not of the people.

Mexican politicians move in a subtle way. Their subtlety is based on an understanding (or a divining, or sniffing out) of the reactions of public opinion, in responding to them, whether by modifying or accepting them, and in adapting programs and decisions to them. This public opinion—expressed not only in the press, but in popular jokes, commentaries, rumors, and of course in economic activities—is always sovereign. For more than forty years, no president has made an important decision that the responsive public has not upheld, or, at least, that has not been supported by the usual pressure groups: the unions, universities, press, chambers of commerce and industry, etc.

Precisely because public opinion represents a minority surrounded by a passive, neutral mass, it tends to express itself with some radicalism—now leaning to the right, now to the left—and to forget that the submerged masses are reacting, too, even if they have no strong political convictions. The Revolution would have been impossible without the people's response. Public opinion may be surprised now and then by a popular reaction that requires a rapid adaptation. An example of this was the people's welcome to President Kennedy in 1963. Two or three hundred thousand people were expected to turn out to greet him; instead, 1 million Mexicans hailed him with enthusiasm. So far, public opinion has always adapted more or less readily to such popular reactions, and the government, in turn, is adept at responding to opinion. And also, the government has shown supreme skill at divining or intuiting the moment when public opinion has failed to express the feeling of the masses and at siding with the masses in order to force public opinion to evolve.

But public opinion is in the minority, and it tends to fossilize into a kind of dogmatism. The country can change more rapidly than public opinion. Since the people's sentiments change with the country, from time to time, government and public opinion are obliged to shift position to adapt to such changes; in other words, government and opinion are both guide and guided. Abrupt changes are the so-called political crises of Mexico. Thanks to them, sovereignty of opinion can claim to represent popular sovereignty.

How, then, can this system be defined? Someone has said that Mexico is an elective monarchy. Someone else said that Mexico has democracy 364 days in the year, and one without it—election day. Be that as it may, Mexico's presidential system gives its chief executive more power than almost any other in the world. The power is conferred mainly by law, but political custom adds to it. Neither the president of the United States nor indeed many dictators enjoy as much power as Mexico's chief executive. Barring re-election and returning oil rights to foreign countries or land to the haciendas, there is almost nothing the Mexican president cannot do, unless public opinion and popular reaction restrain him. Congress passes all the laws the president proposes. Trade unions, farm federations, chambers of commerce and industry, the bankers' club, and the universities may debate or oppose any ministerial decision, but they respect the president's will. Everyone tacitly accepts his power to arbitrate. People may criticize their officials and their laws; they may attack the PRI or make fun of the deputies; but no one attacks the president. The president is not only the direct source of power, which he receives from the people via the PRI, but he is also the living symbol of the nation. Consequently, the man holds the office, but the office makes the man, the personality, the power.

The Revolution was fought to the slogan of "No Re-election

and Effective Suffrage." (This phrase appears above the official's signature on all public documents.) The first principle has been respected; suffrage becomes a little more effective each day—or, if you like, less ineffective. But above and beyond the slogan, the Revolution itself is respected. The presidents do not abuse their power, though they could do so without risk. The freedoms are alive and viable (journalists suppressing a story are censoring themselves or the appropriateness of the item rather than responding to official pressure). Human rights are respected (especially those embodied in the Mexican writ of *habeas corpus*, called *amparo*, by which a judge may forbid any present or future official act with respect to a person asking for the shelter of justice).

The respect for slogans and institutions half a century old, and for rights that could be violated with impunity, demonstrates something that many people overlook in discussing Mexico: that the "establishment," the successive governing teams, place certain convictions above their personal convenience because principles are stronger than corruption or ideological fanaticism. The prevailing conviction may be summarized in one sentence: Mexico is a country yearning to be a nation, wanting to live democratically. This aspiration must be served by anything or anyone in politics.

This has worked, so far—as has Mexico's controlled capitalist system with its touches of a vague kind of socialism, and as the political system has, dominated by one, but not the only, political party. But will it work indefinitely?

Some economists have asked whether the PRI and the government as now organized will be able to continue making decisions which are tutelary in nature without running the risk of finding such decisions inapplicable or of arousing protest.

Mexican society is changing. From 1950 to 1964, the portion of the national income that went to the wealthiest people, about 10 per cent of the population, rose from 49 to 60 per cent. In the same period, the portion received by the poorest 10 per cent dwindled from 26 to 20 per cent. The average income in the wealthiest sector of society has increased from 12 to 18 times' that of the poorest.* This means that the rich have grown richer, and the poor are no better off, even though in absolute terms their living conditions have somewhat improved. If or when the masses become aware of this imbalance, they may lose confidence in the system and protest. In preparation for that inevitable day, the PRI and its leaders have tried to keep the doors open to the opposition, to continue the spread of democracy in the country. But, as we have indicated earlier, they have moved with great caution and very slowly.

To what degree will this policy serve to prepare the ground for new changes in the future? No one can answer this question in concrete terms at the moment, nor can anyone imagine Mexico without the PRI and a powerful executive. Mexico's political situation resembles none other except perhaps Mustafa Kemal's in Turkey (but his regime evolved more rapidly than Mexico's, and the opposition was able to win elections, though not to govern efficiently, and in the end was displaced by a military dictatorship). Until now, the cautious Mexicans have managed to control their country's evolution, at a more leisurely pace and with less risk.

But will the PRI continue to adapt itself to new needs? Will it remain strong enough to keep capitalism under control—as the rich grow richer, more powerful, and more ambitious? Or will it become the rich man's party? Will it deal wisely with the impatience of the poor whenever the poor feel impatient?

Few people ask these questions yet, but some are beginning to feel uneasy. Before the answers can be found, two other questions must first be asked; they express the fundamental preoccupation of the Mexican intellectuals and politicians who are outside the system or who, from within, are trying to change it. The questions are: What was the Mexican Revolution in reality? What is a Mexican?

The Revolution's many phases are interpreted in radically different ways. To some people, the Revolution was essentially nationalistic; to others, it was social; to others, political; to still

* Manuel Germán Parra, "La doctrina de la Revolución Mexicana," *Excelsior* (Mexico, D.F.), May 11, 1965.

others, agrarian and agrarian only. Certainly it broke all theoretical molds, especially the Marxist mold. It was not the outcome of action by an ascendant class seeking political power after having gained economic power, for the middle class, which led it, had been denied economic power under the Díaz dictatorship. Neither did the Mexican Revolution occur as the result of the three previous conditions that Lenin, quoting Engels, considered indispensable to any revolution: the directing classes in the Porfirist society were *not* in a state of decomposition; the exploited classes were *not* conscious of the need for change; there was *not* a theory by which to orient the revolution, and no organization capable of leading the rebellion of the people. The absence of these criteria explains why the Mexican Marxists were never able to interpret the Revolution coherently and why they never had any influence on it. In Mexico, there are three types of Marxists: first, those who might be called mixed, because, though they consider themselves Marxists, they are still loyal to the "thought of the Mexican Revolution" (like Lombardo Toledano, for instance); second, those who consider the Revolution democratic-bourgeois, hence in need of improvement by a strict application of Marxism (Communists of all "lines"); and third, those who might be called "elastic Marxist," who would like to synthesize the concept of the Revolution with the analytical methods of dialectical materialism.

For the great mass of the people, to whom doctrinal speculation is entirely foreign, the Revolution was a parenthesis in their lives at the close of which their manner of living changed, slowly but progressively. The poet Ramón López Velarde spoke of the "newness of the fatherland," because he saw rising from the Revolution a country "not historic, or political, but intimate." He added that "We look at [the Revolution] as accomplished for the life of every one," because it took "years of suffering to conceive a less external, more modest, and probably a more beautiful country." Possibly, the poet interpreted the Revolution correctly: it was a movement that served to quicken Mexico's long, slow march toward its own nationality.

Mexicans claim that their revolution was eminently national, *sui generis*. They rejoice that it came before Russia's or China's and that it can be considered the first agrarian revolution of our epoch, which has seen so many. "The sense of nationality, of fatherland, of a renaissance [is] what makes the Mexicans give back to the Mexicans what was once theirs," one author says.* Many people outside Mexico have questioned whether the PRI and the Mexican political system could be emulated in other countries. Some Spanish leaders, eager to find a solution to their own country's situation, believe that the PRI may be the answer. But they forget that the PRI was born of a revolution that destroyed the oligarchy and that it cost nearly a million lives. They forget, too, that the Mexican Revolution had few repercussions throughout Latin America in its time, probably because the Mexicans had no desire to pass it on, doubtless because they scorned the rest of Latin America—where presidents will not show fight before yielding their offices to the military and where the road to nationality has gone much less far than in Mexico. Even opponents of the Revolution, who were many during and after it, and who were able always to express themselves with complete freedom, recognized that it was and is irreversible. Rightist parties never try to turn back to what existed before; they try merely to keep from moving ahead.

Another Mexican poet, Octavio Paz, has said that the Revolution was "an explosive and authentic revelation of our real nature" and that thanks to it, "the Mexican wants to reconcile himself with his history and his origins. . . . The Revolution began as a discovery of our own selves and a return to our origins; later, it became a search and an abortive attempt at a synthesis; finally, since it was unable to assimilate our tradition and to offer us a new and workable plan, it became a compromise."† The Revolution still lives on in the minds of the Mexicans, and it is the source of the new ideals that have emerged throughout the past fifty years, changing as the aspirations of the groups guiding the country have changed.

For a time after the Revolution, there was almost nothing for conservatives to conserve. But as stability followed upheaval, new interests and things worth conserving emerged. Even so, the Rev-

* Antonio Bahamonde, *México es así* (Mexico City, 1940), p. 65.
† Octavio Paz, *The Labyrinth of Solitude* (New York, 1962), pp. 135, 168.

olution was ever present. Some attempt was made to draw the Revolution and the new conservatism together, with the inevitable result that the revolutionaries themselves split into conservatives and radicals. The radicals held that the Revolution was not yet complete, that it must go on. The conservatives believed that the active revolutionary phase was over and there was no need to move beyond its social achievements, although there was still need for advance in the political order. Both would have liked to skip from the bureaucratic stage, where power resided in the hands of officials, to the popular stage, where power emanated from the people. Luckily for Mexico, the radicals were the bureaucrats, and they kept the principles of the Revolution alive and gradually applied some of its principles that were still on paper.

Changes in the social structure are reflected in the political spectrum. The conservatives in Mexico today accept the Revolution. Though some belong to the PAN, in which they work side by side with the surviving Porfirists and elements of the old bourgeoisie, others are of the new bourgeoisie and are often militant in the PRI. This so-called conservative sector might more accurately be considered progressive, for it has kept pace with Mexico's rapid economic development. It is composed largely of the younger bourgeoisie, the "new group" of industrialists (containing a fair number of foreigners settled in Mexico), who are nationalistic, since they would like to eliminate foreign competition, who accept the unions and the government's social policy, but who take anachronistic positions on economic questions (for example, they favor tariff barriers to protect Mexican industry).

Paradoxically, the organized working class can be regarded as a part of the conservative group. They are content with what they have; their leaders are conformists; and they do not press for social change. This type of trade unionism is gradually losing any ideological content and is beginning to resemble more and more the labor federations of the United States. The bureaucracy that emerged around the *ejidos* is equally conservative; beneath its revolutionary rhetoric, it conceals the hope that the system will go on unchanged.

The most progressive force exists in the middle class, the high government bureaucracy, and the peasant masses united—potentially, at least—in their desire for a further extension of the benefits of the Revolution. These groups include most of the people who are aware of the need that emerged from the Revolution to adapt and reform the agrarian system. Within them, the intellectuals and professionals form a special sub-group, very radical in speech, strongly anti-American, and correspondingly prone to sympathize with the U.S.S.R. Many of the formulas they employ are of a schematic and simplistic Marxist type, but absolutely passive, for they make no effort to approach the mass of the people or to hasten their incorporation into political life.

The Communists have a certain influence among some student minorities as well. It is not the Communist Party itself that is influential—it is a mere skeleton, extremely bureaucratic, and split into three or four factions—but Russian and Chinese anti-American propaganda. The monopoly on cultural life once enjoyed by pro-Communist elements has been fragmented, and they are losing influence: partly because they no longer have the means of seduction—entertaining, publishing, and flattery—or the means of isolating their enemies; partly because the prestige of Castro and the Russians has plummeted since the missile crisis of 1962.

Mexico's society of today may be described as politically developing, economically in rapid development, socially conservative, and culturally disoriented. The cultural disorientation is not so much the result of the intellectuals' attitude as of the fact that the Mexican personality is going through a transitional period. It could not be otherwise in a country that is living through the historical stage of becoming a nation. The intellectuals' attitude is the result, in some way, of their uncertainty about their own personality—an uncertainty similarly caused by the transitional nature of the times. Before, Mexicans knew their country was not a nation and desired it to become one; now the people do not know what kind of nation is emerging, or what kind of Mexican is being molded by it, or even what kind of Mexican they are themselves. Public opinion senses this (although it has not thought it out), and there is even an intuition of it in the submerged masses.

Consequently, Mexico's intellectual activity of the past years —in the novel, films, the essay, painting, music, even political

literature—reveals a loss of the facile assurance evident in Diego
Rivera's frescoes, in the poetry of the Contemporaries, films by
the "Indian" Fernández, Manuel Azuela's novels, the essays of
Alfonso Reyes, or the speeches of Cárdenas. All artistic effort
now revolves around the same question: What is a Mexican?

In 1949, a series of books entitled *Mexico and the Mexicans*
began to be published, and each was greeted with resounding
acclaim. Since then, each time a book appears on the Mexican
psychology, booksellers rejoice in the knowledge that it will sell
like hotcakes. Even before World War II, the philosopher Samuel Ramos (1897–1959) wrote his *Perfil del hombre y la cultura
en México (Profile of Man and Culture in Mexico)*, a work indispensable to an understanding of the country. *El laberinto de
la soledad (The Labyrinth of Solitude)* by Octavio Paz is another book that has influenced the modern generation of Mexican intellectuals.

Why this preoccupation? One answer is that the Mexican is
a person in whom the Indian and the Spaniard are still at war.
In the same way that his religion is an attempted reconciliation of
opposing tenets and practices, his psychology is a not-yet-com-
plete fusion. This is the cause of the individual tragedy of the
mestizo and also of the collective effectiveness of mestizo society.
The Creoles won Mexico's independence. But the two great revolutions—the Reform and the Revolution—were the work of
mestizos who now constitute the majority of the Mexican people.
This fusion of the races, not yet complete, sets the tone of Mexico. As long as the mestizo is considered a crossbreed, he cannot
quite be himself; he lives in a world of contradictions and com-
plexes. (Ramos and Paz have interpreted this phenomenon well,
and I have drawn on their arguments throughout these pages.)
The very hatred that many Mexicans still feel toward Hernán
Cortés is evidence of their split personality. Mexico City is the
only Latin American city that has not honored its discoverer with
a statue or street bearing his name. The word *malinchismo* is used
pejoratively to describe a preference for foreign things; it is most
insulting. José Iturriaga has argued that the Mexican suffers from
a sense that he is a minus value—because of his colonial past, his

status as one of a conquered race, the technical inferiority of his civilization as compared with the conqueror's, and the feeling that his mixed blood came from violence, not love. All the Mexican's virtues and defects are born of this feeling of inferiority.

But clearly the Mexican psychology was not molded by cross-breeding alone. As the novelist Rubén Romero (1890–1952) has said, "Man is hunger." What the Mexican eats influences him—perhaps what he does not eat influences him, too, for a diet of corn and chile, boiled meat, and the fermented juice of the maguey cactus (pulque) is not balanced.

The long denial of freedom to the Mexican at the bottom of the social scale has permanently affected his personality. Before the arrival of the Spaniards, the life of the lowest class was spent in a rigidly theocratic society. Later, the Spanish authorities exerted a similar control, for even when they sought to protect the Indian, they regulated all his acts. Independence did nothing for the masses. The latifundio system of the nineteenth century nullified even the external forms of democracy. Consequently, the Mexicans are still serving an apprenticeship to liberty, and the astonishing thing is that they have learned so rapidly, with no sudden starts or backward steps.

Before the Revolution, a chasm yawned between the upper classes, of aristocratic bent, and the people, who were forced to defend themselves against the upper class as they had defended themselves against the Spaniards and the Aztec lords. Their weapons were silence, humor, and deceit. As long ago as 1840, Mora said that the virtues of the Mexican people must be sought in the masses, not in the privileged classes. The Revolution blended all the classes psychologically—and economically, too. Now the outlines of another differentiation are appearing: the people versus the *nouveaux riches* and the conservatives of the Revolution who became "Americanized" (just as the nineteenth-century Creoles and "aristocrats" had become "Frenchified").

Ramos has said that the Mexican is interested solely in immediate ends; he works for today and tomorrow, never for later. The future is a concern that has been erased from his consciousness. No one ventures into a business offering only long-range returns. Thus, "one of life's most important dimensions has been eliminated: the future." This may explain why the Mexican will vacillate long before he undertakes anything, and why, when he makes up his mind to act, he completes his work quickly and does not care about preserving it. A street, poorly maintained for years and years, may be improved within a few days. Lights are strung up, trees planted, posters put up, after which no one remembers to keep it in good shape and it returns to an even worse state than before. A tract of land, vacant for many years in the middle of a city, will be transformed suddenly with the erection of a building with mosaics and high windows decorating the facade; but soon the mosaics fall off and the panes are broken, and after a while the building is demolished and another is built in its place.

Paz says that the Mexican is timid, introverted, but he compensates by being noisy and aggressive. He celebrates his holidays, of which there are many, with fireworks, blaring band music, and beautiful songs, which can be recognized immediately by their aggressive broken rhythm and high notes. He has a very special kind of humor, sarcastic rather than gay, deadpan, and dry. Death holds an important place in his life; he kills or is killed for no apparent reason. On All Souls' Day, he eats and drinks at the family tomb; he enjoys candy in the shape of skulls. His Spanish is excellent, purer than in Spain, enriched with Nahautl words, and constantly renewed with graphic, imaginative expressions. Listening to the bargaining in the markets is a joy and a lesson in logic and the art of insulting without giving offense.

Paz adds that the Mexicans of the colony learned to be hypocrites, and if they are not now, they are nevertheless timorous and suspicious. They conceal both their anger and their tenderness. Enveloped in loneliness, the individual Mexican is punctilious and irascible. Everything is a defense: silence or words, courtesy or scorn. Toward women, he is ironical and resigned. The fiancé is tender and courtly; the husband is completely different. And of the three parts of religion—dogma, ethics, and rite—says the sociologist Jorge Carrión, the Mexican leans more toward dogma and rite than ethics.

The Mexican combines in his character the contrary traits of a sense of the ridiculous, a desire to be hospitable, and a fondness for individuality—each exaggerated. He lives on two separate planes at once without seeing the inconsistency—the plane of words and the plane of deeds. He is mistrustful and knows he is distrusted; yet he follows two practices based on trust, both of which he values highly: *compadre*-ship and lifelong friendship. *Compadres* are those who have been attendants at a wedding or godfathers at a baptism (merely to be chosen to act at such ceremonies establishes a strong bond). The friend—or *cuate*, meaning brother or twin, in popular parlance—is a friend from childhood to whom one owes loyalty and ever-ready support. Many politicians will protect their enemies and grant position to their adversaries simply because they are *cuates* or *compadres*.

In the Mexican personality there are subtleties that can be found only in people in the process of formation. Possibly Mexico's formative status as a nation and as a people is what gives the country its fascinating character and its strength. The awareness among the masses that their personality is being shaped, and the fact that the system derived from the Revolution compensates for the lack of a sense of the future, has given the country stability and, at the same time, dynamism, and has made Mexico *the* exception in Latin America.

The Mexicans themselves have a phrase for it: *"Como México no hay dos"*—"There are no two Mexicos."

Appendix

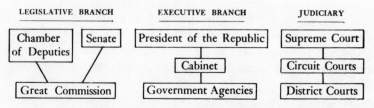

LEGISLATIVE BRANCH	EXECUTIVE BRANCH	JUDICIARY

The basic organization is like that of the United States.

The United States of Mexico is composed of twenty-nine states, the Federal District of Mexico City, and the territories of Quintana Roo and Baja California Sur. The president appoints the territorial governors and the Federal District regent (who holds the rank of secretary of state). State governors are elected by universal popular vote, as are members of the state legislatures.

The 162 members of the Chamber of Deputies are elected every three years by popular vote, with one deputy for every 170,000 inhabitants. The sixty members of the Senate are elected by popular vote every six years, two from each state and one from the Federal District. Both chambers are in session from September 1 to December 31. The Great Commission functions when congress is not in session. This body, representing both chambers, is composed of fifteen senators and fifteen deputies.

The President is elected every six years by popular vote and is not eligible for re-election. If the office falls vacant during the first two years of a mandate, new elections are held. After that, congress elects a successor to fill out the remainder of the term.

The Supreme Court is made up of twenty-one justices, appointed by the president for a term of six years. No justice can be removed except by impeachment. In matters of federal law, the circuit courts are appellate courts that rule on decisions in the district courts. Civil and criminal cases are tried in the municipal and state courts. The sentence of capital punishment does not exist in federal law, and only five of the states have retained it as a permissible sentence for major felonies.

For Further Reading

BLOM, FRANZ. *The Conquest of Yucatan*. Boston, 1936.

CLARK, M. R. *Organized Labor in Mexico*. Chapel Hill, N.C., 1934.

CLINE, HOWARD F. *Mexico, Revolution to Evolution, 1940–1960*. London and New York, 1962.

————. *The United States and Mexico*. Cambridge, Mass., 1963.

COSIO VILLEGAS, DANIEL. *Change in Latin America: The Mexican and Cuban Revolutions*. Lincoln, 1961.

GONZÁLEZ PEÑA, CARLOS. *History of Mexican Literature*. Dallas, 1943.

GUZMÁN, MARTÍN LUIS. *The Eagle and the Serpent*. London, 1930.

LEWIS, OSCAR. *Five Families: Mexican Case Studies in the Culture of Poverty*. New York, 1959.

————. *The Children of Sánchez: The Autobiography of a Mexican Family*. New York, 1961.

MILLON, ROBERT PAUL. *Mexican Marxist: Vicente Lombardo Toledano*. Chapel Hill, N.C., 1966.

PADGET, L. VINCENT. *The Mexican Political System*. Boston, 1966.

PARKES, HENRY BAMFORD. *A History of Mexico*. 3d ed., Boston, 1960.

PAZ, OCTAVIO. *The Labyrinth of Solitude: Life and Thought in Mexico.* New York, 1961.

———. (ed.) *An Anthology of Mexican Poetry.* Bloomington, Ind., 1958.

PRESCOTT, WILLIAM H. *History of the Conquest of Mexico.* New York, 1843.

RAMOS, SAMUEL. *Profile of Man and Culture in Mexico.* Austin, Texas, 1962.

REDFIELD, ROBERT. *Tepoztlan.* Chicago, 1930.

REED, JOHN. *Insurgent Mexico.* New York, 1913.

RICARD, ROBERT. *The Spiritual Conquest of Mexico.* Berkeley, Calif., 1966.

ROEDER, RALPH. *Juárez and His Mexico.* New York, 1947.

ROSS, STANLEY R. *Francisco I. Madero, Apostle of Mexican Democracy.* New York, 1955.

SCHLACMAN, JOSEPH H. *Mexico, Land of Volcanoes.* Milwaukee, 1950.

SCOTT, ROBERT E. *Mexican Government in Transition.* Urbana, Ill., 1959.

SENIOR, CLARENCE O. *Land Reform and Democracy.* Gainesville, Fla., 1958.

SIMPSON, EYLER N. *The Ejido, Mexico's Way Out.* Chapel Hill, N.C., 1937.

SIMPSON, LESLEY BYRD. *Many Mexicos.* Berkeley, Calif., 1952.

TANNENBAUM, FRANK. *Peace by Revolution.* New York, 1933.

———. *Mexico, the Struggle for Peace and Bread.* New York, 1950.

TOOR, FRANCES. *A Treasury of Mexican Folkways.* New York, 1947.

TOWNSEND, WILLIAM CAMERON. *Lázaro Cárdenas, Mexican Democrat.* Ann Arbor, 1952.

VAILLANT, GEORGE C. *The Aztecs of Mexico.* New York, 1941.

VERNON, RAYMOND. *The Dilemma of Mexican Development.* Cambridge, Mass., 1963.

WHETTEN, NATHAN L. *Rural Mexico.* Chicago, 1948.

WOLFE, BERTRAM D. *A Portrait of Mexico.* New York, 1937.

Index